ORDNANCE SURVEY MEMOIRS OF IRELAND

Volume Twenty-three

PARISHES OF COUNTY ANTRIM VIII
1831–5, 1837–8

Published 1993.
The Institute of Irish Studies,
The Queen's University of Belfast,
Belfast.
In association with
The Royal Irish Academy,
Dawson Street,
Dublin.

Reprinted 2018 by Ulster Historical Foundation.

Grateful acknowledgement is made to the Economic and Social Research Council and
the Department of Education for Northern Ireland for their financial assistance at different
stages of this publication programme.

British Library Cataloguing-in-Publication Data.
A catalogue record for this book is available from the British Library.

ISBN 978-0-85389-466-7

Printed by Impressions Print and Label.

Ordnance Survey Memoirs of Ireland

VOLUME TWENTY-THREE

Parishes of County Antrim VIII
1831–5, 1837–8

Ballymena and West Antrim

Edited by Angélique Day, Patrick McWilliams and Nóirín Dobson

The Institute of Irish Studies
in association with
The Royal Irish Academy

CONTENTS

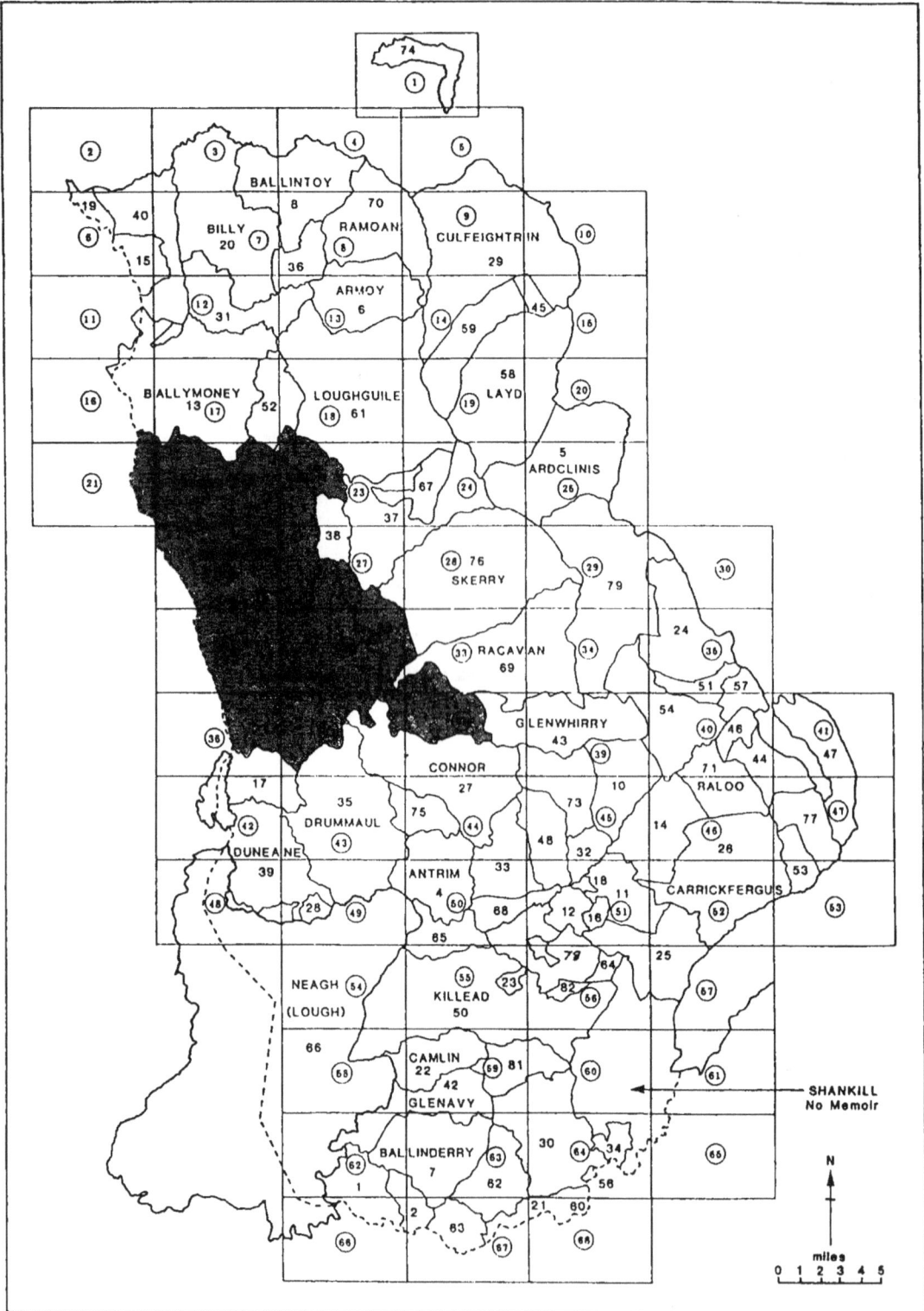

ACKNOWLEDGEMENTS

During the course of the transcription and publication project many have advised and encouraged us in this gigantic task. Thanks must first be given to the Royal Irish Academy, particularly former librarian Mrs Brigid Dolan and her staff, for making the original manuscripts available to us. We are also indebted to Siobhán O'Rafferty for her continuing help in deciphering indistinct passages of manuscript.

We should like to acknowledge the following individuals for their special contributions. Dr Brian Trainor led the way with his edition of the Antrim Memoir and provided vital help on the steering committee. Dr Ann Hamlin also provided valuable support, especially during the most trying stages of the project. Professor R.H. Buchanan's unfailing encouragment has been instrumental in the development of the project to the present. Without Dr Kieran Devine the initial stages of the transcription and the computerising work would never have been completed successfully: the project owes a great deal to his constant help and advice. Dr Kay Muhr's continuing contribution to the work of the transcription project is deeply appreciated. Mr W.C. Kerr's interest and expertise have been invaluable. Professor Anne Crookshank and Dr Edward McParland were most generous with practical help and advice concerning the drawings amongst the Memoir manuscripts. We would like to thank the Director of the Ordnance Survey, Dublin and the keepers of the fire-proof store, among them Leonard Hines. Finally, all students of the nineteenth century Ordnance Survey of Ireland owe a great deal to the pioneering work of Professor J.H. Andrews, and his kind help in the first days of the project is gratefully recorded.

The essential task of inputting the texts from audio tapes was done by Miss Eileen Kingan, Mrs Christine Robertson, Miss Eilis Smyth, Miss Lynn Murray, and, most importantly, Miss Maureen Carr.

We are grateful to the Linen Hall Library for lending us their copies of the first edition 6" Ordnance Survey Maps: also to Ms Maura Pringle of QUB Cartography Department for the index maps showing the parish boundaries. For providing financial assistance at crucial times for the maintenance of the project, we would like to take this opportunity of thanking the trustees of the Esme Mitchell trust and The Public Record Office of Northern Ireland.

Left:

Map of parishes of County Antrim. The area described in this volume, the parishes of West Antrim, has been shaded to highlight its location. The square grids represent the 1830s 6" Ordnance Survey maps. The encircled numbers relate to the map numbers as presented in the bound volumes of maps for the county. The parishes have been numbered in all cases and named in full where possible, except those in the following list: Aghagallon 1, Aghalee 2, Ballyclug 9, Ballycor 10, Ballylinny 11, Ballymartin 12, Ballynure 14, Ballyrashane 15, Grange of Ballyrobert 16, Grange of Ballyscullion 17, Grange of Ballywalter 18, Ballywillin 19, Blaris and Lisburn 21 & 60, Grange of Carmavy 23, Carncastle 24, Carnmoney 25, Cranfield 28, Derryaghy 30, Derrykeighan 31, Grange of Doagh 32, Donegore 33, Drumbeg 34, Grange of Drumtullagh 36, Dunaghy 37, Grange of Dundermot 38, Dunluce 40, Glynn 44, Inver 46, Island Magee 47, Kilbride 48, Killagan 49, Grange of Killyglen 51, Kilraghts 52, Kilroot 53, Kilwaughter 54, Kirkinriola 55, Lambeg 56, Larne 57, Granges of Layd and Inispollan 59 & 45, Magheragall 62, Magheramesk 63, Mallusk 64, Grange of Muckamore 65, Newtown Crommelin 67, Grange of Nilteen 68, Rashee 73, Rathlin Island 74, Grange of Shilvodan 75, Templecorran 77, Templepatrick 78, Tickmacrevan 79, Tullyrusk 81, Umgall 82.

Map of County Antrim, from Samuel Lewis' *Atlas of the counties of Ireland*
(London, 1837)

INTRODUCTION AND GUIDE TO THE PUBLICATION OF
THE ORDNANCE SURVEY MEMOIRS

The following text of the Ordnance Survey Memoirs was first transcribed by a team working in the Institute of Irish Studies at The Queen's University of Belfast, on a computerised index of the material. For this publication programme the text has been further edited: spellings have been modernised in most cases, although where the original spelling was thought to be of any interest it has been retained and is indicated by angle brackets in the text. Variant spellings for townland and lesser place-names have been preserved, although parish and major place-names have been standardised and the original spelling given in angle brackets. Names of prominent people, for instance landlords, have been standardised where possible, but original spellings of names in lists of informants, emigration tables and on tombstones have been retained. We have not altered the Memoir writers' anglicisation of names and words in Irish.

Punctuation has been modernised and is the responsibility of the editors. Editorial additions are indicated by square brackets: a question mark before and after a word indicates a queried reading and tentatively inserted information respectively. Original drawings are referred to in the text, and some have been reproduced. Manuscript page references have been omitted from this series. Because of the huge variation in size of Memoirs for different counties, the following editorial policy has been adopted: where there are numerous duplicating and overlapping accounts, the most complete and finished account, normally the Memoir proper, has been presented, with additional unique information from other accounts like the Fair Sheets entered into a separate section, clearly titled and identified; where the Memoir material is less, nothing has been omitted. To achieve standard volume size, parishes have been associated on the basis of propinquity.

There are considerable differences in the volume of information recorded for different areas: counties Antrim and Londonderry are exceptionally well covered, while the other counties do not have quite the same detail. This series is the first systematic publication of the parish Memoirs, although individual parishes have been published by pioneering local history societies. The entire transcriptions of the Memoirs made in the course of the indexing project can be consulted in the Public Record Office of Northern Ireland and the library at the Queen's University of Belfast. The manuscripts of the Ordnance Survey Memoirs are in the Royal Irish Academy, Dublin.

Brief history of the Irish Ordnance Survey in the nineteenth century and the writing of the Ordnance Survey Memoirs

In 1824 a House of Commons committee recommended a townland survey of Ireland with maps at the scale of 6", to facilitate a uniform valuation for local taxation. The Duke of Wellington, then prime minister, authorised this, the first Ordnance Survey of Ireland. The survey was directed by Colonel Thomas Colby, who had under his command officers of the Royal Engineers and three companies of sappers and miners. In addition to this, civil assistants were recruited to help with sketching, drawing and engraving of maps, and eventually, in the 1830s, the writing of the Memoirs.

The Memoirs were written descriptions intended to accompany the maps, containing information which could not be fitted on to them. Colonel Colby always considered additional information to be necessary to clarify place-names and other distinctive features of each parish; this was to be written up in reports by the officers. Much information about parishes resulted from research into place-names and was used in the writing of the Memoirs. The term "Memoir" comes from the abbreviation of the word "Aide-Memoire". It was also used in the 18th century to describe topographical descriptions accompanying maps.

In 1833 Colby's assistant, Lieutenant Thomas Larcom, developed the scope of the officers' reports by stipulating the headings or "Heads of Inquiry" under which information was to be reported, and including topics of social as well as economic interest. By this time civil assistants were writing some of the Memoirs under the supervision of the officers, as well as collecting information in the Fair Sheets.

The first "Memoirs" are officers' reports covering Antrim in 1830, and work continued on the Antrim parishes right through the decade, with special activity in 1838 and 1839. Counties Down and Tyrone were written up from 1833 to 1837, with both officers and civil assistants working on Memoirs. In Londonderry and Fermanagh research and writing started in 1834. Armagh was worked on in 1835, 1837 and 1838. Much labour was expended in the Londonderry parishes. The plans to publish the Memoirs commenced with the parish of Templemore, containing the city and liberties of Derry, which came out in 1837 after a great deal of expense and effort.

Between 1839 and 1840 the Memoir scheme collapsed. Sir Robert Peel's government could not countenance the expenditure of money and time on such an exercise; despite a parliamentary commission favouring the continuation of the writing of the Memoirs, the scheme was halted before the southern half of the country was covered. The manuscripts remained unpublished and most were removed to the Royal Irish Academy, Dublin from the Ordnance Survey, Phoenix Park. Other records of the Ordnance Survey, including some residual material from the Memoir scheme, have recently been transferred to the National Archives, Bishop Street, Dublin.

The Memoirs are a uniquely detailed source for the history of the northern half of Ireland immediately before the Great Famine. They document the landscape and situation, buildings and antiquities, land-holdings and population, employment and livelihood of the parishes. They act as a nineteenth century Domesday book and are essential to the understanding of the cultural heritage of our communities. It is planned to produce a volume of evaluative essays to put the material in its full context, with information on other sources and on the writers of the Memoirs.

Definition of descriptive terms

Memoir (sometimes Statistical Memoir): an account of a parish written according to the prescribed form outlined in the instructions known as "Heads of Inquiry", and normally divided into three sections: Natural Features and History, Modern and Ancient Topography, Social and Productive Economy.

Fair Sheets: "information gathered for the Memoirs", an original title describing paragraphs of information following no particular order, often with marginal headings, signed and dated by the civil assistant responsible.

Statistical Remarks/Accounts: both titles are employed by the Engineer officers in their descriptions of the parish with marginal headings, often similar in layout to the Memoir.

Office Copies: these are copies of early drafts, generally officers' accounts and must have been made for office purposes.

Ordnance Survey Memoirs for County Antrim

This volume, containing the Memoirs for 6 parishes in west Antrim, is the eighth collection for the county and the twenty-third in the series, covering an area bordering on county Londonderry and separated from it by the River Bann. Included in the parish of Ballyclug are some sections for the grange of Ballyscullion, and some of the drawings in Kirkinriola relate to Dunaghy and Rasharkin.

This volume contains some fine, well-balanced parish descriptions as well as many accomplished drawings. The accounts consist of some early officers' reports returned between 1831 and 1833, the main Memoirs written by James Boyle in 1835 and the Ancient Topography sections by J. Stokes in 1837 and 1838, with additional information provided by John Bleakly's Fair Sheets. There is good evidence for the team nature of the Memoir composition in the Draft Memoir for the parish of Kirkinriola, which contains sections by 5 writers, T.C. Hannyngton, J.R. Ward and another, with notes and queries by James Boyle and Lieutenant R.K. Dawson respectively.

The material describes the main towns and villages of this area and the manner in which Portglenone's market was being usurped by that of Ballymena, a flourishing and prosperous centre of trade at that time, particularly for the sale of linen. Crebilly, in the parish of Ballyclug, was the venue for 2 annual fairs with livestock being brought from as far as the Scottish highlands and the west of Ireland. There is also much detail on the trades and occupations of the inhabitants and the local economy, including mention in the parish of Ahoghill of the cultivation of camomile for sale to druggists. Also in that parish is an interesting account of the Moravian settlement at Gracehill, whose women were renowned for their fine needlework. The schools in this area were particularly numerous, and there are references to several well-endowed academies in Ballymena and around Ahoghill, as well as hedge schools and schools supported by societies. Reference is made to the faction fighting and the party spirit that existed in these parts, especially round Ballymena and Crebilly.

This collection of Memoirs contains some particularly intriguing references to the cultural traditions and beliefs of the area, resulting from fairly close contact with the inhabitants, as can be deduced from James Boyle's first-hand account of Mary McGeary and her tasks which he "picked up at a wake" in Finvoy. There are allusions to the great wealth of traditional knowledge then current amongst the population. Recitation of pedigrees at wakes is recorded in Ahoghill and the genealogy of the O'Haras of Crebilly could be traced back to Noah. There are several stories quoted relating how the wealthy Dr Colville of Galgorm Castle amassed his riches, including one about him selling his soul to the Devil.

Drawings in the Memoir papers are listed below and are cross-referenced in the text; some are illustrated. The manuscript material is to be found in Boxes 1, 3, 11, 12, 13 and 15 of the Royal Irish Academy's collection of Ordnance Survey Memoirs, and section references are given beside each parish below in their printed order.

Ahoghill: Box 1 IV 2, 5 and 4, 6, 7, 8, 1
Ballyclug: Box 3 III 5, 3b and 3a, 2, 4, 1
Finvoy: Box 11 I 2, 1 and 4, 3
Killagan: Box 12 II 3, 1, 2
Kirkinriola: Box 13 III 5, 4, 3, 1, 2
Rasharkin: Box 15 VII 5, 3, 1, 2, 4

Drawings

Ahoghill (sections 3 and 7):

Cave in Moyasset, ground plan with dimensions.

Cove in Killdowney, ground plan with dimensions [by J. Bleakly].

Window in Ahoghill church with dimensions.

Remaining door of stone preaching house near Gortfad.

Fort hill, in Moylarg, section with dimensions.

Fort and cove at Dreen, ground plan.

Map of the standing stones in Ahoghill.

Standing stone in Moylarg, with dimensions.

Standing stone at an ancient burying ground in Galgorm Parks, 2 views with dimensions.

Galgorm chapel, west window with dimensions, doorway, east window and belfry.

Galgorm Castle, front elevation; scaled ground plan of McQuillan's Castle.

Druidical circle in Slievenagh, side view with dimensions of stones, and ground plan.

Giant's Finger Stone in Finkiltagh, with side view and section through top of stone, with dimensions.

Cove in Carndonaghy, ground plan, section and detail of door.

5 coins found in Ahoghill.

Coin and medal of tin and silver alloy.

The Fort hill, scaled ground plan [all by J. Stokes].

Ballyclug (section 2):

Map showing the standing stones in Ballyclug.

Giant's grave in Caherty, view with a person's figure; second view and plan with dimensions.

Todd's Grave in Ballymarlow, with ground plan and dimensions.

Moat in Ballykeel, scaled ground plan and section with dimensions.

Fort in Deerfin, scaled ground plan, section with dimensions, detail of fire hearth and dimensions; small view of fort.

Fort in Ballylessan, scaled ground plan.

Coves in fort in Ballylessan, ground plans and sections with dimensions.

View of interior of Thomas McKeen's Cove, Crebilly, and scaled ground plan [illustrated].

2 stone rings, with side views and dimensions.

3 stone rings, with side views, full size.

Stone ring, both sides, with side view; 2 smaller stone rings with side views, full size.

Salt-cellar of baked clay, with dimensions.

4 flint arrowheads, full size [all by J. Stokes].

Finvoy (section 3):

Cave in Knockans, section.

Giant's grave in Ballymacaldrack, 2 views with dimensions.

Giant's grave in Ballymacaldrack, scaled plan and view of cromlech with dimensions.

Stone monuments including Broad Stone, scaled plan.

The Broad Stone with human figure [illustrated].

The Broad Stone, view with annotations and dimensions; detailed plan.

Stone article, overhead and side view, section with dimensions.

Map of standing stones in Finvoy [all by J. Stokes].

Killagan (section 2):

Half of millstone in Kilmandil burying ground.

Map of standing stones in Killagan.

Rectangular stone with 2 hollows on either side, each side with dimensions and longitudinal section.

3 coins found in Kilmandil.

Stone hatchet found in Kilmandil, with end view.

Flat stone ring found in a cove, with side view and section.

Flint arrowheads, with side view of each, full size [all by J. Stokes].

Kirkinriola (sections 1, 2, 3):

Map of standing stones in Kirkinriola.

Old church of Kirkinriola.

Tomb stone at Kirkinriola showing inscription.

Standing stone in Bottom with dimensions.

Drumfane moat, scaled ground plan and section with dimensions.

Mound in Bottom with dimensions, scaled ground plan.

Fort called the Castle in Killyflugh, scaled ground plan and section.

Fort in Carnlea, scaled ground plan and section with dimensions.

View of Ballymena from the north.

Ancient Irish ornament of bronze with remains of painting on enamel [illustrated].

Ornament of beaten gold, showing decoration, with dimensions [illustrated].

Coin or medal found near Ballymena, both faces [illustrated].

2 ancient pins found near Ballymena, with annotations and dimensions.

Articles of green and red glass, found at a standing stone, with section and dimensions.

3 arrowheads with dimensions, one with both sides with dimensions, Dunaghy parish.

A sword of brass with dimensions.

Ornament of gold, parish of Rasharkin, 2 views and section, full size.

Spanish coin found in Finvoy.

Anvil of bronze found near Ballymoney, 2 views with dimensions.

Fragment of ancient mould for casting spearheads found near Ballymena, 2 views with dimensions [all by J. Stokes].

Plan of old church of Kirkinriola with annotations and dimensions; detail of window.

Portion of the west end of old church of Kirkinriola, with masonry [both by T.C. Hannyngton].

Rasharkin (sections 1 and 2):

Map of the standing stones in Rasharkin.

Lisnacannon Fort, scaled ground plan and section with dimensions.

Stirrup-shaped ornament found in Glenbuck, with section and dimensions.

Brass pin found with ornament, full size.

Cave in Pharoah's Fort, scaled ground plan with dimensions.

Cave in Anticur, ground plan with dimensions.

Coin found in Bellaghy, both faces, full size [all by J. Stokes].

Pharoah's Fort, ground plan with dimensions.

Artificial cove in Anticur, ground plan with dimensions [both by J. Bleakly].

Parish of Ahoghill, County Antrim

Statistical Report by Lieutenant T.C. Robe,
April 1833

NATURAL STATE

Name

Archdall (*Monasticon*), speaking of Rath-murbuilg, says, "Probably this is Magherchill, 3 miles south west of Ballymenagh." By this he clearly means what is generally known by the name of Ahoghill. In the ecclesiastical annals of the diocese of Connor, published in Lock's *Ecclesiastical Register*, it is stated that the rectory of Hoonhohill, alias Magherahowel, situated in the territory of Killultagh in the Claneboy district, belonged to the Priory of St John of Jerusalem. Colgan calls it Achadh-na-coille i e. "the field of the church" and Magerahill would have the same meaning (Machaire-chille). It is still frequently called Magherahoghill by the inhabitants. Another derivative gives *Achadh Thuathail* i.e. campulus Tuathalli "Toole's field."

Situation

It is situated about the middle of the west side of the county of Antrim, adjacent to the River Bann, and extending eastwards from thence to the town of Ballymena, the principal part of it being in the barony of Lower Toome, but comprising likewise part of the baronies of Upper Toome, Kilconway and Lower Antrim.

It is a rectory of the diocese of Connor, in the gift of the Crown. 21 townlands, situated on the side of the range of hills sloping towards the Bann, were on the 7th September 1825, by virtue of an act of parliament 11th and 12th of George III, created into a perpetual curacy for the exercise of ministerial duties; it is called the curacy of Portglenone. The curate receives his salary from the rector. Except for ministerial duties and the provision of things necessary for divine service, the parish of Ahoghill remains entire.

Boundaries and Extent

It is bounded on the north by the parish of Rasharkin and grange of Dundermot, the latter only for a very small extent at the north east corner; on the east by the parishes of Kirkinriola and Ballyclug; on the south by the parishes of Connor and Drummaul, and the grange of Ballyscullion <Ballyscullen>. On the west it is bounded by the River Bann, which separates it from the county of Londonderry.

It extends from east to west from Ballymena to the River Bann about 8 British miles and from north to south 7 miles. The parish contains 35,288 British statute acres.

Divisions

Ecclesiastically it is divided into 2 parts, viz. the parish of Ahoghill properly so called, and the curacy of Portglenone, the line of division being the summit of the elevated ridge which runs through the parish from north to south, the eastern side being the parish of Ahoghill. For civil purposes it is divided into 73 townlands, 1 of which is in the barony of Kilconway, 1 in that of Lower Antrim, 6 in Upper Toome and the remainder in Lower Toome. In the ecclesiastical division, 21 townlands are in the parish of Portglenone and the remainder in Ahoghill.

NATURAL FEATURES AND NATURAL HISTORY

Surface and Soil

An elevated ridge traverses the parish from north to south, at about one-third of its breadth from the Bann. The Main river also runs through it parallel to this ridge and about half-way between it and the eastern boundary of the parish, thus dividing it into 3 portions. There is nothing particularly striking in the appearance of the hills, the greatest elevation of which is at Tully between Ahoghill and Portglenone, the height of which is only 660 feet.

The soil is in general light and unfit for growing wheat. The general crops are potatoes, flax and oats. In the townland of Ballykennedy an individual has very successfully cultivated camomile.

Turbary is very abundant in detached patches throughout the parish. In many places it is of a very good quality.

Rocks

The only description of rock is basalt, which crops out in numerous places on the west slope of the central ridge. On the east side the declivity is less and consequently the rocks are not as frequently exposed to view, but their nature is the same wherever they occur. The stone is quarried for the ordinary purposes of building and of road making. There is a good quarry for building-stone near Ballymena.

MODERN TOPOGRAPHY

Towns and Villages: Ahoghill

The village of Ahoghill is a very small insignificant place, situated a little to the south of the centre of the parish. It has a small market once a month and 3 fairs annually. A manor court is held here once a month by appointment from the Lord Bishop of Down and Connor; its jurisdiction extends only to 2 pounds. Here is the parish church, a Presbyterian meeting house, 2 Seceding meeting houses and a Roman Catholic chapel, which last is a fair distance to the south of the village.

Portglenone

Portglenone is a much more considerable town, situated on the Bann, over which there is a stone bridge of 7 arches. It has a weekly market on Tuesdays and a fair on the first Monday in every month. A manor court is held here once a month for the manor of Cashel, by appointment from Lord O'Neill. Its jurisdiction extends to 20 pounds British.

Close to the south of the town is a good house with extensive plantations about it, the property of the Bishop of Down and Connor, at present occupied by his son the Revd Archdeacon Alexander.

There is a good school on Erasmus Smith's foundation. It has a chapel of ease or curacy church, a Presbyterian meeting house and a Roman Catholic chapel. The last is about half a mile

south of the town, on the road to Randalstown <Randliston>.

Galgorm and Cullybackey

Galgorm, a long straggling village about 2 miles from Ballymena, on the road to Ahoghill. It is only remarkable for its castle, an antiquated looking building, a residence of the Earl of Mountcashel, but seldom occupied by him. It was built by a Dr Colville about the year 1696, whose daughter married an ancestor of Lord Mountcashel. The castle appears to have been built partly in imitation of an ancient defensible residence. The walls of the court exhibit a rude attempt at bastioned fronts but the greater part of the front enclosure has been removed, and that in the rear is as much encumbered with offices as to render it difficult to discern the original design. On the right hand side of the approach to the house are the ruins of a small chapel. Its appearance presents nothing remarkable.

A court for the manor of Straboy alias Fortescue is held at Galgorm once a month, by appointment from Lord Mountcashel. Its jurisdiction is to the extent of 4 pounds 6s 8d.

There is also a court held in Ballymena for the manor of the same name, which is partly in Ahoghill. Its jurisdiction is only 2 pounds. W. Adair Esquire is the lord of the manor.

Cullybackey is a small village on the left bank of the River Main, over which there is a stone bridge. It has neither fairs nor markets. There are 2 Presbyterian meeting houses here.

Moravians at Gracehill

Gracehill <Grace Hill>: this is a Moravian settlement, situated on the right bank of the Main river,

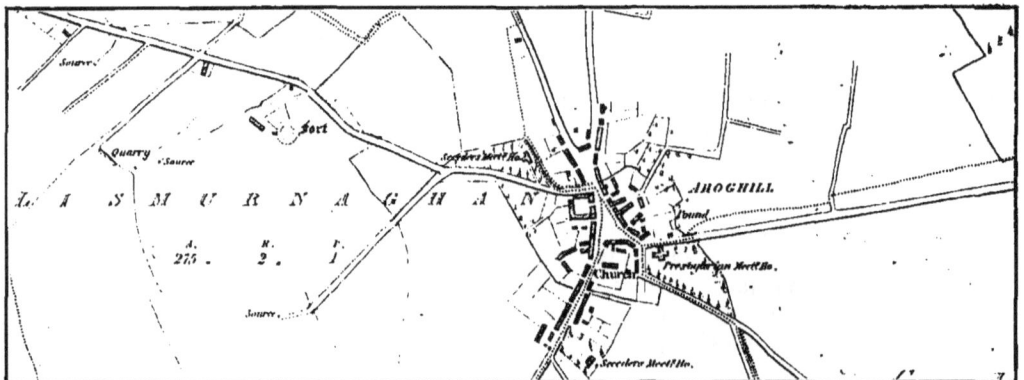

Map of Ahoghill from the first 6" O.S. maps, 1830s

in the townland of Ballykennedy. It was established in 1755. The number of the community is about 700, of whom nearly 300 reside at the settlement. The principal buildings form 3 sides of a square, the centre of the principal side being the church, having at either end, under the same roof, houses for the minister and warden. To the north of the church, in the same line with it, is the house for the single sisters, whose time is chiefly occupied in ornamental needlework, the deservedly high reputation of which always commands a ready sale. The corresponding building is an academy for boys, which is very well conducted under the superintendence of a clergyman of their own persuasion. The other buildings in the square are a boarding school for girls, an inn, a house for the single brethren where a savings bank is open once a week, and a shop. The houses for the rest of the community are disposed in 2 streets in the production of the sides of the square.

The members, with the exception of the clergy, are chiefly mechanics, and are remarkable for their quiet orderly behaviour and industrious habits. Of the society itself, it is sufficient in this place to say that it is an episcopal church, professing the Lutheran doctrine, differing very little from the Established Church except in the form of the liturgy. A very erroneous, but exceedingly general opinion, has prevailed that Moravians profess all things in common and that the produce of their labour is all put into a general stock. This is by no means the case: the estate is the property of the community, the warden being the manager of it, but each occupier, whether of house or land, pays rent as in ordinary cases, and the produce is entirely his own. The income of the community is applied to the repairs of the buildings, the support of the clergy and of the poor, and for missionary purposes.

Manufactures

The only manufacture carried on is linen, which is made in the houses of the peasantry. The Main river affords an abundant supply of water for the purposes of bleach greens and, as may be supposed, there are several along its banks. A very large establishment of this sort has been lately erected at Lisnafillon near Gracehill.

Roads

The communications are very numerous and generally good, of which the principal are: the mail road from Belfast to Coleraine, the western one from Ballymena to Ballymoney, that from Randalstown to Coleraine by Ahoghill and that between the same places by Portglenone. These 4 roads run from south to north. In the cross direction there are roads from Ballymena to Toome Bridge and to Portglenone, and very numerous cross ones.

NATURAL FEATURES

Rivers, Bogs and Woods

The Bann skirts the parish on the west. It is navigable for boats but only for short distances. The Main river which traverses the parish is not navigable.

There are several large bogs in different parts of the parish.

The woods round the Bishop of Down's house at Portglenone are the only ones of any extent.

SOCIAL ECONOMY

Population

The population is about 20,000, chiefly the descendants of Scottish settlers.

ANCIENT TOPOGRAPHY

Antiquities

There are no antiquities worthy of note, except the numerous mounds or forts and the castle of Galgorm already mentioned. [Signed] T.C. Robe, Lieutenant Royal Engineers, 18th April 1833.

Memoir by James Boyle, October 1835

NATURAL FEATURES

Hills

The Killymurrys ridge, extending from the parish of Ballymoney to Lough Neagh, traverses the western side of the parish from north to south, and parallel to the River Bann. This does not present a striking appearance, being neither bold in its formation nor exceeding 660 feet in height above the level of the sea. It is also but partially cultivated and its aspect, particularly towards its summit and on its western side, is bare and desolate.

The highest point is Tully hill, in the townland of Slieveanagh and about 2 miles south east of Portglenone. Its summit is, towards the south of the parish, much diversified by numerous minor features. The fall eastward is more gradual and smooth than towards the west, where it is abrupt, broken and in many places rocky, from the outbreaking of the basalt. It finally terminates in numerous beautifully undulating and parallel little ridges or features, becoming gradually lower as they approach the Bann. On the east side its descent terminates at the Main river, and on this side the ground is also towards its base somewhat broken. The average elevation of this ridge above the sea is 520 feet and above the Bann 470 feet.

The ground along the eastern side of the parish is a low ridge, not exceeding an average elevation of 350 feet above the level of the sea, and from this it undulates gently towards the Main river on its western side, the average elevation of which in this parish is 176 feet above the level of the sea.

The principal points in this parish are Tully, 660 feet, Black hill, 513 feet (on the Killymurrys ridge) and Fenagh Hillhead, 456 feet, and Crank hill, 413 feet above the level of the sea, on the east side of the parish.

Lakes and Rivers: The Bann

There are no lakes in this parish. The principal rivers in this parish are the Bann, the Main, the Braid and the Clogh.

The Bann, which flows for 7 and a third miles along the western boundary of this parish, forming the boundary between the counties of Antrim and Londonderry, flows from the southern extremity of Lough Beg, which is [blank] miles distant from its mouth and 47 feet above the level of the sea at low water. The southern extremity of Lough Beg is also within 500 yards of the north west extremity of this parish. After flowing for [blank] miles in a northerly direction, forming a part of the boundary between the counties of Antrim and Londonderry, and passing by the town of Portglenone and through that of Coleraine, it discharges itself into the sea within the tideway, [blank] miles north of the latter town and after an entire course of [blank] miles.

In its course along this parish it is navigable for boats of 60 tons burthen and drawing from 5 to 6 feet of water; and much of the heavy goods, such as timber, iron, coals, slates, received at Portglenone are brought down it in lighters. It is usefully situated for navigation, but might be rendered much more valuable, as all the merchandise consumed in the neighbourhood might be brought by water from Belfast, there being a canal from that town to Lough Neagh, which is united to Lough Beg. It is not usefully situated for machinery, there not being sufficient fall, as also from the ground along it being low and frequently inundated. It is usefully situated for irrigation and drainage, and by its inundations, which are

frequent and in winter continue for some days, it enriches the flooded country. It subsides of itself. No deposit of any consequence, except a sort of slime which is rather beneficial, is made by it.

Its extreme breadth is 350 feet, least breadth 176 feet and average breadth 210 feet. Its greatest ordinary depth is 25 feet (this is towards its source). Its shallowest part in the channel is 3 and a half feet and its average depth in the summer 7 feet. Its average velocity or fall is not more than 1 foot in its course along this parish. It neither facilitates nor impedes communication. Its bed is soft and clayey, its banks very low and the scenery along them, except at Portglenone, bleak and uninteresting, the ground being flat, boggy and marshy.

Main River

The Main takes its rise in the parish of Killagan, at an elevation of 290 feet above the level of the sea and, pursuing a southerly course for 4 miles, it enters the northern side of this parish, through which it flows for 7 and a half miles, and descends to a level of 108 feet. It finally, after an entire and southerly course of 35 miles, discharges itself into Lough Neagh, 1 and three-quarter miles south of the town of Randalstown, through which it flows. Its height above the sea on entering this parish is 263 feet and its average fall is 1 foot in 258 feet.

Its course is a little broken by a ledge of rock which intersects it at Dunminning, near the northern extremity of the parish, and also by several artificial carriers for the purpose of turning off water for machinery, but the fall produced by any natural interruption is inconsiderable. That at Dunminning causes a sufficient fall of water to propel the machinery in that neighbourhood, which would otherwise be wanting. A carry is erected on this ledge and, though it is necessary for the purposes of machinery, it is the cause of serious injury to the lands along the banks of the river near its source (see Rivers, grange of Dundermot).

This river is subject to frequent and sudden floods, which do mischief to the lands in this parish north of the carry just mentioned, but during the rest of its course they are harmless, there being sufficient fall to carry off the water. Its bed is rocky, stony and gravelly towards the north of the parish, but soft towards the south. Its average breadth is 36 feet and average ordinary depth 2 feet 6 inches. It is very usefully situated and valuable for machinery, drainage and irrigation. In its course through the parish it propels the machinery of 8 bleach greens. Its banks are for the most part high and the scenery along them is pleasing and interesting, the ground being much diversified and chiefly planted. It neither facilitates nor impedes communication.

Clogh River

The Clogh river, which takes its rise in the mountains in the parishes of Ardclinis and Skerry, at an elevation of about 1,200 feet above the level of the sea, flows westerly for 1 mile along the northern boundary of this parish and discharges itself into the Main at an elevation of 263 feet above the sea. Its average fall in this parish is about 1 foot in 400 feet, its average breadth 17 feet and average ordinary depth 2 and a half feet. Its bed is soft and its banks low. It frequently overflows them, being subject to high and sudden floods; and from the check given to the discharge of its waters by its flowing at right-angles into the Main, and the trifling fall of these rivers, it does considerable injury to the level grounds along its banks and requires some time to subside. From its inconsiderable fall, it is not, in this parish, usefully situated for machinery, drainage or irrigation.

Braid River

The Braid river takes its rise in the mountains in the parish of Tickmacrevan and, after a south westerly course, enters on the southern boundary of this parish, at which point it is about 140 feet above the sea; and after flowing westerly for 2 and a third miles, it discharges itself into the Main, at a distance of 10 miles from its mouth and at an elevation of 110 feet above the level of the sea. Its average fall in this parish is 1 foot in 210 feet, its average breadth 57 feet and average natural depth 3 feet. From the height and number of its sources it rises rapidly and frequently, but does not, in this parish, do any injury. It is usefully situated for machinery, drainage and irrigation. Its bed is gravelly and its banks low. It does not tend to impede or facilitate communication.

This parish is amply supplied with soft spring water for domestic uses. It abounds, particularly in the hills, with springs. There are not any hot or mineral springs in the parish.

Bogs

The bogs in this parish extend over a considerable portion of its surface, and are to be found at elevations of from 60 to 600 feet above the sea and 10 to 560 above the River Bann. The bogs in the hills are less cut than those in the lower parts of the parish. Their substratum is usually either rock or blue clay, and their depth varies from 7 to 18 feet. They seem to be growing, as the bog near the surface is very soft and spongy, and the fir timber with which they abound is invariably nearer the bottom than the surface. In the mountains there is usually only 1 layer of stumps, though a few instances of 2, one standing on the other, have occurred. The stumps are very large, stand upright, and mostly seem to have been burnt or subjected to fire, as a sort of charcoal is found on them. Very few trunks are found, and those which are, lie indiscriminately. The stumps and trunks are of the finest description of pine timber, being very hard and close grained. Very little oak is found in the mountains.

In some parts of the lower grounds, particularly along the River Bann, some of the bogs are nearly cut out. Their subsoil is a sort of tough whitish clay, such as bricks are made of. In this, oak blocks are firmly and thickly imbedded, and sometimes to a depth of 6 feet; and on the surface, as well as sometimes in the clay, oak trunks lie indiscriminately and in considerable numbers. They appear to have been broken down at the same height, and on one occasion, where the bog had been cut away, a stump was discovered which bore evident marks of having been hagged [hacked]. The nearer the Bann, the timber is whiter and of a superior and valuable description (see Woods).

Very little fir is found on the subsoil or in the cut-out bog, but in those which have only been partially cut, fir and a little beech and sallow are found, the first in considerable quantities. Some of these bogs are 15 feet deep. They seem to be growing, as the timber is at a considerable depth. Very few trunks of fir are found. The stumps are broken at the same height and stand upright. There is seldom more than 1 layer, and the trees have probably averaged 16 inches in diameter at the butt.

Woods

The tradition that "a man could have walked on the trees along the Bann from Coleraine to Toome" is borne out by the great quantity of oak, hazel, ash, birch, alder and holly brushwood still remaining in this parish. There is scarce a townland in which there is not some underwood, but there is more of [it] on the western side and along the Bann than in the other parts of the parish. It is very low and cattle are allowed to graze in it. Hazel principally abounds and holly is only found in the rocky districts.

Another evidence of the former existence of

woods in this parish is the circumstance of oak blocks or stumps being found imbedded in the banks and bed of the Bann, and also at depths of from 1 to 6 feet in the whitish clay in its vicinity. Some of these stumps are upright and a few of them inclined. A few trunks are found. They are said to be from 14 inches to 2 feet in diameter. They lie indiscriminately, do not always occupy the same plane with the stumps, and seem to have been broken down. Their timber is white and sound, and of an excellent quality. There is not now any natural timber or wood, except the brushwood growing in the parish.

Climate

The south and south west winds, particularly the latter, prevail in this parish, the former blowing for nearly 9 months in the year. [Insert marginal note: This is contradictory]. To these winds, which are usually followed by rain, the western side of the parish is very much exposed, as may be seen by the stunted appearance of the trees exposed to it and their invariable inclination to the north east. There is but little protection from hedgerows, and the cabins are usually hid in the gorges or behind the little hills. The west side of the parish is also, from its proximity to the Bann and its uncultivated state, very subject to rain and fogs. Sowing in this side commences in March and potato setting continues during the month of May. Harvest commences in the beginning of September and is generally over by the first week in October. Potato digging commences about the end of October and is finished by the end of November.

On the eastern side of the parish the climate is much earlier and the air purer, particularly towards the south and along the Main. It is protected from the winds to which the west side is exposed by the high ridge which traverses the centre of the parish and, owing to its more cultivated state, it is comparatively free from fogs and less subject to rain. The crops are therefore earlier. Sowing commences a fortnight sooner and the harvest 3 weeks earlier than on the western side.

Modern Topography

Towns: Portglenone

This parish contains the town of Portglenone and the villages of Ahoghill, Gracehill, Cullybackey and Galgorm.

Portglenone is 129 and a half miles north of Dublin and 9 miles west of Ballymena. It is situated in the diocese of Down and Connor, province of Ulster, parish of Ahoghill and north east circuit of assize. It is seated on the River Bann which flows by the town, and near the bridge over that river, which forms the communication between the counties of Antrim and Derry. Its extreme length is 560 yards and breadth 150 yards. It is pleasantly situated at the base of a hilly ridge which traverses the parish parallel to the river, and there is a considerable quantity of planting extending for some distance along the latter and almost encompassing the town.

History

Origin of Portglenone

Portglenone owes its origin to a castle which was erected by Queen Elizabeth in the year 1572, close to the present town, on the edge of the Bann and near a ferry which was formerly on that river. This castle was for the purpose of acting as a check on Phelim O'Neill and curtailing his then increasing territories and power. It was garrisoned by 44 soldiers under a Captain Stafford, who remained in it until the colonisation of the country by the English, which soon after commenced. 14 townlands were given to Captain Stafford for his services, and many of his soldiers preferred remaining in the country to returning to England. Houses for the accommodation of soldiers were built about the castle and the inhabitants of the country soon began to build there also, and from this the origins of the town may be dated.

On the 6th of April 1687 Portglenone was set on fire and burnt by the red hot balls fired from the castle in the advanced guard of King James' army which came this way from Dungannon, on going to besiege the city of Derry. The action continued to the next day, when the Protestants were defeated and about 150 killed on each side. The Protestants were commanded by Sir Arthur Rawdon and the Irish by Gordon O'Neill.

Portglenone was soon after rebuilt, but on the country being subdued and colonised by the Presbyterians, the English having fled from it to the castles in the county of Derry, which took place between 1618 and 1621, the castle was suffered to fall into decay and finally dismantled 15 years after the battle of the Boyne. The foundations can now with difficulty be traced.

Modern Topography

Streets and Houses

Portglenone consists of an oblong square [blank] yards long and [blank] yards wide, and from this 2 small streets extend, one at each extremity. It

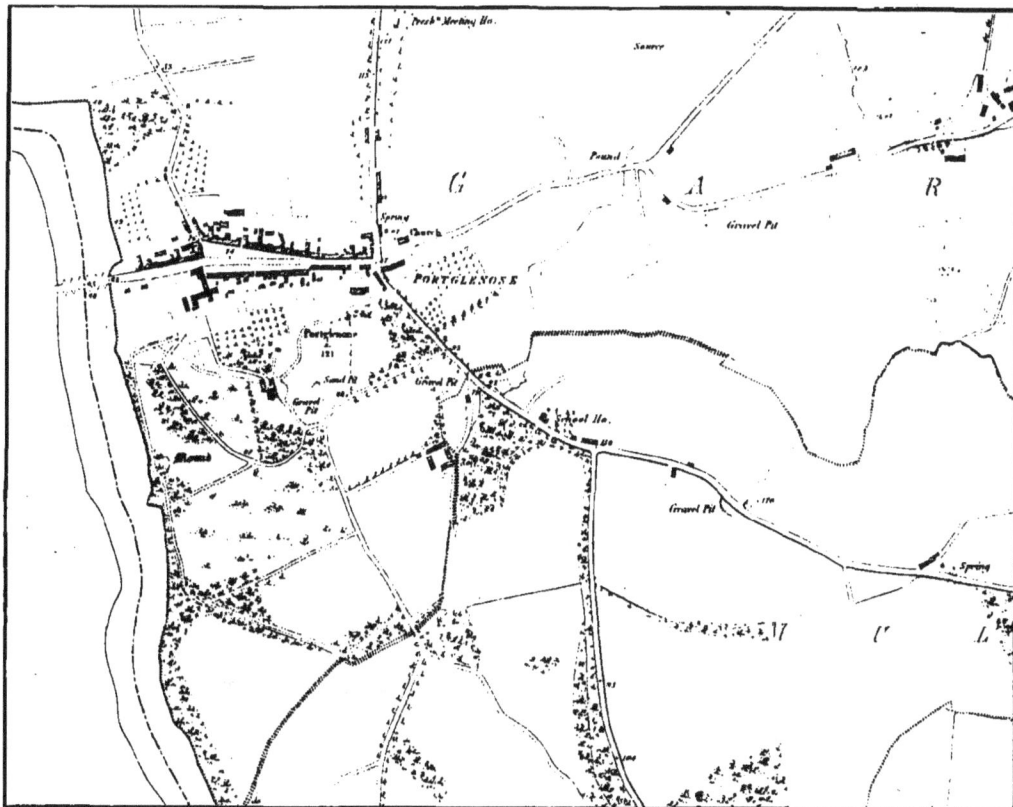

Map of Portglenone from the first 6" O.S. maps, 1830s

contains 138 houses, of which 4 are 3-storeys high, 73 2-storey and 61 1-storey high. They are all built of stone and mostly thatched. There is little regard paid to neatness or uniformity in their erection, and though there are some comfortable 2-storey houses, their want of uniformity takes away from their appearance. They are mostly also occupied by persons in business. The 1-storey cabins are in general of a wretched description, all thatched, and filthy and comfortless in their appearance. They are mostly occupied by labourers or tradesmen. The streets are dirty, though from their slope they might be easily kept clean (see tolls and rates).

A few houses have been lately built near the centre of the town. They are 2-storey and suited for persons in business.

Public Buildings

The public buildings consist of: the church, which stands at the eastern end of the town. It is a plain old building without tower, steeple or any ornament. It is 57 feet long, 21 feet wide, contains 21 seats and would accommodate 150 persons. It

was built about the year 1761 and is in but middling repair.

The Presbyterian meeting house, which stands near the east end of the town, is a rude old building which was erected about the same time as the church. It is 96 feet long by 27 wide, has a large gallery, and would accommodate about 1,500 persons.

The Ebenezer Methodist chapel is nearly opposite the Presbyterian meeting house. It is a simple little brick house, neatly finished but without pews. It is 35 feet long, 20 feet wide and would accommodate about 100 persons. It was built by subscription in 1834 and cost 120 pounds.

The court house was built about the year 1795 by Lord O'Neill, for the purpose of holding manor courts in. Petty sessions are also held in it every second Tuesday [insert marginal correction: Wednesday]. It is a plain low building 40 feet long and 22 feet wide. It is also used as a schoolhouse.

There is a 2-storey house near the centre of the town, fitted up as a police barrack. It affords accommodation for 16 men.

The bridge over the Bann consists of 7 semicircular arches. Its length across or over the water-way is 246 feet and its breadth within the parapets 22 feet. It is a perfectly plain structure and is in tolerable repair. It was built about 36 years ago.

There are 2 self-termed hotels, but more properly inns, which afford tolerable accommodation.

SOCIAL AND PRODUCTIVE ECONOMY

Population

Portglenone contains 773 inhabitants, of whom about 121 are engaged in dealing or business, 37 as tradesmen or mechanics and the remainder of the adult population as servants or labourers (see Table of Trades and Occupations). They are in general sober, peaceable and industrious. There are not any private gentlemen, and they are all of the middle or lower class. They are generally considered moral and economical in their habits.

Library

There is a library under the Sunday School Society, containing about 300 volumes of useful works, to which there are many subscribers in the town and its vicinity; and there is also a small religious lending library, chiefly containing religious tracts. They are no doubt calculated to improve the moral habits of the people and it is considered they will do so.

Markets and Fairs

A weekly market is held on Tuesdays for the sale of meal, yarn, potatoes, flax etc., which articles are not exposed in any great quantity and the market is small.

A market is held on every second Tuesday for the sale of linen and the articles before mentioned. This market was established about 40 years ago and flourished until of late years, when it commenced decline and is now very trifling, not more than 100 webs being now brought to each market, while formerly there were commonly 2,000. This is owing to its proximity to Ballymena and Kilrea, as the weavers preferred going to the former market; and those who give out mill-spun yarn to the manufacturers in the country live chiefly in that town, and those who are near Kilrea, and too far from Ballymena, take their linen to the former place.

A fair is held in Portglenone on the first Tuesday in every month. All kinds of cattle, except horses, are exposed for sale, but not in any great numbers. The spring and winter fairs are considered the largest. Some black cattle and pigs are bought up by dealers for exportation. The farmers

bring their farm produce to market in their own carts and cars. No tolls or customs are levied. They formerly were, but have been for some years abolished.

Supply of Goods

Portglenone is not very well supplied with butcher's meat, particularly in spring. This loss is little felt, there being few who regularly use fresh meat. There is a tolerable supply of poultry, milk, butter, eggs and fruit, but little or no vegetables. Very few cattle are stall fed or grazed (except for milk) about the town. There is no market gardening and ground for pasture usually lets at from 2 pounds to 3 pounds per acre.

Building Materials

Pine is the timber mostly used. It is brought by water from Belfast. It costs there about 3 pounds per ton and its carriage about 7s 6d per ton. Stone (whinstone) abounds everywhere about the town. Bricks are made in its vicinity and cost from 6s 6d to 10s per thousand. Lime is brought from the county Derry and when laid down stands on average 1s 2d per barrel. Slates are brought from Belfast by water and cost when laid down 4 pounds 17s 6d a thousand. Countesses are the kind used.

Insurances and Conveyances

There are neither fire nor life insurances. There are no coaches. A car conveying 4 passengers leaves Portglenone every Saturday morning for Ballymena market and returns in the evening. The fare for going and returning is 1s 6d for each passenger.

Carriage of Goods

There are 4 regular carriers to Belfast, each having 2 carts and horses. They leave Portglenone on Thursdays and return on Monday; the charges per cwt is 1s 5d. Timber, iron, coals are brought by water from Belfast. Previous to the canal being cut from Belfast to Lough Neagh, these articles were brought by water from Newry. The lighters which bring these articles are from 40 to 60 tons burthen, and in fair weather can perform the trip there and back in 4 days. The usual charge is 7s 6d per ton.

General Remarks

There are no hospitals or dispensaries. There are no endowed schools nor provisions for the poor.

The people are not of the class prone to amusement. There are not any places of public amusement.

7 post cars are kept for hire; 8d per Irish mile is the charge.

The people are obliging and civil and hospitable so far as in their power.

Progress of Improvement

So far as the appearance of the houses goes, the town is improving, but in commerce it is not. Ballymena absorbs the trade of the surrounding country and Portglenone is too near it to thrive. Its main support was the linen markets and fairs held in it. The reasons for the decline of the former has been stated, and the cause of the latter declining was the dreadful party riots which latterly occurred at them, waylaying being carried on to a great extent; and many respectable persons being beaten, others were deterred from attending the fairs.

Another injury to the business of Portglenone is the number of little villages and clusters of cottages throughout the country. Each of these now possesses at least 1 grocery and 1 spirit shop, which a few years ago were only found in the towns. The reduction in the price of licences is the cause of these, and those who formerly had to go some distance to town can now procure their necessaries nearer home. These little shops have taken away considerably from the business of the towns.

MODERN TOPOGRAPHY

Ahoghill

The village of Ahoghill is situated near the southern side of the parish, on the main road from Randalstown to Ballymoney. It is 137 miles north of Dublin and 4 miles south west of Ballymena. The situation of the town is in a slight hollow on the east side of the Killymurrys hills, at an elevation of 220 feet above the sea. There is nothing interesting in its appearance, nor that of its immediate neighbourhood, and on the contrary the town is irregular and dirty, and most of the houses of an inferior and comfortless description.

Ahoghill consists of 1 principal and 1 smaller street. The former is 330 yards in length, of a tolerable width, but crooked and dirty. It contains 90 houses, of which 18 are 2-storey and the remainder 1-storey cabins. All are built of stone and mostly all thatched. There are not more than half a dozen good houses in the village. The 1-storey cabins are bad and in very middling repair.

They are occupied by labourers and the 2-storey by people in business (see Table of Trades and Occupations). It is said Ahoghill was built soon after the battle of the Boyne, but it is not [known ?] as to what determined its site.

Ahoghill formerly possessed an excellent monthly linen market, which has been given up about 5 years ago, partly from the decline in the linen trade at that time, and what remains of it was absorbed into Ballymena.

3 annual fairs are held in it on the following days: 4th June, 26th August and 8th October. Horses and cattle of all kinds are sold in these fairs, in tolerable numbers. A few pigs and black cattle are bought up for exportation by dealers. The tolls paid are 6d for every entire horse, 3d for every horse, 2d for every cow, 1d for every sheep, goat and pig.

Ahoghill is not improving, but rather the reverse, nor are there any new houses building.

Public Buildings

The public buildings in the village are: the parish church, which was built many years ago. It was raised and roofed in the year 1828. It is perfectly plain, without tower or any ornament, except a little wooden cupola on the top of the western gable, from which is suspended a bell. It is 51 feet long, 24 feet wide and would accommodate about 186 persons.

The Presbyterian meeting house stands on the eastern side of the town. It is a clumsy old building in the form of a cross, the extreme dimensions of which are 62 feet by 72 feet. It was rebuilt in 1762. It has a spacious gallery and would accommodate 1,000 persons.

The first Seceders' meeting house stands at the southern extremity of the village. It is a plain substantial building 50 feet long by 36 feet wide and capable of accommodating 400 persons. It was rebuilt in 1806.

The other Seceders' meeting house stands on the northern side of the town. It is a plain building, the extreme dimensions of which are 60 feet by 44 feet. It was built in 1796. It might accommodate 800 persons.

These houses are all comfortably fitted up internally.

Gracehill

The pretty village of Gracehill is situated in the townland of Ballykennedy, near the south east side of the parish and on the main road from Ballymena to Portglenone. It is 3 miles west of the former and 7 and a third miles west of the latter of these towns. The Main river also flows at a short distance from the village. Gracehill is prettily situated in a fertile part of the country, and the planting in which the village is almost secluded adds considerably to the surrounding scenery.

It owes its origin to a Moravian settlement which took place in this townland in the year 1755, when a lease of it of lives renewable forever was obtained at a reasonable rent from the late Earl O'Neill, by the company of joint proprietors of the community of Moravians, or United Brethren as they style themselves. Several families, principally artisans, then came over from England, and among them were several Germans and other foreigners, and the building of the village then commenced. The church and the houses on either side of it were first built, the former by subscription. The latter were intended as workshops for weavers who were set agoing in them, but one is now converted into the academy and the other into the sisters' house. Money was obtained by loan for the purpose of erecting these buildings (see Social Economy of Gracehill). The rest of the village was soon after built. It is not increasing nor decreasing.

Houses

Gracehill consists of 2 parallel rows of houses, in the centre of which is a handsome enclosed square surrounded with lofty beeches. In its centre is a pound, and a walk extends around it inside the enclosure. Its dimensions are 230 feet square and houses extend along 3 of its sides. The houses on its western side include the church, at one end of which is the boys' academy and at the other end the sisters' house. On the northern side is the ladies' boarding school and a neat hotel, and on the southern side is the savings bank and 2 other neat 2-storey houses. The high road to Toome passes along the eastern side of the square. The houses on the west are whitened but those on the other side are not roughcast, and they are all uncommonly neat and uniform. From the angles of the square little streets extend north and south parallel to each other.

Gracehill altogether contains 30 1-storey and 17 2-storey houses. The latter are comfortable and neat and are, except those mentioned, occupied by persons in business. The former are small but neat, cleanly and comfortable, and are mostly occupied by mechanics (see Table of Trades), and all bespeak industry, comfort and neatness. There is a penny post office in connection with the post office in Ballymena, and a savings bank (see Appendix).

Public Buildings

The public buildings consist of: the church, which was built by a general subscription among the Moravians in 1755. It stands on the west side of the square and is surmounted by a tasteful cupola, in which there is a clock. The church is plain but neat, 58 feet long and 34 feet wide, and has a gallery at either end. In one of these is a well-tuned organ. In the body of the house the seats are forms with backs but comfortable.

The academy is at the southern end and within a few feet of the church. It is 2-storey, 140 feet long and 34 feet wide, and contains accommodation for the master and his family, 6 ushers and 50 boarders. The rooms are airy and healthy, and the establishment kept in the nicest order.

At the northern end, and close to the church, is the sisters' house, a plain, uniform 2-storey building 80 feet long and 33 feet wide, and containing accommodation for 40 ladies and boarders, and their governess. The house was built in 1755 and converted into its present use at that time.

The ladies' boarding school stands on the north side of the square. It is a plain 2-storey house, forming 2 sides of a square and presenting a front 40 feet long and 20 feet wide, and was built in 1795. There is a nice garden attached to it.

The inn stands on the same side of the square and next the road. It is a neat 2-storey house and is comfortable and well kept. There are neat gardens and some fine orchards in the rear of the houses at Gracehill, and these, with the trees in the square and along the road, serve almost to hide it.

The inhabitants are honest, peaceable and well educated, being moral and religious, and neither minding nor interfering in anything but what tends to their improvement.

Cullybackey

The little village of Cullybackey is very prettily situated on the River Main and towards the eastern side of the parish. The ground undulates beautifully about the town. There is also some planting on the banks of the river, which are lofty and steep. It is a pity more attention was not paid to cleanliness and uniformity in the village, as there are some very tasteful and comfortable cottages in it, but as it is, it is very dirty and irregular.

It contains 42 1-storey and 9 2-storey houses, most of which are thatched, some being very neat and some the reverse. The poorer class are mostly labourers. The rest are engaged in dealing or as mechanics (see Table of Trades).

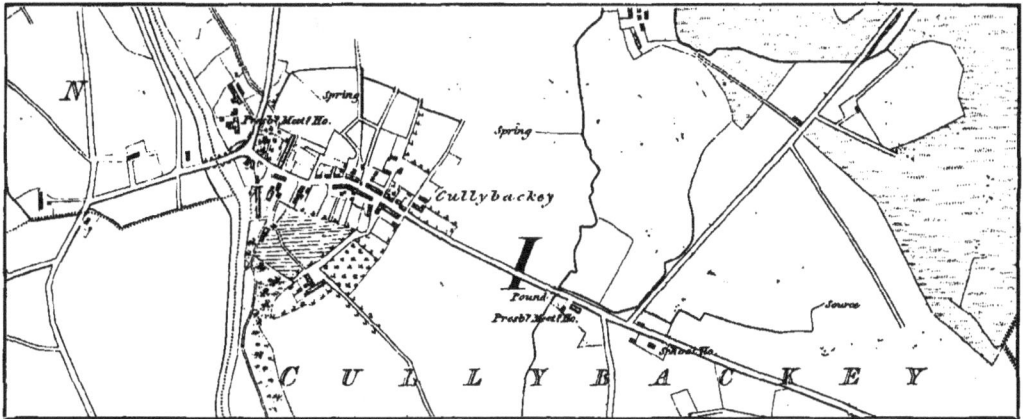

Map of Cullybackey from the first 6" O.S. maps, 1830s

Public Buildings

The public buildings consist of: the Presbyterian meeting house, which stands at the western side of the town. It is a clumsy old structure, consisting of the main aisle which is 76 feet long and 22 feet wide, and a lesser aisle at its western side which is 34 feet long and 32 feet wide. On the summit of the latter is a little belfry bell and vane. It has spacious galleries, the only access to which is by the stone staircases outside. It contains 98 seats and would accommodate 700 persons. It was erected in 1737.

The Covenanters' meeting house is near the western end of the village. It is a simple old building 51 feet long and 24 wide, and has a gallery with stone staircases outside. It contains 50 seats and would accommodate 350 persons.

The bridge over the Main is at the western end of the village. It is a plain structure 130 feet long and 30 feet wide, and consists of 7 semicircular arches.

Galgorm

The village of Galgorm is situated on the main road from Ballymena to Portglenone, 1 and a half miles west of the former and 7 and three-quarter miles east of the latter of these towns. It merely consists of a single row containing 41 1-storey and 3 2-storey houses, which extend along the road for about a third of a mile. It is a place of no importance and presents nothing interesting in its appearance.

There is neither fair nor market nor post office, and the only building is the court house which was erected in 1821 by Lord Mountcashel, the proprietor, for holding manor courts and courts leet for the recovery of debts not exceeding 4 pounds 6s

8d by civil bill, Henry Raphael, seneschal. The manor courts are held 12 times and the courts leet twice a year. They are for the manor of Straboy alias Fortescue, in which the village is situated.

The people are mostly engaged in agriculture; a few are engaged as dealers or mechanics (see Table of Trades and Occupations).

The court house is a plain, little 1-storey building 30 feet long and 18 feet wide. It is also used as a school.

Public Buildings in the Parish

The public buildings in the parish consist of the church, Presbyterian meeting house, Ebenezer chapel, court house and bridge in the town of Portglenone; the church, Presbyterian and 2 Seceding meeting houses in the village of Ahoghill; the church and academy in the village of Gracehill; the Presbyterian and Covenanter meeting houses and bridge in the village of Cullybackey; and the court house in the village of Galgorm. These buildings have been already described under the head of "Public Buildings" in the town or village in which they are situated.

The other public buildings in the parish are: the Independent meeting house, which is situated in the townland of Tullaghgarley: is a simple edifice 30 feet long and 20 feet wide, and capable of accommodating 300 persons. It was erected by subscription in 1826.

The Seceders' meeting house, which is situated in the townland of Garvaghy and within a quarter mile of the town of Portglenone, is a plain building 51 feet long and 37 feet wide; rather low but in good repair and capable of accommodating 500 persons. It was built by subscription in 1823.

The Roman Catholic chapel, which stands in the townland of Slievenagh, three-quarters of a mile south of Portglenone, is a plain building, the extreme dimensions of which are 66 feet by 20 feet. It has spacious galleries and is comfortably seated and fitted up internally. It might accommodate 1,000 persons. It was built by subscription in 1782.

The second Roman Catholic chapel is situated in the townland of Lismurnaghan and about a third of a mile south west of the village of Ahoghill. It is a plain building 58 feet long and 18 feet wide, and capable of accommodating about 800 persons. It was built by subscription in 1770.

Bridges

The bridge over the Main, on the road from Ballymena to Portglenone, is 76 feet long and 20 feet wide, and consists of 5 small semicircular arches.

The bridge over the same river, on the road from Ballymena to Rasharkin, is 140 feet long and 20 feet wide, and consists of 5 semicircular arches.

The bridge over the same river at Dunminning is 50 feet long and 19 feet wide, and consists of 3 semicircular arches.

The Glaraford bridge over the Clogh river, and on the mail coach road from Ballymena to Ballymoney, consists of 1 large circular-segment arch and is 60 feet long and 17 feet wide. This bridge is too high and narrow and is not in a very sound state. It is also at an angle of the road where there is a very awkward turn.

Gentlemen's Seats

Portglenone House, the residence of the Revd Robert Alexander, rector of the parish and son of the Bishop of Meath: it was built by the bishop in 1823. The house is modern in its construction, very spacious and 3-storeys high. It is situated on the banks of the Bann and within a third of a mile of the town of Portglenone. There is a good garden and hothouses and suitable offices at a short distance from the house. The demesne extends over about 250 acres and is for the most part walled. It is beautifully diversified and there is a considerable quantity of planting which is judiciously disposed. There are some very fine copper beeches, yews and cypresses near the house. These were planted by the celebrated Bishop Hutchinson, who was one of the bishops tried by James II and whose residence stood near the present house.

The Glebe, the residence of Revd George Kirkpatrick, curate of the parish, is a roomy,

comfortable and modern 2-storey house, situated in the Glebe townland. The view from it is extensive and there is some young planting about the house.

Mount Davis, the residence of Alexander McMannus Esquire, J.P., is a modern 2-storey house situated in the townland of Carndonaghy, about 1 mile south of the village of Cullybackey and on the Main river, the banks of which are beautifully diversified and planted. There is a good deal of ornamental planting about the house.

Fenaghy, in the townland of the same name and on the opposite side of the river from Mount Davis, is a neat 2-storey house, the residence of Mrs McMannus.

Near Fenaghy is Low Park, the seat of John Dickey Esquire. It is 1-storey and prettily situated.

Galgorm Castle, the property of Lord Mountcashel and the residence of George Joy Esquire, his agent: it has lately undergone considerable alterations and improvements, and is now rather a handsome building. It is square, 3-storey and seems to have been built in imitation of an ancient defensible residence. It was originally built in 1696 by a Dr Colville, whose neice married an ancestor of Lord Mountcashel, by which means the castle and estate came into the Mountcashel family (see notes, appendix). The castle is rather too near the road and the lawn is therefore confined. It is 1 and a half miles west of Ballymena.

Hillmount, the residence of Robert Young Esquire, is seated on the banks of the Main, in the townland of Craigs. The house is 2-storey.

Ballybollen, the seat of Ambrose O'Rourke Esquire, is situated in the townland of the same name, at the southern extremity of the parish.

Lisnafillon, the seat of William Beggs Esquire, is situated in the townland of the same name, 2 miles west of Ballymena and near the village of Gracehill. The house is 2-storeys.

Gloonan Cottage, the seat of Alexander O'Hara Esquire, J.P., is situated in the townland of Killane and half a mile north east of the village of Ahoghill.

Hillhead, the residence of William Gihon Esquire, J.P., is situated in the townland of Brocklamont, one-third of a mile west of Ballymena. The house is 2-storey and is prettily situated on a rising ground. There is also a good deal of planting and shrubbery about it.

Mount Pleasant, the residence of the Revd Alexander Houston, is situated in the same townland. The house is comfortable and 2-storey.

Leghinmore, the residence of John Dickey

Esquire, is also situated in the same townland, half a mile south of the town of Ballymena. The house is 2-storey.

Dromona, the residence of William Cunningham, is situated on the River Main, in the townland of Moylarg.

Bleach Greens

There are 9 bleach greens in this parish, 8 of which are on the River Main.

Leghinmore bleach green extends over 13 acres 2 roods. Its machinery, which is situated on the Braid river, is propelled by 2 water wheels, one of which is 15 feet in diameter and 3 feet 6 inches broad and is driven by undershot water; the second is 14 feet in diameter, 2 feet broad and is driven by undershot water.

The other mills are on the Main river. The first (towards the north) is Gruba mill, which is propelled by an overshot water wheel 44 feet in diameter and 3 feet 6 inches broad. The bleach field extends over 20 acres 1 perch.

The machinery of Fanaghy mills is propelled by 3 undershot water wheels. One of these is 16 feet in diameter and 5 feet broad; the second is 11 feet in diameter and 4 feet broad; and the third 10 feet in diameter and 10 feet 4 inches broad.

The machinery of Craigs beetling mill is propelled by an undershot water wheel 18 feet in diameter and 8 feet 4 inches broad.

The machinery of Lower Craigs mill is propelled by an undershot water wheel 14 feet in diameter and 5 feet broad.

The machinery of Hillmount bleach green is propelled by 3 undershot water wheels. One is 18 feet in diameter and 5 feet broad; the second is 14 feet in diameter and 5 feet 10 inches broad; and the third 12 feet in diameter and 4 feet broad. The bleach field extends over 14 acres 1 rood.

The machinery of Cullybackey bleach green is propelled by 4 breast water wheels. 3 of them are 16 feet in diameter and 4 feet 6 inches broad, and the fourth 13 feet in diameter and 2 feet broad. The bleach field extends over 2 acres 2 roods 24 perches.

The machinery of Low Park beetling mills (the oldest on the river, having been built about the year 1760) is propelled by 2 undershot water wheels. One 16 feet in diameter and 5 feet broad, the other 16 feet diameter and 13 feet broad.

The machinery of Lisnafillon bleach green is propelled by 3 breast water wheels, having a fall of water of 12 feet. 2 of them are 18 feet in diameter and 6 feet broad, the third is 15 feet in diameter and 6 feet broad. The house containing

the machinery is 260 feet long and 32 feet wide, and the bleach field extends over 39 acres.

Mills

There are 7 corn mills and 4 flax mills in this parish.

Corn mills: Cullybackey townland, undershot wheel 14 feet by 3 feet.

Straid townland, breast water wheel 13 feet by 2 feet.

Gortgole townland, overshot water wheel 14 feet by 2 feet.

Bracknamuckley townland, breast water wheel 14 feet by 2 feet.

Drumranklin townland, breast water wheel 13 feet by 2 feet.

Camdonaghy townland, breast water wheel 14 feet by 2 feet.

Carnearny's townland, breast water wheel 13 feet by 3 feet.

Flax mills: Carnearny's townland, breast water wheel 13 feet by 2 feet.

Straid townland, breast water wheel 13 feet by 2 feet.

Gortgole townland, undershot wheel 13 feet by 1 foot 10 inches.

Aughnacleagh townland, breast water wheel 13 feet by 1 foot 10 inches.

There is 1 small brickfield along the Bann, in the townland of Killygarn.

Communications

There is scarce a road in the parish the direction of which might not be much improved, as, though many of them are circuitous, it is not for the purpose of avoiding hills. The Killymurrys ridge, which traverses the centre of the parish, necessarily renders the roads over it very hilly, but they might be rendered much less so. The main roads are in general in but middling order, being rough as hilly roads generally are, from the winter torrents, which generally find their way down them, acquiring increased velocity as they proceed. The materials commonly used are whinstone, greenstone and the softer kinds of basalt, all of which are abundant. Unfortunately the latter is too frequently used, probably from a mistaken motive of public economy, or a dishonest one of private gain on the part of the contractor. The roads through the bogs are among the best, if not the best, in the parish, as they are nearly level and mostly well drained, from the bog along their sides being cut away.

The principal main roads are: the mail coach

road from Ballymena to Ballymoney, of which there are 4 and a half miles in the parish. It is rather level and is kept in tolerable repair at the expense of the county. Its average breadth is 24 feet.

The road from Ballymena to Portglenone, which is wretchedly hilly and much of it in very bad order: its direction might be much improved and a good line of road would be of significant service, owing [to] the constant communication between these towns and to which the present road offers a formidable barrier. There are 8 and a half miles of this road.

The road from Randalstown through Portglenone to Rasharkin, which traverses the western side of this parish for 7 and a quarter miles: this road is hilly and not in good repair. Its direction as to avoiding the hills might be much improved.

9 miles of the road from Randalstown to Kilrea through Ahoghill and Rasharkin village pass through the centre of the parish. This road is hilly and in bad order. Its direction might be improved.

4 miles of the road from Portglenone to Cushendall pass through the northern side of the parish. It is very hilly and in bad order.

The average breadth of these roads is 20 feet. They are kept up at the expense of the baronies through which they pass.

The by and crossroads are sufficient in every respect.

Bridges

The principal bridges are: that over the Bann at Portglenone (see towns in this parish); 3 over the Main (see Public Buildings in this parish); and 1 over the Clogh river.

There are not any ferries, nor would they be of much service. There are 2 fords in the Bann, which are only passable in very dry weather, and they are even then 4 and a half feet deep. One of these is about 200 yards above Portglenone bridge and the other about 2 miles below it. They are rarely used and are not of any service.

General Appearance and Scenery

The general aspect of the western side of the parish is, particularly in winter, bleak and desolate. This may be attributed to partial cultivation of the ground, the wretched appearance of the cottages and the almost total want of planting. In this district of the parish, except immediately about Portglenone, there is nothing to cheer the eye. The prospect of the neighbouring county of Derry, the Bann, Lough Neagh and

the distant hills in Tyrone and Down is very beautiful.

On the eastern side of the parish the appearance of the country improves, particularly towards the River Main, along the banks of which there is a good deal of thriving planting and some pleasing rural scenery. The cottages also, on this side of the parish, are much more comfortable and the fields afford evidence of an industrious and improved state of husbandry.

Social Economy

Early Improvements

The first settlement which took place in this parish was in the reign of Queen Elizabeth in 1572, when the castle of Portglenone was garrisoned by 44 English soldiers under Captain Stafford. The second settlement took place between the years 1615 and 1618, and during the reign of James I, when several Scottish families, who came over during the persecution in Scotland and landed on the coast of this county, settled in the eastern districts of this county. The third settlement took place immediately after 1642, when many of the Scots who came over to Carrickfergus with General Munroe located in this parish. And a fourth, but less extensive, settlement took place soon after the battle of the Boyne, when several of King William's soldiers, who had formed part of the garrison of Portglenone Castle, got possession of some lands in this parish and settled in them. The present inhabitants are almost all the descendants of these settlers, particularly of the second and third settlements.

It is probable that the second settlement was the earliest step towards improvement, though this parish was well off for religious houses, there being no less than 3 monasteries and a church in it, namely the monasteries of Maddymassag, Killycoolan and Templemore, and the church in Gortfad, in which St Columb is said to have preached.

Since the last settlement, the parish seems to have improved rapidly, and several Presbyterian congregations were in a comparatively short time established.

The more recent causes of improvement have been the establishment of schools and the spread of useful and religious information. The number of sects in the parish (there being 8) has also shown that the clergy have not been inactive, and the activity of one in trying to accomplish proselytism is generally followed by the exertions of the rest to prevent it.

Progress of Improvement

Among the improvements which have taken place may be noticed the stop put [to] the merrymakings at the wakes of Presbyterians, as their clergy are now obliged to forbid the custom of offering whiskey or refreshments at them; and in their stead the reading of the Scriptures has been substituted. Cock-fighting, card-playing and dances, which formerly were numerously attended, are now, except the latter and it very seldom, never known among that body; and the other sects are imitating their example. Fairs are not now attended for amusement, and many other similar amusements have been given up. To them have succeeded the establishment of book clubs throughout the country, and much useful religious knowledge is diffused by these and the Sunday School libraries. The introduction of Sunday schools has excited a strict observance of the Sabbath; and except a few along the Bann (and they are improving), the inhabitants of this parish are perhaps among the most moral in the country.

They are, particularly in the more eastern districts of the parish, comfortable in their circumstance and manner of living, and much resemble the Scots in their habits, customs and dialect. They are rather dogged, obstinate and blunt, and have a degree of familiarity and equality in their manners and notions which to a stranger is very disagreeable.

More than half the population are engaged in some branch of the linen manufacture, which at present affords them good wages. There never has been, within memory, more flax sown than in the present year, and it never promised to pay better. The rest of the population are principally engaged in agriculture.

Obstructions to improvement: none.

Local Government

There is 1 stipendiary magistrate, John Gore Jones Esquire, stationed at Portglenone. There are 4 other magistrates: Alexander McMannus Esquire of Mount Davis, near the village of Ahoghill; Alexander O'Hara of Gloonan Cottage, Esquire; William Gihon of Hillhead, Esquire; and George Joy of Galgorm Castle, near the village of Galgorm. These magistrates, from their influence as landlords and gentlemen, ought to be respected and useful, and their residences are conveniently situated.

A chief constable and 20 constabulary are stationed in Portglenone. There are 4 constabulary in Ahoghill village and 4 in Cullybackey. There are not any revenue police nor troops.

A manor court, for the recovery of debts under 20 pounds Irish [insert addition: British] currency by civil bill, and a court leet, the former once a month and the latter twice a year, are held in Portglenone for the manor of Cashel, by appointment from Lord O'Neill, Peter Aicken Esquire, seneschal.

A second manor court and courts leet are held in the village of Ahoghill, the former 12 times and the latter twice a year, by appointment from the Bishop of Down and Connor, in which debts not exceeding 2 pounds are recoverable, Peter Aicken Esquire, seneschal.

A third manor court, for the recovery of debts not exceeding 4 pounds 6s 8d, and courts leet for the manor of Straboy alias Fortescue, are held, the former 12 times and the latter twice a year, at the village of Galgorm, by appointment from Lord Mountcashel, Mr Henry Raphael, seneschal.

A portion of this parish near Ballymena is under the jurisdiction of the manor court of that town. The highest sum recoverable is 2 pounds.

Petty sessions are held on every second Wednesday in the town of Portglenone and on the intermediate Wednesdays in the village of Ahoghill.

Party Riots

The only outrages which occur are party riots; and until a short time since, they had been so frequent as to call for the appointment of a stipendiary magistrate and increased police force, and a company of infantry were quartered in Portglenone, which was the seat of disturbances. However, since the 19th May no outrages or riots have occurred, and the troops have been withdrawn. Several of both parties were sentenced to imprisonment, and 1 to transportation, at the last Ballymena sessions for rioting, waylaying etc., and the country is now pretty quiet.

There is not now any illicit distillation. It formerly was carried on to some extent. There are few fire or life insurances.

Dispensaries

The only dispensary in this parish is that in Ahoghill. Its establishment has been too recent to cause any visible improvement in the health of the people. There is no doubt but their comforts have been increased by it, as many now receive medicine and advice who could not otherwise have procured it. More good might yet be done by it if the salary allowed the medical man would enable him to devote himself exclusively to it, as the district of country which it embraces is extensive (see [Ahoghill Dispensary]).

Schools

The introduction of schools, particularly of Sunday schools, has done a great deal of good, and led to a very perceptible change in the morals of the people and in their observance of the sabbath.

They are very desirous of information, as is evidenced by the number of little book clubs which they have of themselves got up through the parish, and they are anxious to have their children instructed (see Table of Schools).

Poor

The only provision for the poor, except the usual collections on Sundays, is an annual grant of 10 pounds from the Bishop of Meath for a certain number of poor females on his estate in this parish.

Religion

By the revised census of 1834 there are in this parish 985 Episcopalians, 12,918 Presbyterians, 4,120 Roman Catholics, 767 Moravians, 955 other Dissenters, such as Methodists.

The rector is supported by his tithes, which amount to 11,000 pounds per year. The curate of the parish has the Glebe House (in which he resides) and 40 acres of the glebe, which contains 175 acres 2 roods 23 perches, for his support. 21 townlands on the west of the parish were, on the 7th September 1825, by virtue of an act of parliament 11 and 12 of George III, created into a perpetual cure called the curacy of Portglenone. The curate who has the charge of them receives 150 pounds per annum from his rector and resides in the town of Portglenone. Except for ministerial duties, the parish of Ahoghill remains entire.

3 of tne Presbyterian clergymen are in connection with the Synod of Ulster. They receive their support from their stipend. 2 of them have third-class congregations and receive each 50 pounds per annum regium donum. The other has a second-class congregation and receives 75 pounds per annum regium donum.

3 clergymen are Seceders and in connection with the Secession Synod. They receive their stipend and, having third-class congregations, 50 pounds per annum regium donum.

There is 1 Coventanter and 1 Independent minister. They are paid their stipend, but do not accept the regium donum.

The Methodist clergyman receives a salary of 40 pounds per annum from the Methodist Society.

The Moravian clergyman is paid by his flock who make their payments quarterly. [Beginning of line erased] of their community. These lands are included in the townland of Ballykennedy, which they hold on a lease renewable for ever from Lord O'Neill.

The priest has 2 chapels in this parish. He performs in each of them every Sunday. His income is derived from his flock in a variety of ways.

Habits of the People

The houses in the eastern side of the parish are of a neater and more comfortable description than those on the western side, particularly along the Bann, where they are dirty and comfortless. Those along the Bann are all thatched, some of them of brick, but most of stone and generally consist of 1 apartment, very few having more. They generally receive light from 1 or 2 glazed windows. As they approach the eastern border of the parish, the houses present a much neater appearance and are cleanly and comfortable internally. They are built of stone, mostly thatched, and generally contain a kitchen and sleeping apartments. They are all 1-storey and are well lit.

The people along the Bann do not live as well as those along the east of the parish, as they use more potatoes and less meal and animal food. Meal, potatoes, bacon, milk, some baker's bread, salt herrings and a little tea constitute the food of the manufacturing class and small farmers. The labouring class consume very little bacon, baker's bread or tea. Turf is their only fuel and it is abundant.

The Presbyterians and Protestants dress very well, the Roman Catholics not quite so well, but they are much improved of late years, as formerly many might be seen coming to chapel both bare-headed and bare-footed, which is never the case now.

They are long lived, there being at present many persons in the parish who are above 90 years of age. 6 is the usual number in a family. They marry very early: within the last 9 months, a boy of 15 was married to a girl of 17, and a girl of 14 was married to a boy of 18. They were all Presbyterians and had the consent of their parents.

Amusements

They cannot be said now to have any amusements. Dancing is almost totally given up, and card-playing, cock-fighting almost totally abolished, owing to the exertions of their clergy.

On Easter Mondays they assemble in a field called the Green, where they have the play called "the round ring", for a description of which see Memoir of Ballymoney parish. This Green used formerly to be well attended and kept up for 2 days, but it now lasts only 1 day and is only attended by the young people.

The ancient customs observed at Hallow Eve are now given up, as is also going to fairs, which were formerly much resorted to as places of amusement. Wakes are still attended, but by the Roman Catholics only, for the purpose of amusement. They have a custom of playing trumps or Jew's harps at them, and they also perform a variety of tricks and low plays at these places. The Presbyterians have adopted the more rational amusement of reading useful books, which they procure from their book clubs, and attending schools for the instruction of sacred music.

They have no patrons' days nor local customs, except occasionally burning fire on St John's Eve. They have no peculiar games nor legendary tales, but they have a custom, particularly at wakes, of which the Roman Catholics are very fond, namely of reciting their pedigree, which invariably ends in tracing themselves, or rather their family, back to some important or very wealthy person, whose property has now gone to another family and which they always say should be their own. Singing hymns at funerals has been substituted for the Irish lays. There is no ancient music nor peculiarity of costumes.

Emigration

About 15, on average, annually emigrate to America, and few return. Canada is the part of America usually resorted to, and spring is the usual season for embarkation. Emigration has declined very much of late years.

Not more than from 15 to 20 young men, Roman Catholics, now go annually to harvests; this practice is also declining greatly. The principal reasons for it are: first, there not being the same encouragements as formerly; secondly, the farmers and others are unwilling to hire as servants a person who has been in the habit of going to the harvests, as it gives them roving and unsettled notions, besides their acquiring bad habits; and it is now considered a disreputable action, and none who value their character or good name pursue it.

Remarkable Events

None except those recorded under the head of Towns.

[Insert note: I have left this blank, as I shall soon be able to procure information which will fill it up [signed] James Boyle].

Appendix to Memoir

HISTORY

Historical Notes

Captain Stafford received a grant of 14 townlands from Queen Elizabeth, as a remuneration for his services. 7 of these of he sold to the Hutchinson family, by whom they came into the O'Hara family, and Hamilton O'Hara's widow has since sold them to the Bishop of Meath. The remaining 7, Eccles Stafford some time since sold to the Miss Thomsons of Greenmount, in whose possession they now are.

There are few of the Stafford family now in the county Antrim. There are several of the name, but in more humbler rank in life, in the neighbourhood of the village of Bellaghy in the county Derry.

There formerly was a ferry over the Bann, about 30 perches above the present bridge. It is fordable in summer. The neighbourhood of this ferry on both sides was the principal scene of the action alluded to, and on the edge of the river, in the Derry side, there is still a hawthorn bush which, it is said, marked the spot where Captain Magill of King William's army was killed and is buried.

Legend of Galgorm Castle

The legend connected with Galgorm Castle and its former proprietor Dr Colville, by whom it was built in 1696 and from whom, by marrying his niece, it came into the possession of an ancestor of Lord Mountcashel, is as follows.

Dr Colville had been in Scotland, where he principally received his education. He was a curate of the Established Church, but through love of money sold his soul to the Devil for the full of a boot of guineas. The Devil came to make good his part of the bargain by paying the money, but the doctor very roguishly cut the foot out of the boot and held it over the mouth of a lime-kiln. The Devil continued to pour on without being able to fill the boot and was obliged to sweep the seas to obtain enough, and did not discover the trick until the kiln was almost full. He, however, filled it and

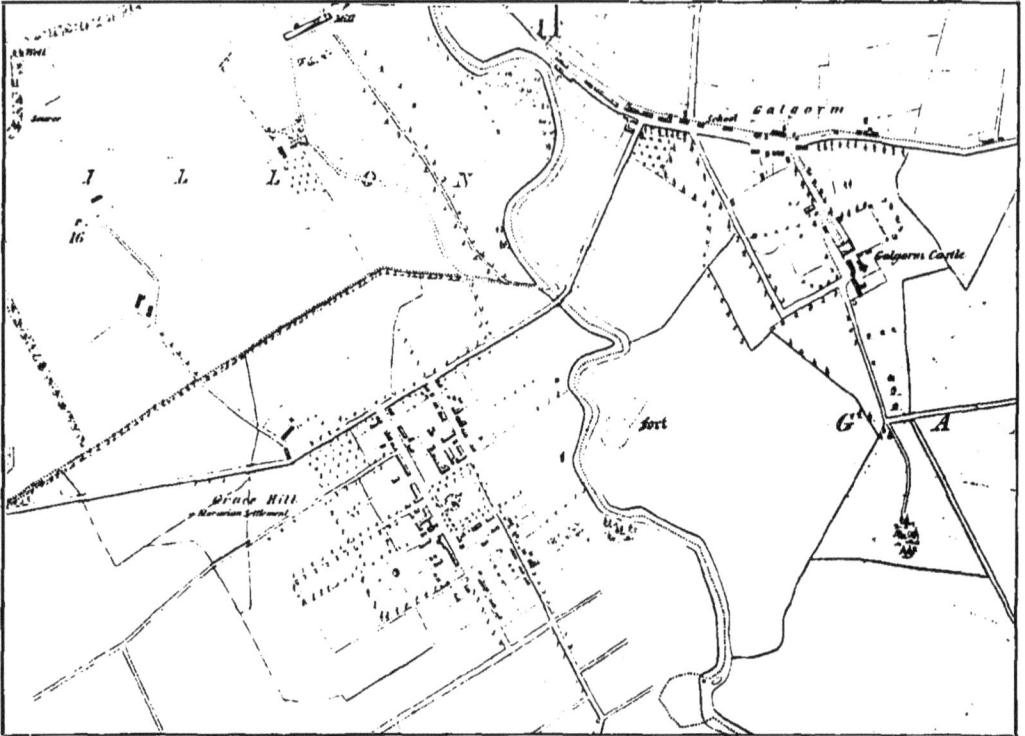

Map of Galgorm and Gracehill from the first 6" O.S. maps, 1830s

demanded of the doctor to make good his part of the bargain. The doctor said he would, if he would only allow him to read the Bible until a little candle he held should be burned. To this the Devil also consented, but the doctor immediately blew out the candle, put it into the Bible and then closed all in an iron chest which he threw into the sea, and by this measure not only gained the gold but saved his soul.

This legend is commonly told and believed to this day, but the following account as to the manner in which the doctor made his money is more probable. He had been a curate of the Established Church and was stationed in Connor. When in Scotland he became acquainted with a gentleman of large property, who unfortunately killed another, while in a fit of passion. The gentleman fled to this country and remained for many years in disguise with the doctor, who used to go over at certain times and receive his rents. He finally died while with the doctor and left him all his property, amounting to an immense sum, and with this the doctor purchased his property in this country and built Galgorm Castle.

Social Economy

Moravians at Gracehill

The Moravian settlement took place here in the year 1755, when the townland of Ballykennedy, containing 363 acres 1 rood 21 perches, was purchased by the joint proprietors or committee of Moravians or United Brethren. They first built the church and the house south of it (now the academy) but then intended for weavers and consequently divided into numerous small rooms. The money was obtained by loans advanced on the property. The remaining houses and dwellings were soon after built, and among them the sisters' house, which affords a respectable and comfortable asylum for 40 single ladies or females, who, having lost their friends or being reduced in circumstances, find this a desirable refuge. The number is limited, and the strictest investigation as to character etc. takes place previous to their admission. A governess superintends and directs them and the establishment. They are boarded, but maintain themselves by their work which is so well known under the name of the "Moravians' work." It fetches a very high price, being so much more desirable than any other, and also bears washing. Several articles of it have lately been sent to Queen Adelaide.

The utmost neatness and regularity prevails in this establishment and a strict discipline is kept up. A married person would not on any account, or under any circumstances, be permitted to sleep or stay in the establishment, and there are several other similar regulations. There is, however, no restraint on them as to their quitting the establishment, which they may do when they think proper.

Several German and English mechanics came over with the original settlement from England, but except the Revd C.J. Harke and 2 of the ushers, there are not any foreigners now in this settlement.

The boys' school was established in 1805. The boys are all under the ages of 7 and 15, none being admitted after 14. This school is rather initiatory, as it does not pretend to prepare boys for college but only for other schools, and those educated here generally go next to Dungannon school.

The ladies' school was established in 1795. It is superintended by Miss Liley and comprises the usual routine of ladies' education.

No intercourse is allowed between the males and females. They sit at different sides of the church and are buried at different sides of the graveyard. The situation and plan of the latter place is well chosen and laid out. It is in the rear of the sisters' house, from which it is distant about 100 yards. It is surrounded by a row of lofty trees and a double row extends along the sides of the walk in the centre. This walk serves to divide the males' from the females' burying ground. The graves, or rather the stones (which are laid flat), are all numbered, and no grave is ever opened a second time. The names of several Germans and Swedes are to be found on these stones.

A short time since, the Moravians raised among themselves the sum of 300 pounds, which they gave for a fine-toned organ in their church, the former one having gone out of order. The singing is very sweet and there is a good deal of it in their service. Their clergyman (the Revd W. Malalieu) is paid by the congregation, which amounts to 767 individuals. The payments are made quarterly.

The tenants on the property amount to 51. They are among the most industrious and moral people in the country. The agent to the proprietor, Mr Lee, resides in Gracehill. The affairs are managed by a number of delegates who reside in England, and also by a synodical assembly on the Continent, consisting of the clergy and elders, who meet once in 10 years.

The rent paid is not considered or appropriated as profit, but towards paying off the original sum lent for erecting the buildings.

This little community is flourishing and its members may be looked on as among the most virtuous models of society. There is much of the Quaker simplicity in their dress and habits, and, like them, they do not interfere in the more public affairs of life.

Savings Bank

NB The savings bank in Gracehill has accidently been omitted. It was established in 1831. It is principally resorted to by the class for whose benefit such institutions are intended, namely servants and labourers, though many affluent farmers are depositors. No classification of the callings of the depositors is preserved. It is thriving (see [below]).

Portglenone: Table of Trades and Callings

Attorneys 1, apothecaries and surgeons 3, bonnetmakers 2, bakers 3, blacksmiths 3, clockmakers 1, carpenters 2, ciergymen 4, constabulary 21, cartmakers 1, dressmakers 3, flax dressers 1, grocers 11, innkeepers 2, hucksters <huxters> and lodging house keepers 8, haberdashers and milliners 4, labourers (agricultural and domestic) 38, magistrates (stipendiary) 1, linen inspector 1, linen sealmaster 1, masons 4, nailors 2, physicians 1, publicans 9, postmaster 1, surgeons and apothecaries 3, shoemakers 4, schoolmaster 1, tailors 2, painters and glaziers 2, woollen drapers 4, wheelwrights 2, weavers 1, total 147.

Gracehill: Table of Trades and Callings

Bakers 1, butchers 1, carpenters 2, clergymen 2, grocers and woollen drapers 1, innkeepers 1, heddle makers 2, total 10.

Ahoghill: Table of Trades and Occupations

Apothecaries and surgeons 2, bakers 1, blacksmiths 1, carpenters 1, grocers 3, hucksters 2, innkeepers and publicans 5, lodging houses 3, mantua makers 2, police (constabulary) 4, shoemakers 2, tailors 1, clergyman 1, total 28.

Cullybackey: Table of Trades and Occupations

Blacksmiths 2, carpenters and toolmakers 2, grocers and spirit sellers 1, grocers 2, spirit sellers 2, shoemakers 1, tailors 1, total 11.

Galgorm: Table of Trades and Occupations

Carpenter 1, grocer and spirit seller 1, glazier 1, spirit seller 1, stonecutter 1, seneschal 1, total 6.

Ahoghill Dispensary

Table of cases for the year 1834.

Asthmatic complaints 9, apoplexy 1, died, anomalous complaints 18, constipation of the bowels 26, consumption 4, 1 died, cholera morbus 4, convulsive affections 3, caries of the tibia 1, cancer 1, dyspeptic complaints 40, dropsy (11 operations for [?] it) 13, 3 died, diarrhoea 9, diabetes 1, external injuries 24, fever 91, fungus of the antrum 1, fungus of the faeces 1, whooping <hooping> cough 12, herpetic eruptions 7, hernia 1, itch 8, liver complaints 13, opthalmia 9, pleuritic complaints 5, inflammatory affections 5, palpitation of the heart 1, rheumatism 1, scrofulous complaints 5, stricture of the oesophagus 1, toothache and extraction of teeth 6, worms 6, [total cases 327], 12 died.

Lists of patients for the year 1834: individuals assisted at the dispensary 328, number visited at their houses 110, number of visits paid 318, number dismissed and cured 300, number died 12.

Gracehill Savings Bank

A statement of the funds of the Gracehill Savings Bank for the year 1834.

Sums received of depositors within the year ending 20th November 1834 584 pounds 9s 3d; sums actually paid to depositors, including interest, 803 pounds; total amount of deposits on the books on the 20th November 1834 2,118 pounds; average amounts of each deposit 1 pound 4s 6d; total number of depositors 162; average number of depositors (annually) 56.

Of the depositors in this bank since its commencement, 129 deposited sums not exceeding 20 pounds, 25 deposited sums not exceeding 50 pounds, 7 deposited sums not exceeding 100 pounds, 1 deposited a sum of 150 pounds.

Benevolence: Establishments for the Indigent

[Table] Dispensary, object: affording medicine and medical advice gratis to the poor; the dispensary is open on Mondays and Thursdays and patients are visited. The affairs are managed by a treasurer and 2 secretaries. 300 are annually relieved or cured; 328 received medicine and advice and 110 visited at their houses; 14 died this year. Funds: from the grand jury of the county 30

pounds, fines from magistrates 2 pounds 17s 6d, [total] 32 pounds 17s 6d; annual subscription 43 pounds 8s 3d. Expenses: physician's salary 40 pounds, allowances for house and extras 20 pounds, total 60 pounds. Relief afforded: medicines and medical advice; when founded: 1833.

Table of Schools

[Table contains the following headings: name, situation and description, when established, income and expenditure, physical, intellectual and moral education, number of pupils subdivided by age, sex and religion, name and religion of master or mistress].

Gracehill Ladies' Academy, in a neat 2-storey house built for the purpose in the village of Gracehill, established 1795; income: terms for private tuition 26 pounds per annum; intellectual education: music, drawing, French, history, geography, grammar, writing, arithmetic, needlework; moral education: catechism of selections from the Scriptures with expositions, lectures from the clergy daily (Authorised Version of Scripture); number of pupils: 8 under 10 years of age, 4 from 10 to 15, 2 above 15, total 14, 9 Protestants, 5 Presbyterians; mistress Miss Lilly, Moravian Protestant.

Gracehill Academy (boys' boarding school), in a suitable, airy and commodious house in the village of Gracehill, established 1805; income from pupils 26 guineas per annum, 1 guinea for entrance; intellectual education: no boy is admitted after the age of 14; the course of education comprises all that is necessary for a preparatory education for a more advanced school such as Dungannon, to which those who enter college usually go; moral education: lectures on the Scriptures from the Revd C.F. Harke, the headmaster, a catechism compiled from the Scriptures (Authorised Version); number of pupils: 16 under 10 years of age, 34 from 10 to 15, total 50, 37 Protestants, 13 Presbyterians; master the Revd C.F. Harke, headmaster, 6 assistants, all Moravian Protestants.

Erasmus Smith's school for males and females, in a handsome 2-storey house built at the expense of Erasmus Smith's foundation, cost 460 pounds; it contains apartments for the master and mistress, and separate rooms for boys and girls; there is 1 and a half acres of land attached for the use of the master; this school is half a mile south of Portglenone and in the townland of [blank], established 1813; income from Erasmus Smith's foundation 48 pounds; expenditure: master's salary 30 pounds, mistress' salary 18 pounds, [total] 48 pounds; intellectual education: the males are taught reading, writing, arithmetic, geometry, the books and cards being those issued from the institution; females are taught spelling, reading, writing, arithmetic and sewing, similar books; moral education: visits from the clergyman, Sunday schools, Scriptures daily (Authorised Version of them) and similar catechism on Saturdays and Sundays; number of pupils: males, 14 under 10 years of age, 14 from 10 to 15, 6 above 15, 34 total males; females, 35 under 10 years of age, 31 from 10 to 15, 7 above 15, 73 total females; total number of pupils 107, 27 Protestants, 36 Presbyterians, 44 Roman Catholics; master and mistress John Patman and Rebecca Patman, Protestants.

Under the Board of National Education, in a house built by subscription in the townland of Gortgole, established 1833; income: from the Board of National Education 8 pounds, from pupils 9 pounds; intellectual education: books issued by the Board of National Education; moral education: visits from the priest, Douai and Authorised Version at stated hours; number of pupils: males, 27 under 10 years of age, 27 total males; females, 14 under 10 years of age, 14 total females; total number of pupils 41, 3 Protestants, 38 Roman Catholics; master Patrick Mulholland, Roman Catholic.

Under the Board of National Education, in a house built by subscription in the townland of Largy, established 1832: income: from the Board of National Education 8 pounds, from pupils 6 pounds 15s; intellectual education: books issued by the Board of National Education; moral education: visits from the priest, Douai and Authorised Version at stated hours; number of pupils: males, 36 under 10 years of age, 5 from 10 to 15, 31 [sic] total males; females, 26 under 10 years of age, 1 from 10 to 15, 37 [sic] total females; total number of pupils 58, all Roman Catholics; master James McLaughlin, Roman Catholic.

Under the Kildare Place Society, in a house built by subscription in the townland of Cullybackey, established 1825; income from pupils 30 pounds; intellectual education: some of the Kildare books, *Murray's Grammar, Thomson's Arithmetic, Crocker's and Gibson's Mensuration*; moral education: visits from the clergy, Sunday school, Authorised Version of Scriptures, shorter catechism on Saturdays; number of pupils: males, 26 under 10 years of age, 14 from 10 to 15, 2 over 15, 42 total males; females, 15 under 10 years of age, 9 from 10 to 15, 24 total females; total number of pupils 66, 6

Protestants, 54 Presbyterians, 6 Roman Catholics; master Daniel McFall, Presbyterian.

Under the Kildare Place Society, in a house built by subscription in the townland of Glenhugh, established 1828; income from pupils 16 pounds; intellectual education: some of the Kildare books, *Murray's Grammar, Thomson's Arithmetic*; moral education: visits from the clergy, Sunday school, Authorised Version of Scriptures, shorter catechism on Saturdays; number of pupils: males, 10 under 10 years of age, 6 from 10 to 15, 16 total males; females, 22 under 10 years of age, 2 from 10 to 15, 24 total females; total number of pupils 40, 6 Protestants, 28 Presbyterians, 6 Roman Catholics; master Samuel Kirkpatrick, Presbyterian.

Under Kildare Place Society, in a house built by subscription in the townland of Moyasset, established 1828; income from pupils 17 pounds; intellectual education: some of the Kildare books, *Murray's Grammar, Thomson's Arithmetic*; moral education: visits from the clergy, Sunday school, Authorised Version of Scriptures, shorter catechism on Saturdays; number of pupils: males, 14 under 10 years of age, 7 from 10 to 15, 21 total males; females, 14 under 10 years of age, 5 from 10 to 15, 19 total females; total number of pupils 40, 9 Protestants, 31 Presbyterians; master James Drummond, Presbyterian.

Under the Kildare Place Society, in the manor court house in the village of Galgorm, established 1822; income: from Lord Mountcashel (annually) 5 pounds, from pupils 22 pounds; intellectual education: some Kildare books, Manson's works, *Dublin Reader, Gough's Arithmetic, Crocker's Mensuration*; moral education: visits from the clergy, Sunday school, Authorised Version of Scriptures, shorter catechism on Saturdays; number of pupils: males, 20 under 10 years of age, 6 from 10 to 15, 26 total males; females, 5 under 10 years of age, 2 from 10 to 15, 3 above 15, 10 total females; total number of pupils 36, 33 Presbyterians, 3 Roman Catholics; master Hugh Rea, Presbyterian.

[Subtotals]: income from private or benovolent individuals 69 pounds, from pupils 100 pounds 15s; number of pupils: males, 137 under 10 years of age, 52 from 10 to 15, 8 above 15, 197 total males; females, 131 under 10 years of age, 50 from 10 to 15, 10 above 15, 191 total females; total number of pupils 288, 41 Protestants, 182 Presbyterians, 155 Roman Catholics.

Under the London Hibernian Society, in a house built by subscription in the townland of Garvaghy West, established 1832; income: from the London Hibernian Society (annually) 3 pounds 3s, from pupils 21 pounds; intellectual education: spelling, *Dublin Reader, Gough's Arithmetic*, writing, *Murray's Grammar*; moral education: occasional visits from the clergy, Sunday school, Shorter Catechism and Authorised Scriptures *daily*; number of pupils: males, 18 under 10 years of age, 7 from 10 to 15, 4 above 15, 29 total males; females, 16 under 10 years of age, 5 from 10 to 15, 21 total females; total number of pupils 40, 10 Protestants, 30 Presbyterians; master Matthew Johnson, Presbyterian.

Under the London Hibernian Society, in a house built by subscription in the townland of Garvaghy East, established 1832; income: from the London Hibernian Society (annually) 4 pounds, from pupils 20 pounds; intellectual education: spelling, *Dublin Reader, Gough's Arithmetic*, writing, *Murray's Grammar*; moral education: occasional visits from the clergy, Sunday school, Shorter Catechism and Authorised Scriptures daily; number of pupils: males, 18 under 10 years of age, 6 from 10 to 15, 3 above 15, 27 total males; females, 19 under 10 years of age, 5 from 10 to 15, 24 total females; total number of pupils 51, 9 Protestants, 42 Presbyterians; master John Andrews, Presbyterian.

Under the London Hibernian Society, in a house built by subscription in the townland of Tinnyhannon, established 1825; income from pupils 18 pounds; intellectual education: spelling, *Dublin Reader, Gough's Arithmetic*, writing, *Murray's Grammar*; moral education: occasional visits from the clergy, Sunday school, Shorter Catechism and Authorised Scriptures daily; number of pupils: males, 10 under 10 years of age, 5 from 10 to 15, 15 total males; females, 30 under 10 years of age, 15 from 10 to 15, 45 total females; total number of pupils 60, 58 Presbyterians, 2 Roman Catholics; master William Campbell, Protestant.

Under the London Hibernian Society, in the court house, which is given gratis, in the town of Portglenone, established 1832; income: from the London Hibernian Society (annually) 1 pound 15s, from pupils 20 pounds; intellectual education: spelling, *Dublin Reader, Gough's Arithmetic*, writing, *Murray's Grammar*; moral education: occasional visits, Sunday school, Scriptures (Authorised Version daily) Shorter and church catechism on Saturday; number of pupils: males, 11 under 10 years of age, 5 from 10 to 15, 3 above 15, 19 total males; females, 19 under 10 years of age, 8 from 10 to 15, 17 total females; total number of pupils 36, 8 Protestants, 20

Presbyterians, 8 Roman Catholics; master Arthur Barnes, Covenanter.

Under the London Hibernian Society, in a house built by subscription in the townland of Aughnaheely, established 1831; income: from the London Hibernian Society (annually) 2 pounds, from pupils 7 pounds; intellectual education: spelling, *Dublin Reader, Gough's Arithmetic*, writing, *Murray's Grammar*; moral education: occasional visits from the clergy, Sunday school, Shorter Catechism and Authorised Scriptures daily; number of pupils: males, 18 under 10 years of age, 8 from 10 to 15, 1 above 15, 27 total males; females, 19 under 10 years of age, 6 from 10 to 15, 25 total females; total number of pupils 52, 2 Protestants, 43 Presbyterians, 7 Roman Catholics; master Arthur Barnes, Covenanter.

Under the London Hibernian Society, in a house built by subscription in the townland of Killycarry, established 1827; income: from the London Hibernian Society (annually) 7 pounds 10s, from pupils 12 pounds; intellectual education: spelling, *Dublin Reader, Gough's Arithmetic*, writing, *Murray's Grammar*; moral education: occasional visits from the clergy, Sunday school, Shorter Catechism and Authorised Scriptures daily; number of pupils: males, 41 under 10 years of age, 8 from 10 to 15, 49 total males; females, 11 under 10 years of age, 4 from 10 to 15, 15 total females; total number of pupils 64, 10 Protestants, 21 Presbyterians, 33 Roman Catholics; master George Weir, Presbyterian.

Under the London Hibernian Society, in a house built by the Kildare Place Society in the townland of Connaghligar, established 1824; income: from the London Hibernian Society (annually) 4 pounds, from pupils 6 pounds; intellectual education: spelling, *Dublin Reader, Gough's Arithmetic*, writing, *Murray's Grammar*; moral education: occasional visits from the clergy, Sunday school, Shorter Catechism and Authorised Scriptures daily; number of pupils: males, 12 under 10 years of age, 3 from 10 to 15, 15 total males; females, 8 under 10 years of age, 1 from 10 to 15, 9 total females; total number of pupils 24, 4 Protestants, 20 Presbyterians; master Samuel Marr, Presbyterian.

Under the London Hibernian Society, in a house built by subscription in the townland of Milltown, established 1830; income: from the London Hibernian Society (annually) 4 pounds, from pupils 10 pounds; intellectual education: spelling, *Dublin Reader, Gough's Arithmetic*, writing, *Murray's Grammar*; moral education: occasional visits from the clergy, Sunday school,

Shorter Catechism and Authorised Scriptures daily; number of pupils: males, 28 under 10 years of age, 5 from 10 to 15, 33 total males; females, 25 under 10 years of age, 2 from 10 to 15, 27 total females; total number of pupils 60, 48 Presbyterians, 12 Roman Catholics.

[Subtotals]: income from public societies or benevolent individuals 95 pounds 8s, from pupils 214 pounds 15s; number of pupils: males, 295 under 10 years of age, 99 from 10 to 15, 19 above 15, 411 total males; females, 265 under 10 years of age, 96 from 10 to 15, 10 above 15, 376 total females; total number of pupils 775, 84 Protestants, 464 Presbyterians, 217 Roman Catholics.

Under the London Hibernian Society, in a house built by subscription in the townland of Tullinch; income: from the London Hibernian Society 5 pounds, from pupils 4 pounds; intellectual education: Kildare books, *Dublin Reader, Manson's and Universal spelling [book]*; moral education: occasional visits, Scripture daily, and catechisms (Authorised Version) on Saturday, Sunday school; number of pupils: males, 6 under 10 years of age, 4 from 10 to 15, 19 total males; females, 8 under 10 years of age, 4 from 10 to 15, 12 total females; total number of pupils 22, 5 Protestants, 11 Presbyterians, 6 Roman Catholics; [name of teacher blank], Presbyterian.

Under the Kildare Place Society, in a [crossed out: very] nice house built by subscription [crossed out: cost 46 pounds] in the townland of Ballybeg, established 1828; income: from [blank] Adair Esquire of Loughanmore (annually) 5 pounds, from pupils 14 pounds; intellectual education: Kildare books, *Dublin Reader, Manson's and Universal spelling [book]*; moral education: occasional visits, Scripture daily, and catechisms (Authorised Version) on Saturday, Sunday school; number of pupils: males, 14 under 10 years of age, 5 from 10 to 15, 19 total males; females, 12 under 10 years of age, 4 from 10 to 15, 16 total females; total number of pupils 35, 2 Protestants, 28 Presbyterians, 5 Roman Catholics; master John Walker, Presbyterian.

[Subtotals]: income from public societies or benovolent individuals 105 pounds 8s, from pupils 232 pounds 16s; number of pupils: males, 315 under 10 years of age, 108 from 10 to 15, 19 above 15, 440 total males; females, 288 under 10 years of age, 104 from 10 to 15, 10 above 15, 402 total females; total number of pupils 832, 91 Protestants, 503 Presbyterians, 228 Roman Catholics.

Private school, in a good house built by subscription (and cost 46 pounds) in the townland of Aughnaleesh, established 1835; income from pupils 20 pounds; intellectual education: *Manson's and Universal spelling and reading books, Gough's Arithmetic*; moral education: Authorised Version of Scriptures daily, Shorter Catechism occasionally; number of pupils: males, 31 under 10 years of age, 12 from 10 to 15, 43 total males; females, 29 under 10 years of age, 8 from 10 to 15, 37 total females; total number of pupils 80, 3 Protestants, 70 Presbyterians, 7 Roman Catholics; master Joshua Scott, Presbyterian.

Private school, in a house built by subscription in the townland of Mobuy; income from pupils 14 pounds; intellectual education: *Manson's and Universal spelling and reading books, Gough's Arithmetic*; moral education: Authorised Version of Scriptures daily, Shorter Catechism occasionally, and Sunday school; number of pupils: males, 20 under 10 years of age, 5 from 10 to 15, 25 total males; females, 13 under 10 years of age, 4 from 10 to 15, 17 total females; total number of pupils 42, 2 Protestants, 32 Presbyterians, 8 Roman Catholics.

Private school, in a house built by subscription in the townland of Slavenagh; income from pupils 8 pounds; intellectual education: *Manson's and Universal spelling and reading books, Gough's Arithmetic*; moral education: Authorised Version of Scriptures daily, Shorter Catechism occasionally, and Sunday school; number of pupils: males, 13 under 10 years of age, 8 from 10 to 15, 21 total males; females, 6 under 10 years of age, 3 from 10 to 15, 9 total females; total number of pupils 30, 3 Protestants, 27 Presbyterians; master James Scott, Presbyterian.

[Overall totals]: income from public societies or benevolent individuals 105 pounds 8s, from pupils 274 pounds 15s; number of pupils: males, 379 under 10 years of age, 133 from 10 to 15, 19 above 15, 529 total males; females, 336 under 10 years of age, 119 from 10 to 15, 10 above 15, 466 total females; total number of pupils 986, 99 Protestants, 622 Presbyterians, 243 Roman Catholics.

Benevolence: Establishments for the Indigent

17 schools wholly or partly supported by benevolence; object: the removal of ignorance; management: sundry societies; number relieved: 850 pupils receiving instruction; funds: from public bodies 4 pounds 8s, from private individuals 63 pounds; annual expenses: salaries, the teachers receive all viz. 110 pounds 8s; relief afforded: 822 children receiving instruction; when founded: at sundry times.

Savings bank, object: to enable the working classes to amass the fruits of their industry; management: committee of management, 9 directors, 1 accountant, 1 secretary and treasurer, 1 actuary; number relieved: 162 on the books on the 20th November 1834; funds from public bodies: interest paid by government deposits; from private individuals: 2,106 pounds amount of deposits on the books on the 20th November 1834; expenses: house rent 2 pounds, actuary's salary 3 pounds; relief afforded: sums drawn by depositors increased by compound interest; when founded: 1831.

Bequest, object: the support of a certain number of reduced females; distributed by his agent; number relieved: fluctuating; funds: from the Bishop of Meath 10 pounds annually.

Establishments for Mental and Bodily Disease

Dispensary, management: 1 treasurer and 2 secretaries; number relieved 300; funds from public bodies: from the county grand jury 30 pounds; from private individuals: fines from magistrates 2 pounds 17s 6d, subscriptions 43 pounds 8s 3d, total 46 pounds 5s 9d; expenses: surgeon's salary 40 pounds, extra salary 10 pounds, house allowance 10 pounds, [total] 60 pounds; annual expenses of patients 80 pounds 19s; when founded: 1833.

Memoir by J. Stokes [before July 1837]

ANCIENT TOPOGRAPHY

Ecclesiastical: Templemoyle Burial Ground

In the townland of Galgorm Parks, at the side of the Main river and on the summit of an elongated hill, there was formerly an ancient burial ground. Decayed boards of the coffins interred in it have been frequently dug up. There is nothing now to indicate it but a standing stone and a holy well. The former is represented in drawing[s]. The latter stands about 20 yards off and is nearly closed up. Pilgrimages were formerly made to it but they have long since ceased.

The burial ground itself is called Templemoyle. It extended an acre and a half along the top of the hill. The standing stone is situated half-way. An extensive cove was formerly at the western side, but is now filled up. No trace of any building or of the surrounding wall is recollected. As for the standing stone, its present situation is not the original one. It was removed by the grandfather of

the present tenant from the place where it, along with another, both stood as the entrance to the burial ground, and placed where it now is as a rubbing post for cattle. The other is embedded in a ditch.

From its very clumsy form it is probable that this graveyard was similar to some of the ancient burial places in the parish of Bovevagh, county Londonderry, which are in like manner set round with standing stones with 2 rude clumsy ones standing as an entrance. Its use may have continued from pagan to Christian times, aided as it was by the superstition of the holy well. The standing stone is not set deeper in the ground than about 8 inches; see drawing[s]. No church ever stood at this yard.

Graveyard at Craigs

In the townland of the Craigs there is an old graveyard in the centre of a field and covering about half a rood. It was once nearly half an acre in extent, but has been diminished by partial enclosure and cultivations. It is now in an open pasture, and on it there are still graves of irregular form with rough stones set at the head and foot of each. Infants are occasionally interred here. No graveyard wall is visible, nor are there traces of any ever recollected to have been seen.

At the distance of a few yards from the southern end, on overturning a small standing stone about 2 feet high, 4 silver coins were found, about a size intermediate between that of a shilling and a sixpence. They were not enclosed in anything. They were found in 1834 and were sold to a watchmaker in Ballymena.

This graveyard is believed to have been the spot where they originally intended to have built the parish churchyard situated at Ahoghill. It is remarkable that it stands almost exactly in the centre of the united parishes of Ahoghill and Rasharkin, i.e. it is nearly equidistant from the boundary of both. It stands on the side of a bleak stony hill.

Old Church at Galgorm Castle

The old church at Galgorm Castle stands closely surrounded by trees and a little distant from the front of the house. [Insert note: See Modern Topography for information regarding this castle]. The closeness of the plantation around it prevents every general view, but [the] drawing contains the windows, doors etc. It had originally 4 windows, but of these only 2 remain complete, namely one in each gable. The others are so dilapidated that their form cannot be distinguished. The door is at the western end of the southern wall. The carving visible at the foot of the fluting on each side is very much decayed. As for the masonry, it does not appear ancient, and the mortar also is not good. The dimensions outside of the building are 47 feet in length by 27 in breadth. The walls are 2 and a third feet thick. They stand north east and south west. The interior contains at the east window a portion of the floor 14 feet in length, raised 2 feet 9 inches above the rest.

As the history of the castle is connected with that of the church, see drawing[s] for a front view of the former.

Old Church in Ahoghill

There was a very old church in the village of Ahoghill. The present one, i.e. the parish church, stands on the foundations. It was burned down in the rebellion of 1641. As far as a few feet from the ground the stones of the present church are the same. It is believed to have been rebuilt about the year 1700. The architecture is now completely modern. The above drawing represents the style of the windows: [drawing of window, 6 feet across]. For further particulars, see Modern Topography.

This was the fourth church erected in the county Antrim. [Insert note: This is tradition]. The first was in Connor, the second in Ballymena, the third in Skerry, the fourth in Ahoghill, the fifth in Rasharkin, the sixth in Kildollagh.

Graveyard

Hugh Weir, 1697, appears to be the oldest stone in the yard. They are disposed generally east and west, and the stones of each name are always grouped together. The following families are interred: Taylor, Weir, Chaine, Mark, Spence, Speers, Stirling, Nicholl, Walker, Watson, Leetch, Stewart, Morell, Nelson, Clement, Cumming, Shaw, Cowan, Cleaver, Mill, Wilson, Fullerton, Kinnard, Wylie, Nickel, Kenny, Speers, Ogilby, Connor, McAulay, Morrow, Gault, Oudde, Picken, Mooney, McDonnell, Clark, Mehassey, Caul, McAlary, Meek, McNeill, Leman, McCreight, McKee, Carson. McCreight was Presbyterian minister of Cullybackey and died in 1757 aged 66.

There are no crosses or holy wells in the neighbourhood.

Old Churches

An old church formerly stood at a distance of 20 perches from the graveyard in the Craigs already described. It was formerly the parish church of Rasharkin and was next in age to Ahoghill, being the fifth place of worship erected in the county. It was destroyed in the rebellion of 1641. Its name was in Irish "Donelly's cell."

An old church stood also in Gortfad. It belonged to the Culdees and it is believed that St Columkille very often preached there. An ancient thorn-bush called after his name was cut down about 70 years ago. The graveyard is now contracted to the area of half a rood in the corner of the field. It is covered with long grass, but still shows the marks of graves. The last burial in it took place 16 years ago.

About 60 years ago a stone "preaching house", as it was called, stood in the centre. The remaining fragment of it stands in a neighbouring ditch and is 3 feet high, 2 feet wide and 13 inches thick, of regular form. It was double the length, or rather height, as it [is] now standing on one end.

The adjacent cut [drawing] represents the small building of which it was once a part. It was made of 5 stones, 1 being laid on the top. The sides were 6 feet high. It is believed that a priest in ancient times stood in this place and preached to the surrounding crowd.

The site is in a retired picturesque place at the distance of three-quarters of a mile from Portglenone. It is surrounded on the east by a ridge of hills.

Altar Green

In the townland of Tullynahinnion, and in a narrow ravine, there is another ecclesiastical place. It is called the Altar Green, and it is believed that an old church stood either at it or at an adjacent graveyard, which will be presently described.

The Green was a small holm along the edge of the stream that runs along the ravine. Next to the stream there was formerly a pile of stones 4 perches long and three-quarters of a perch broad. The side next to the water was regularly built and sloped outwards. In the rest of the building they lay in a confused manner. Many are said to have been of large dimensions. Some fragments of iron were found.

The direction of this pile was parallel to that of the stream, and was but a few feet distance. It was destroyed in 1832 and the Green converted into a field. Nearly a dozen of large standing stones were taken from different parts. No burials ever took place here. As for the altar, it was a square pile of stones about 4 feet high, raised by the Catholic priests to celebrate mass on during the prevalence of the Penal Laws.

In the townland of Finkiltagh, and at the distance of half a mile north east, there was formerly a graveyard, now entirely destroyed and obliterated. Bones and gravestones were frequently found in it.

In the townland of Killycoogan, and 1 and a half miles west from the Altar Green, there was formerly a graveyard. The remains of a church, believed to have been of an age coeval with the introduction of Christianity, also stood in it. It has been destroyed.

Military: Castle

The castle of Portglenone stood at the distance of 15 chains from the edge of the Bann river and at the western end of the street. Nothing of it now remains. It was, at the time it was pulled down, merely a very old-fashioned dwelling. It was taken down about 14 years ago. The fortifications which it originally had were long ago removed. It was built in the reign of Queen Elizabeth by Captain Stafford, to whom was granted an adjacent large tract of land.

At the time of the seige of Derry, his descendant Colonel Stafford succeeded in preventing the Irish from crossing the Bann at this place. [Insert note: This is merely the tradition of the country]. They attempted a ford situated 13 chains south of the site of the castle, but were repulsed by the fire of a battery erected by him immediately on the shore at the Antrim end of it. It was manned by himself and a party of militia raised from his tenantry. The battery remains still in the form of a small ridge about 10 feet high, 20 broad and a chain and a half long. The Irish fired from the Derry side with another battery.

McQuillan Castle

The castle of Rory Oge McQuillan stood in the townland of Galgorm, at the side of the Main river, in the midst of low flat ground. The traces of foundations are still visible. It was burned down in the wars that succeeded the rebellion of 1641. It is said that it was to this place the McQuillan family fled, after their expulsion from Dunluce Castle by the MacDonnells <McDonalds>. It appears to have been built on a Danish fort.

The foundations are on the top of a circular platform a chain and a half in diameter and 15 feet above the level of the adjacent field. They are surrounded by the trace of a ditch, and have on the eastern side an irregular triangular eminence 90 feet long and about half the height of the platform.

The 2 eminences are divided by the ditch. The castle foundations are indicated by a hollow on the top of the former; see drawing[s]. A single fragment of the walls still remains. They were 9 feet thick all around and were pulled down by the present tenant, who rooted out all the stones except that single fragment. On the other eminence the castle chapel formerly stood. It was in the form of a cross.

Except fragments of burned timber, showing that the house had been destroyed by fire, nothing very remarkable was found. Previous to its entire destruction the walls stood only 4 feet high. The masonry at the fragment already mentioned, and which is 3 feet by 3 feet, is of stone cemented together with hard grouted mortar. Some of them are of the black composition that occurs among those of the Cranfield chapel.

At the distance of 100 perches there was once a cave of some extent, now stopped up.

Pagan: Druidical Circles

In the townland of Slievenagh, and immediately adjoining Archdeacon Alexander's demesne, there are, on the top of a small rocky knoll, the remains of a druidical circle. In the year 1822 it was planted with fir, at which time a search in it for gold was made and many of the principal stones were removed. A cromlech stood at the northern end, based upon a great three-sided block embedded in the ground; see drawing[s]. Only 3 stones of this monument have been left. All the stones of the circle except those marked "b" are completely covered over with ivy, weeds and creeping plants. The exceptions do not rise a foot above the surface. In 1817 many silver coins were found here.

At the distance of 6 chains south west of the Giant's Finger Stone in the townland of Finkiltagh a druidical circle formerly stood. It was 1 chain in diameter. 6 of the stones still remain, but the people are carrying them away for building. They stand close to one another upon the original circumference and are overgrown with grass, weeds, nettles and brambles; so much that a drawing of them would be uninteresting. They are of various forms and are from 3 to 5 feet high. There are intervals between each of but a few inches. They extend to the length of 15 feet.

Cairns

In the townland of Finkiltagh there was formerly a large cairn now destroyed. When it was cleared away, a very neatly formed paved hearth was found in the centre. The dimensions are not remembered.

Some circles of stones are said to have been found in the bog of Lisnahunshin, near the dried up lake known by the name of Lough Tamin.

Standing Stones

On the side of a hill in the townland of Lisnahunshin, and commanding a very extensive view, there is a standing stone, now, however, overturned, known by the name of the Bullock's Track. It had a cavity in one side, resembling in form a bullock's hoof, to which the superstitious resorted for the cure of warts, by dipping their fingers or limbs in the rain water collected in it. It was lately upset by a treasure seeker who dreamed of money at the bottom, and the cavity is consequently now concealed. It is a block of an irregular triangular shape, 5 feet 8 inches long, 3 feet 4 inches wide and 2 feet thick.

In the adjacent townland of Finkiltagh, in the bottom of a valley and at the edge of a little stream, there is another called the Giant's Finger Stone. For drawing and dimensions of it, see drawing[s]. These 2 appear to be connected with one in the townland of Moylarg, which is 5 feet 4 inches high, 2 feet 5 inches broad and 1 foot 8 inches thick. It is near the edge of the Main river; see drawing[s].

Along the southern side of the parish there are 2 others not so large, one in the townland of Killycurry, the other in that of Corbally. The former is 3 feet 2 inches high, 1 foot 2 inches broad and 1 foot thick. The latter is 2 feet high, 1 and a half feet broad and 1 and a half feet thick. The former was originally twice as high, the half of it having been broken off. It stands on high ground overlooking the county Derry. The latter is in a low situation and at the side of the high road to Mount Davis.

The form of the Giant's Finger Stone is peculiar.

There is one a few yards from Cullybackey bridge, in the ditch at the roadside. It is 4 feet high, 5 feet broad and 2 feet thick.

Fort Hill

The Fort hill in the townland of Moylarg, and at the side of the Main river, is an abrupt eminence rising from its edge to the height of 70 feet and having a flat summit. A shallow ditch, evidently similar in nature to those of ordinary Danish forts, cuts off a part. The space between it and the river is known by the name of Fort, and is an irregular

triangle 1 and three-quarter chains long from the ditch to the vortex or point of it. It is surrounded on 2 sides by the precipice, sloping suddenly into the river. In the margin there is a section [drawing]. The ditch is 30 feet broad, the rampart is made of earth and 10 feet high. See drawing for a plan. [Insert marginal note by C.W. Ligar: A plan of this fort should be given, 20th July 1837].

Forts

In the townland of Dreen, and adjacent to the Main river, there is, on the sloping side of a hill, an earthen fort of the ordinary form. In it a cove opens from the parapet, 11 and a half feet long, 4 and a half high and 3 feet wide. It is built in the usual manner. At the end there is an entry from the side into a second room in the interior of the fort, but the roof appears to have fallen in, in consequence of having been undermined by rabbits. It is situated at the north side of the entrance and east of the fort. In the margin there is a small sketch of the whole. The cove is marked "A": [outline of fort].

In the adjacent townland of Moyasset there is an earthen fort of the same form as the above, containing also a cove opening from the parapet at the north side of the entrance and eastern side of the fort. The stones are all taken out, but the trench in which they stood fully remains. This trench is in the form of an L, that is, it consists of what were 2 long passages set at right angles. Each was originally about 40 feet long and 6 feet high. The first room, however, is not all contained within the parapet, as in the cove at Dreen. It proceeds directly towards the centre of the fort.

Coves

In the townland of Carndonaghy, and in the grounds of Mount Davis, there is in a small eminence a collection of remarkable coves, a ground plan of which is given in drawing[s]. The stones round the doorways are remarkable for the precision with which they are laid. The threshold of the one marked "A" is not on a level with the floor within, but is raised several inches above it. It is probable from this that the floor was once raised higher, as a door thus constructed is a very awkward one. No one could be obtained willing to clear the 2 doors marked "B" and "C." They were afraid of loosening the stones of the wall and so bringing down the whole building. However, those who were beyond them before they were choked described them as leading into rooms nearly circular.

At Gracehill there was formerly a cove, consisting of 1 long passage divided at intervals by low-browed doors. It is now stopped up. These 2 coves were each of them connected with forts. The last was near a fort of ordinary form. The first is on an eminence apparently artificial and probably once a fort, but from being fenced round, planted and otherwise altered, it has now lost all resemblance to it.

All the other forts of the parish are less than the usual size and earthen, with but 1 parapet and ditch. With some exceptions, the people are converting them into manure.

Miscellaneous: Discoveries in Bogs

Lough Tammin, in the townland of Lisnahunshin, was drained 25 years ago by order of the landlord Lord O'Neill. There had been in it an artificial island, circular and containing about 10 square perches. It was made of poles of timber. On it there was found the remains of a small wooden hut, containing in the inside a hearth with some bones and 2 swords. A canoe was also obtained. It cannot be presently ascertained in whose hands these articles are at present. It is believed that this island was inhabited by robbers of the name of McQuillan. The lake is small. It is now covered with grass.

In 1833 an ancient gold ornament was found in the bog of Drumraw. [Insert query: What kind of ornament was it?]. It was sold to Archdeacon Alexander for 2 pounds 5s. The weight was half an ounce and 10 grains. It is not now in his possession.

There have not been found many coins in the parish. The most remarkable, i.e. the one marked David of Scotland, was found in the bog of Teeshan, see drawings. Some were found near Columkille's graveyard.

In Carneany a remarkable moat was destroyed some years ago, and from the interior a curiously carved earthen urn dug out. For further particulars of it, as well as a drawing, refer to Mr Boyle. It is in the possession of the Adair family, who reside near the town of Antrim.

A great number of quern-stones have been found from time to time on the several farms adjoining the Fort hill, with many "thunderbolts" i.e. stone-cutting instruments or hatchets. None have been preserved.

Drawings of Antiquities

Map showing the relative positions of the standing stones and monuments of Ahoghill, scale 3 miles to 1 inch.

Standing stone in Moylarg, main dimensions 5 feet 4 inches by 1 foot 8 inches.

Standing stone at an ancient burying ground, townland of Galgorm Parks, 2 views, height 4 feet.

Galgorm chapel, views of west window, 4 feet by 5 feet, east window from the inside, belfry and doorway, main dimensions 8 feet by 3 feet 2 inches.

Front of Galgorm Castle, showing its style of architecture.

Plan sketch of McQuillan's Castle, scale a quarter inch to a chain.

Druidical circle in the townland of Slievenagh, with dimensions; plan, 54 feet across, scale 40 feet to an inch.

The Giant's Finger Stone in Finkiltagh, main dimensions 7 feet by 7 feet, side view and section.

Door in cove, 1 foot 6 inches high, with plan and section.

5 coins found in the parish of Ahoghill, both faces: David of Scotland, Edward?, Mary Queen of Scots, unidentified coin, Charles II.

Coin, both faces; medal apparently of an alloy of silver and tin.

The Fort hill, plan with orientation, scale a quarter of an inch to a chain.

Draft Memoir, with Queries and Answers by Lieutenant R.K. Dawson and T.C. Hannyngton, 1834

NATURAL STATE

Locality

It is situated on the west side of the county Antrim and about midway between the north and south extremities. The greater portion of the parish is in the barony of Lower Toome, but it extends on the north into the barony of Kilconway, on the north east into that of Lower Antrim and on the south into Upper Toome.

It is bounded on the north by the parish of Rasharkin and the grange of Dundermot, on the east by Kirkinriola and Ballyclug, on the south by Connor, Drummaul and the grange of Ballyscullion, and on the west by the River Bann, which divides it from the county Londonderry.

Its greatest length is 7 miles and breadth 5 and a half miles, average length and breadth 6 by 4 miles. It contains 35,418 acres 36 perches, including 145 acres 9 roods 15 perches of water.

NATURAL FEATURES

Hills

An elevated ridge extends through the parish from north to south. There is nothing particularly striking in the appearance of the hills. The highest point is a hill called Tully in Slievenagh townland, 2 miles south east of Portglenone. The summit is 660 feet above the level of the sea. It may be well to remark that the rise of this ridge is much more gradual and smooth on the east side; on the west it is abrupt <abrubt> and broken by the outcropping of basalt. It is very poorly cultivated. It abounds in springs.

Lakes

There are 3 lakes, or rather ponds, situated within a mile of each other in the north of the parish. The largest is not more than 300 yards from the west bank of the Main river. These are only mill-ponds: one supplies the Dunminning mills, one the Gruba and one the Craigs Castle.

River Bann

The River Bann flows along the west side of the parish for 7 miles. It is navigable for boats of 60 tons, from 5 to 6 feet draught <draft> of water.

The Bann is navigable for boats of 60 tons, drawing from 5 to 6 feet of water, as far down as Portna in the winter months. In summer there is a rapid about 500 yards above Portglenone bridge, which they cannot pass except during a peak in the river. This barrier is formed by some detached stones and mud. These boats trade to Belfast and bring down coals, iron, slates, in fact anything the merchants may require. They are manned by from 4 to 6 seamen and are generally fore and aft-rigged vessels.

Where the river first issues from Lough Beg, there is a ferry called the New ferry. A large flat-bottomed boat is employed here, capable of conveying a carriage and horses, half a dozen bullocks, or a score of sheep at once. It is not worked with oars: a chain is passed through bulkheads along the boat's gunwale and made fast at both sides of the river. 2 men pulling on this chain shoot the boat across the stream with ease. One end of the boat drops down and forms a gangway by which a horse and cart can enter.

The banks of the river are low and afford abundance of clay for the manufacture of bricks, of which a number are made. They are sold at from 6s 6d to 10s per thousand, according to quality. Ferry charges: horse and car 1s, horse 6d, foot passenger 1d.

River Main

The Main river traverses the parish from north to south for 5 miles. The fall is not great, but from the constant supply of water it is well adapted for the purpose of machinery. It is not navigable. It frequently overflows its banks.

The banks of the Main river from Dunminning to near Gracehill are high. Consequently it does not overflow its banks till it reaches the flat ground south of Gracehill and is joined by the Braid river. Here it forms a large sheet of water, frequently during winter months. The deposits are beneficial.

There are 4 natural falls on the river in this parish. The most important occurs at Cow Park mills. It is a fall of about 20 feet. At Craigs mill there is one of about 10 feet.

Bogs

There are several large tracts of bog, generally exalted, being from 500 to 600 feet above the sea. They contain a considerable quantity of wood, principally of oak and fir. Birch is found in small quantities. [Insert query by R.K. Dawson: It is stated that "there are several large tracts of bog"; more particulars wanted as to their names, extent, height above the river; have the trees been broken at the same height, do they lie in the same direction?]

Woods

There are no natural woods, but a good deal of plantation about the dean's at Portglenone. This is all fir and not yet arrived at perfection. There are a few old trees about the house itself. The whole of the ground above Portglenone bears evident marks of having been under wood at no very distant date.

Climate

This parish differs little from the surrounding parishes. The upper parts are damp and subject to fogs. Towards the bottom of the southern side the crops ripen sooner than in Kirkinriola, so the inhabitants assert. In reality there can be but little or no difference. The prevailing winds are south west: for instance, trees planted in an exposed situation will all have an inclination towards the north east, and the outside trees, towards the south west, are stunted in their growth and do not grow more than two-thirds of the height of the centre ones. This may be assigned as the cause of the east side of the range of ground which runs through the parish being much better cultivated than the ground on the west. On this side all, or nearly all, the cottages will be found hid in the gorges and behind the little hills, to find shelter from the wet south west wind. It may be said to blow 9 months in the year.

Table of Occupations

Ahoghill, trades and callings: surgeons 1, spirit shops 5, grocers 3, tailors 1, houses of entertainment 3, bakers 1, shoemakers 1, blacksmiths 1.

Cullybackey, trades and callings: surgeons 1, spirit shops 5, grocers 2, bakers 0, carpenters 2, blacksmiths 2, houses of entertainment 1.

Gracehill, trades and callings: grocers 2, carpenters 3, shoemakers 1, bakers 1, hotelkeepers 1, heddle <headel> makers 2. [Insert note: Heddles are used in weaving].

Portglenone, trades and callings: apothecaries 3, bakers [illegible], bonnet makers 2, booksellers 0, carpenters 2, clockmakers 1, drapers 2, grocers 8, houses of entertainment for the poorer class 5, hardware shops 1, innkeepers 2, leather cutters 0, milliners <miliners> 6, tailors 2, painters and glaziers 2, cartmakers 1, whiskey shops 9, wheelwrights 2, tailors 0, shoemakers 4, saddlers 0.

MODERN TOPOGRAPHY

Towns

Portglenone, situated on the River Bann, joined to the county Derry by a good stone bridge. There is only 1 3-storey house in the town. The street is wide but very dirty. [Insert query by Dawson: What is the style and character of the houses generally? [Answer by T.C. Hannyngton]: The houses in Portglenone are principally low and wretchedly roofed. The town lies low and close to the River Bann, and is consequently very damp. The street is flat and very dirty, there being no fall to carry off the water].

Ahoghill is a small thriving village towards the centre of the parish. It has a good monthly market for linen on Fridays, the first Friday in the month, also 2 tolerable houses (carmen's inns) for the reception of travellers, Dubourdieu. [Insert query: Is it really thriving and does it wear the appearance of being so? [Answer] Ahoghill is by no means a thriving village now. It was before the markets removed to Ballymena. It is small and dirty. Many of the houses are roofless. It is well supplied with excellent spring water].

Cullybackey, a small village at the east bank of the Main river: there is a good stone bridge over

the River Main here, also a fine bleach mill and corn mills. It is a neat village.

Galgorm, a long straggling village about 2 miles from Ballymena on the road to Ahoghill.

Gracehill, a Moravian settlement on the west bank of the Main river, about half a mile south of its junction with the Braid river: it was established in 1755. The number of houses both public and private is 40 and the number of inhabitants 400. A savings bank is held in the house, of the single brethren. The members of the community, with the exception of the clergy, are principally mechanics, such as cabinet makers, carpenters, shoemakers, bakers, stocking weavers and weavers of linen and cotton. Each family has, besides, land for keeping a cow and raising potatoes. Gracehill is 1 mile and a half south west of Ballymena.

Places of Worship

Ahoghill: Protestant church, one of the oldest churches in the parish, is 51 feet by 24, has 31 seats and would accommodate 186 persons.

Covenanters' meeting house is 60 feet by 30, has 91 seats and would accommodate 914 persons.

Roman Catholic chapel, large, would accommodate 800 persons.

Cullybackey: Covenanters' meeting house is 51 feet by 24, has 50 seats and would accommodate 350.

Presbyterian house, built in 1727, is 37 by 24, 98 seats and would accommodate 686.

Portglenone: Protestant church, a small old building in bad repair, contains 21 seats and would accommodate 150 persons, is 57 feet by 21, built 1707.

Presbyterian meeting house, an old building, would accommodate 1,500 persons, is 69 feet by 27.

Methodist New Connection, built in 1834, 35 feet by 20, a brick house and cost 120 pounds.

Seceding meeting house, built in 1823, is 51 feet by 27, would accommodate 500 persons.

Roman Catholic chapel is as large as the Presbyterian house and would accommodate about the same number. [Insert query: When was it built, what did it cost and what number of persons will it accomodate? [Answer] 1,500].

Bleach Mills

On the Main river in the parish of Ahoghill, between Dunminning and Gracehill, there are 9 bleach mills.

First, Gruba mill, has 1 water wheel 44 feet in

diameter, 3 feet 6 inches buckets, an overshot wheel.

Second, Fanaghy mill, has 3 wheels: 1 wheel 16 feet in diameter, 5 feet buckets; one 11 feet, 4 feet buckets; one 10 feet, 2 feet buckets, undershot.

Craigs mill has 1 water wheel 18 feet in diameter, 8 feet, 4 across the buckets, an undershot wheel.

Lower Craigs mill has 1 wheel 14 feet diameter, 5 feet buckets, undershot.

Cullybackey mill has 4 water wheels: 3 of them 16 feet in diameter, 4 feet 6 inches buckets; one 13 feet diameter, buckets 2 feet 9 inches.

Low Park mills, the oldest mill on the river, built about 1700, has 2 wheels: one 16 feet diameter, 5 feet buckets; one 16 feet diameter, 3 feet buckets, undershot.

Hill Mount Green mill has 3 water wheels: one 18 feet diameter, 5 feet buckets; one 14 feet diameter, 5 feet 10 inches buckets; one 12 feet diameter, 4 feet buckets, all undershot.

Lisnafallan mills have 3 wheels: 2 of them 18 feet diameter, 6 feet buckets; one 15 feet diameter, 6 feet buckets, breast wheels, fall of water 12 feet.

Leighanmore mill, close to Ballymena, has 2 wheels: one 15 feet diameter, 3 feet 6 inches buckets; one 14 feet, 2 feet buckets, undershot, 6 feet fall.

In all there are 9 mills in the parish, with a plentiful supply of water and still a sufficient supply for as many more wheels.

Corn and Flax Mills

Corn mills: 1 in Cullybackey, water wheel diameter 14 feet, buckets 3 feet, undershot; 1 in Straid, half a mile south of Gracehill, diameter 13 feet, 2 feet 8 inches buckets; also a flax mill, wheel the same dimensions, supplied by a small stream from the high ground.

Public Buildings

The places of public worship consist of 2 Protestant and 1 Moravian church, 4 Presbyterian and 2 Seceding meeting houses, and 2 Roman Catholic chapels. The parish church is in the village of Ahoghill and the chapel of ease in Portglenone.

There are 2 [insert marginal query: 3?] Presbyterian meeting houses in Cullybackey village, 1 in Portglenone and 1 in Ahoghill. In the latter village are situated the 2 Seceding meeting houses and 1 Roman Catholic chapel. The second Roman Catholic chapel is situated about a mile south of Portglenone.

There are 4 bridges, 3 over the Main river and 1 over the Bann at Portglenone.

Gentlemen's Seats

Bishop of Down at Portglenone, Archdeacon Alexander.

Mount Davis, [blank] O'Rourke Esquire. [Insert query: What is the Christian name of Mr O'Rourke who lives at Mount Davis? [Answer] It is not Mr O'Rourke who lives at Mount Davis. It is Captain McMannus. Ballyboys is the name of Mr O'Rourke's place. I do not know Christian name].

Mount Pleasant, William Houstan. [Insert query: Is Houstan the name of the gentleman who lives at Mount Pleasant? [Answer] Yes].

Hillmount, the proprietor of the bleach green of the same name.

Galgorm Castle, occupied by John Joy Esquire, an antiquated looking building, belonging to the Earl of Mountcashel, but seldom occupied by him. It was built by a Dr Colville in 1696, whose daughter married an ancestor of Lord Mountcashel. The castle appears to have been partly in imitation of an ancient defensible residence. The walls of it each exhibit a rude attempt at bastioned fronts, but the greater part of the front enclosure has been removed and that in the rear so encumbered with offices as to make it difficult to discover the original design.

[Insert query: The name Mount Stafford appears on the Index map: is it the name of a gentleman's house, and who resides there? Answer: Occupied by Mr Adams, a timber merchant].

Manufactories

The River Main affords an abundant supply of water for bleaching. There are 9 of such establishments situated on its banks. There are no other manufactories in the parish except some brickfields near the Bann.

Communications

The roads are very numerous and generally good. The principal are: the mail road from Belfast to Coleraine; the western road from Ballymena to Ballymoney; that from Randalstown to Coleraine; from Ballymena to Toome Bridge and Portglenone, besides several crossroads, most of which are kept in good repair.

General Appearance and Scenery

There is nothing striking in the parish. In winter it presents a very desolate appearance. On the Main water between Dunminning and Gracehill there is some pleasing rural scenery, but this cannot be seen from any part of the parish. It lies low. The spot must be visited.

[Insert note: Under the head General Appearance and Scenery, more might be said of the banks of the rivers which afford many pleasing views and the general appearance of Gracehill would admit of fuller description. This Memoir appears rather meagre on the whole and I shall be glad of further particulars to help to fill it up. [Signed] Robert K. Dawson, Lieutenant Royal Engineers, 9th December 1834].

SOCIAL ECONOMY

Ahoghill Dispensary

Founded in 1833, supported by voluntary subscription and the grand jury of the county, the county paying a sum equal to that raised by the subscription. Salary of the medical man 40 pounds per annum. It has added much to the comfort of the poor. More good might still be done if the salary would admit of the surgeon devoting his whole time to it. To enable him to live, he is obliged to practise for himself, and the one employment clashes with the other. In one quarter 129 visits were paid. Days for the poor to attend Monday and Friday. [Table] Average number of patients in 3 months 130; patients cured 71, still on hand 39. Fever in the spring the most prevalent, dropsy next, only 2 cases of consumption.

Epidemic diseases are very rare, but rheumatic affections are very common.

Schools

There is a good school in Gracehill, at which on average 48 boys are educated. 6 ushers are employed. No boys are admitted after 14 years of age and 50 is the limited number of scholars <scolars>.

Portglenone school, founded in 1813 by Erasmus Smith: 40 males are educated annually and 30 females. The master receives 20 pounds per annum and the benefit of an acre and a half of ground. The mistress receives 10 pounds per annum. They both have accommodation in the schoolhouse.

There are various small hedge schools all throughout the parish. There is also a ladies' school at Gracehill, at which the average number is 10 boarders.

Religion

The parish is a rectory in the gift of the Crown.

The greater portion of the inhabitants are Presbyterians. There are about 700 persons belonging to the Moravian establishment in Gracehill. They hold the townland of Ballykennedy on a lease renewable for ever from Earl O'Neill. This is let out again to the members of the community and profits are applied to the repairs of the public buildings, the maintenance of their clergy etc.

PRODUCTIVE ECONOMY

Manufacturing

Bleaching linen is extensively carried on along the banks of the Main water. This and spinning and weaving, together with making bricks, are the only manufactures of the parish. The single sisters of the Moravian brethren are celebrated for their ornamental needlework.

Fairs and Markets

There is a weekly market in Portglenone and a monthly market in Ahoghill. In the latter town are 3 fairs annually, and in the former a monthly fair every month.

Rural Economy

The soil is in general light. The general crops are potatoes, flax and oats. Wheat is not cultivated. In the townland of Ballykennedy, and close to the Moravian school, is a garden containing [blank] acres, devoted exclusively to the growth of camomile, which has attained a high degree of celebrity amongst the druggists of the country.

Uses made of the Bogs

Their principal use is for fuel. A few individuals mix it with lime for manure. It is considered good for this purpose.

General Remarks

The parish of Ahoghill is the largest in the county Antrim, but not a profitable one in proportion to its size. It is well adapted for bleaching, which is in fact the only wealth it possesses. Much more can be made by flax than the tillage of such poor ground. It is much exposed, being a high detached ridge running between 2 rivers, the Bann and the Main. If hedgerows were planted, the farmer would soon find the benefit they would give: his corn would not be shaken or blighted by the winds and his cattle would have something to screen them also.

The parish is well off for spring and river water

and fuel. Material for building is also plenty. It abounds in basalt and bricks. Notwithstanding, the roads are now in a bad condition, particularly that between Ballymena and Portglenone. The cottages are low and terribly dirty. The poor have no idea of the comfort of cleanliness. The bane of the parish is high party spirit. The Protestants are the strongest party.

Fair Sheets by John Bleakly, May to July 1837

Modern Topography

Church

The church is situated in the centre of the village of Ahoghill. Its dimensions interiorly is 79 by 23 and a half feet, with ornament; above a belfry, in which is a bell. It contains 27 pews viz. 22 single and 5 double pews. 10 of the single pews are each 8 feet 7 inches by 3 and a half feet; the other 10 are each 8 feet 7 inches by 3 feet 9 inches; and 2 at the communion end, each 2 and a half by 9 and a half feet. The 5 double pews are each 9 and a half by 8 feet 7 inches and the aisle is 5 feet wide. All boarded, in good repair, with 7 Gothic windows viz. 3 at each side and 1 on east end 5 and a half feet wide. The other windows are each 3 feet 2 inches wide. Wall in front is 6 feet high. The oldest tombstone inscription visible is dated 1697. 5th May 1837.

Seceding Meeting House

The Seceding meeting house of the Revd Frederick Buick was built AD 1806. Total dimensions interiorally is 52 by 30 and a half feet. It contains 51 single pews and 1 double pew, which is 9 by 4 and a half feet. 24 of the single pews are each 7 feet 9 inches by 2 and a half feet and 27 single pews each 5 feet 10 inches by 2 and a half feet. The aisle is of earth, 6 feet wide. The floor is of earth. 8 windows viz. 6 are arched and 2 are oblong, and 3 doors viz. 1 on each end and 1 on the side. 2 are each 4 feet wide and one 3 feet wide. This meeting house is not in good repair. The oldest tombstone is dated 1829, Sarah Gordon.

Church and Meeting House

The church at Portglenone is said to have been erected in AD 1735, which date is on a marble font in the church granted by the Revd Mr Leslie.

The Presbyterian meeting house at Ahoghill was recently built in 1788. See stone on front of meeting house.

Ancient Topography

Artificial Cave

There is an artificial cave on the farm of James McClure in the townland of Moyasset, which runs 40 and a half feet north and south, with a chamber which runs east 10 feet by 3 feet wide and 4 feet high. The entrance or mouth is at this end. The north chamber is 4 feet wide by 3 feet high. Entrance into second chamber is 2 by 1 and a half feet and 5 feet high, and 5 feet broad at broadest end. The stone, like those of other caves, rudely put up and is situated in a cornfield, and was closed up at the mouth until this day with a large stone which is now removed. It is said by the proprietor to have extended a considerable length further eastward. [Ground plan, main dimensions 38 and a half by 10 feet, "T" shape]. From James McClure, farmer.

Forts

There is a fort on the farm of Samuel Paul of Broughdown; 2 forts in Tullygrally, 1 on Adam Harbeson's farm and 1 on Thomas Richy's farm; a fort on the farm of John McAlister, but dug up, in Tullygowan; and 1 on the farm of John Christie in Killybeg; and 1 on William McCibbin's farm, Ballymontenagh; and 1 on John McMaster's farm.

Standing Stone

There is a standing stone in Moylarg, on the farm of Mr Cunningham near the river and bleach mill. This standing stone is 5 feet 8 inches high by 2 feet 5 inches broad on the broadest span. Nothing remarkable nor any tradition respecting it.

Caves

Cave on the farm of Robert Blackley, Brocklamont, but closed up; and one on the farm of Patrick Hatton in same townland but closed up. Cave in McKeastown townland, Ballyminister, on Michael Hagan's farm, closed up.

Sword Hilt

The hilt of an ancient sword was found 10 years ago in the bottom of a pump in the town of Ahoghill, and is now is the possession of John Dallis, a tailor in the village, and is of iron.

Cave

Cove on Mr Joy's property on the Cove hill, nearly closed; nothing remarkable about it. 19th June 1837.

Irish Hill and Scout Hill

The Irish hill is so called from the Irish army being encamped on it during Cromwell's war. It is a large hill situated in the townland of Tullygrally, on the road leading from Ballymena to Randalstown. An ancient castle of the O'Hara family stood in the flat near the stream, in the townland of Staght McConnor, between the Irish hill and the Scout hill. This castle was kept by the Irish, in which was 3 young ladies of the O'Haras, whom the Irish stripped naked and kept as prisoners, until the Scotch army, who were then stationed in the Scout hill, took possession of the castle by putting a number of hats on poles near the castle, for which the Irish took for men by night, and their guards fled from the castle, when Halladay and 2 of the Youngs rescued the ladies and took the castle. The Irish and Scotch armies fought in scouting parties between these 2 hills, from which the hill takes its name. From John Bartholomew, farmer, Tullygarby. 28 June 1837.

Camp Hill

The Camp hill is a planted fort on the property of Mr John Dickey, in townland Ballea. On this hill the Royal Scotch and Tay fencibles were encamped the year after the rebellion of 1798. All the prisoners who were leading men of the rebellion who were taken prisoners were 9 in number, namely Tom Archer, who was gibbeted on the moat for 2 years in townland Ballykeel; James Montgomery and Charles Montogomery with John McCleery, Eagleson, Ryan, Dunn, Boyle and Craig were all hanged on the moat. James and Charles Montgomery and John McCleery were beheaded, after being hanged and their heads put up on the market house in Ballymena. Archer was the most courageous. Ryan and Dunn were Roman Catholics and the rest Presbyterians. From Tom Blair, caretaker to Mr Casement.

Gold Ornament

An ancient gold ornament or necklace was found in the moss of Drumraw, 1 foot under the surface by George Holmes, farmer in Drumraw, 4 years ago near the house, but was sold to Archdeacon Alexander's daughter for 2 pounds 5s 0d; weight half an ounce and 10 grains. From George Holmes.

Forts

The 2 forts on James Hill and John Adams' farm: one is destroyed and the other undisturbed. The parapet of one is of stone and earth.

Undisturbed fort on Charles Martin's farm, same townland, but dug up in part.

The fort on Widow Kyle's farm, Garvaghey, is undisturbed, very high parapet and on a heathery hill, is of earth.

Standing Stones

Opposite this hill in Tullynahuncon townland there are 3 standing stones, each 3 feet high but no regular shape, on the farm of Robert Hilton. The hill is called Cloughcurragh. These stones are said to have been placed <plaiced> as headstones. From Alexander McMullan and Ennis McDonald, farmers.

Burial Ground and Discoveries

Ancient burial ground in Finkiltagh are 2 stones each 3 feet high and 9 feet apart, supposed to have been put up as gateposts on Peter McCloskey's farm.

Circle of stones in Finkiltagh on James Simpson's farm, near the flax mill: *worth drawing.*

An iron pot with a few iron articles found on the farm of Ennis McDonald, Finkiltagh, 60 years ago but all lost. From Ennis McDonald. 4th July 1837.

Forts

There is a fort of earth on Robert Barkly's farm in townland Tullygarby, demolished. Fort on Widow Andrew's farm, townland of Garvahy; 1 on Archie Dysert's farm and 1 on Paddy McIlvenon's farm, same townland. Fort on John Crawford's farm, Lisroddin. One on Robert Kyle's farm, Bracknamucklagh. 2 forts in Morbury: 1 on Archie Lewis' farm and 1 on William McKendry's farm. 2 forts on Lisnahulcheon: 1 on Henry Maddigan's farm and 1 on Daniel Fulton's farm. 3 forts in Lisnagarron: 1 on John McDonald's farm, 1 on Bernard Lord's farm and 1 on Bernard Kennedy's farm. One on John Mark's farm, Gortaherron. One on Thomas McMaster's farm, Killylish.

Burial Ground

Ancient burial ground about 20 perches south east of the schoolhouse in townland of Craigs, on Edward Taylor's farm.

Artificial Island and Standing Stone

An artificial island in Loughtammon now digged up, both island and lake, in townland of Lisnahuncheon.

Standing stone called the Bullock's Stone, from the track of a bullock hoof on it, but now turned over and sunk, in townland of Lisnahuncheon.

Caves

Tory Holes in Lisnahuncheon bog, but closed up.
A cave on James McClure's farm, Moyasset, but closed up.
Cave on Samuel McIlroy's farm, Drumrankin, but closed up.

Ancient Trough

An ancient wooden trough of black oak found in 1855 by James Burns, but now destroyed. Supposed to have been used in a brewery or distillery, in townland of Lisroddin.

Forts and Caves

A fort on Robert Knowles' farm, of Cardonaghy, and a cove, but closed up. A fort in Dreen, on John McIlroy's farm, and a cave, but closed up. A fort on John Kyle's farm, Garvaghy East. A fort and cove on Andrew Carson's farm, Ballybeg, but closed up. A fort on William Davis' farm, Cardonaghy. A fort on Charles Martin's farm, Drumraw, and 1 on James McCartney's farm, same townland. Fort on Daniel Kernan's farm, Carmaigraw. Fort on Hugh Quinn's farm, Killygarron. 3 forts in Castletown: 1 on James Brown's farm, 1 on John McMeehan's farm and 1 on Alexander McClure's farm. 3 forts in Lisnahuncheon, on rundale. A fort in Tullygowan, on John McAlister's farm.

There is a fort of earth on David Lagan's farm, in the townland of Craignageeraght, and 1 on Robert Nichol's farm in the same townland; 1 in Ballybeg, on Andrew Carson's farm; 1 in Lumnaherry, on Samuel Millar's farm; 1 on the farm of William Dunlop in Ballynafir; 1 in Slavenagh, on James McKowen's; 1 in Gloona, on Hugh Kernaghan's farm; 1 in Lismornaghan, on John Higgins' farm; 1 on Hugh Kernaghan's farm in Moyasset; 1 in Galgorm, on George Raphael's farm; 1 on the farm of Betty Nichol in Ballyconnolly; also 1 on John Maxwell's farm, Aughnahoy, also a cave on the farm of Andrew Fleming, now closed up, in same townland; also an old graveyard opposite the Roman Catholic chapel on Archdeacon Alexander's farm in Slavenagh; also 1 at the Roman Catholic chapel in same place; a fort in Killyleese, on Thomas McMaster's farm.

A cave is said to have been at Gracehill, in the townland of Ballykennedy, 8 years closed up.

Also a fort in which is a cave at Mount Davis, on the farm of Alexander McManus Esquire, in the townland of Cordanaghy.

Galgorm Castle

Galgorm Castle is said to have been erected by Dr Colville <Colvin>. The date of its original erection cannot be ascertained. Roary Ogue McQuillan's castle is said to have stood on the bank of the river a little below Galgorm Castle in same townland. The walls of the old church at Galgorm Castle are 2 and a half feet thick. Dr Colville's grave is elevated 3 feet above the level of the church floor, dimensions 20 by 14 feet.

Standing Stone and Discoveries

The Long Stone opposite William Marshall's door on the roadside in the townland of Killycurry is only 3 feet 2 inches high and 14 inches broad on the face. About 2 and a half feet is said to have been broken off the top.

About 12 years ago Felix Scullion of Castletown found 2 silver candlesticks, with a few gold coins, but sold them all.

The schoolhouse at Killycurry is 32 by 16 feet inside, but unoccupied at present.

Forts

Fort on Hugh Kernaghan's farm, in which was a cave, but long since demolished.
A fort in William Burnett's farm, Ballylummin.

Standing Stones

There is a standing stone a few yards from Cullybackey bridge, in the ditch at the roadside. This stone is 4 feet high 5 feet broad and 1 foot thick.

There is also a small standing stone in the Sawpit Field, on the farm of John Millar in Broughclone.

Forts and Caves

There is a fort of earth on the farm of John McIlroy near Mount Davis in the townland of Dreen, undisturbed. There is a cave in the parapet of this fort: *worth drawing*.

There is a cave on the farm of Peter Harbeson, in a cornfield in the townland of Killdowney, the mouth or opening in a hedge, but now closed up.

The fort on the farm of Thomas Richey is undisturbed. There is a cave in this fort, but closed up, in the townland of Tullygrally.

The cave in McKeestown on Michael Hagan's farm, townland of Ballyminister, is closed up 2 years.

There is a cove in Killdowney on the farm of John Murdock which runs thus: [diagram indicating direction of cave] and is 3 feet wide by 4 feet high. The entrance into the second room is 1 and a half feet wide by 1 foot high, but nearly filled with water except the outside room. [Ground plan, main dimensions 17 by 5 feet, "L" shape]. 7th July 1837.

SOCIAL ECONOMY

Ahoghill: Trades and Occupations

Village of Ahoghill [table contains the following headings: number of house, trade or occupation, number of storeys, slated or thatched].

1, labourer <laborer>, 1-storey, thatched.
2, pauper, 1-storey, thatched.
3, labourer, 1-storey, thatched.
4, besom <bisom> maker, 1-storey, thatched.
5, cobbler <cobler>, 1-storey, thatched.
6, pauper, 1-storey, thatched.
7, walls of a new house.
8, linen weaver, 1-storey, thatched.
9, shoemaker, 1-storey, thatched.
10, labourer, 1-storey, thatched.
11, linen weaver, 1 and a half-storeys, thatched.
12, linen weaver, 1-storey, thatched.
13, widow, 1-storey, thatched.
14, widow, 1-storey, thatched.
15, pauper, 1-storey, thatched.
16, carpenter, 1-storey, thatched.
17, smith's forge, 1-storey, thatched.
18, linen weaver, 1-storey, thatched.
19, stone mason, 1-storey, thatched.
20, labourer, 1-storey, thatched.
21, widow, 1-storey, thatched.
22, labourer, 1-storey, thatched.
23, empty house, 1-storey, thatched.
24, labourer, 1-storey, thatched.
25, smith's forge, 1-storey, thatched.
26, farmers' and carmen's inn, 2-storeys, slated.
27, tailor, 1-storey, thatched.
28, widow, 1-storey, thatched.
29, linen weaver, 2-storey, thatched.
30, grocer and publican, 1-storey, thatched.
31, stokerman, 2-storeys, thatched.
32, labourer, 2-storeys, thatched.
33, labourer, 2-storeys, thatched.
34, publican, 2-storeys, thatched.
35, dispensary and petty session house, 2-storeys, slated.

36, linen weaver, 1-storey, thatched.
37, labourer, 1-storey, thatched.
38, black hole, 1-storey, stone-roofed.
39, linen weaver, 1-storey, thatched.
40, linen weaver, 1-storey, thatched.
41, huckster, 1-storey, thatched.
42, linen weaver, 1-storey, thatched.
43, shoemaker, 1-storey, thatched.
44, carpenter, 1-storey, thatched.
45, labourer, 1-storey, thatched.
46, schoolmaster, 1-storey, thatched.
47, wheelwright, 1-storey, thatched.
48, labourer, 1-storey, thatched.
49, empty stables, 2-storeys, thatched.
50, linen weaver, 1-storey, thatched.
51, minister, Seceder, 2-storeys, slated.
52, linen weaver, 1-storey, thatched.
53, labourer, 1-storey, thatched.
54, publican, 1-storey, thatched.
55, linen weaver, 1-storey, thatched.
56, meeting house, Seceding, 1-storey, slated.
57, labourer, 1-storey, thatched.
58 and 59, tailor, painter and glazier, same door, 1-storey, thatched.
59, labourer, 1-storey, thatched.
60, labourer, 1-storey, thatched.
61, linen weaver, back house, 1-storey, thatched.
62, grocer, 1-storey, thatched.
63, blacksmith, 1-storey, thatched.
64, widow, 1-storey, thatched.
65, empty, 2-storeys, slated.
66, police barracks, 2-storeys, slated.
67, church, Established Church, 1-storey, slated.
68, publican, 1-storey, thatched.
69, labourer and lodging house, 1-storey, thatched.
70, bakery, 1-storey, thatched.
71, labourer, 1-storey, thatched.
72, linen weaver, 1-storey, thatched.
73, carman, 1-storey, thatched.
74, surgeon, 1-storey, thatched.
75, linen weaver, 2-storeys, slated.
76, reedmaker, 1-storey, thatched.
77, linen weaver, 1-storey, thatched.
78, meeting house, Presbyterian, 1-storey, slated.
79, butcher, 1-storey, thatched.
80, old maid, 1-storey, thatched.
81, labourer, 1-storey, thatched.
82, labourer, 1-storey, thatched.
83, labourer, 1-storey, thatched.
84, empty house, 1-storey, thatched.
85, publican, 2-storeys, slated.
86, farmer and publican, 2-storeys, slated.
87, carpenter, 2-storeys, slated.

88, farmer, part 1-storey, part 2-storeys, thatched and slated.

89, grocer, 1-storey, thatched.

90, blacksmith, 2-storeys, thatched.

91, weigh-house and schoolhouse, 2-storeys, slated.

92, labourer, 2-storeys, thatched.

93, linen weaver, 1-storey, thatched.

94, flax dresser, 1-storey, thatched.

95, linen weaver, 1-storey, thatched.

96, widow, 1-storey, thatched.

97, labourer, 1-storey, thatched.

98, besom maker, 1-storey, thatched.

99, workman in a stable, 1-storey, thatched.

100, linen weaver, 1-storey, thatched.

101, linen weaver, 1-storey, thatched.

102, linen weaver, 1-storey, thatched.

103, pensioner, 1-storey, thatched.

104, linen weaver, 1-storey, thatched.

105, labourer, 1-storey, thatched.

106, labourer, 1-storey, thatched.

107, farmer, 1-storey, thatched.

108, grocer, 1-storey, thatched.

109, meeting house, Seceding, 1-storey, slated.
4th May 1837.

Emigration in 1835

List of persons who have emigrated from the parish of Ahoghill during the year 1835. [Table contains the following headings: name, age, religion, townland of origin, port emigrated to].

Thomas McKeen, 44, James McKeen, 10, Jane McKeen, 8, Presbyterians, from Galgorm to New York.

Robert Ritchie, 30, Presbyterian, from Galgorm to Quebec.

John McFall, 30, Roman Catholic, from Galgorm to Quebec.

John Ruddan, 50, Margaret Ruddan, 60, Presbyterians, from Aughnahoy to New York, returned.

Hugh Kernahan, 22, Nancy Kernahan, 20, Jane Kernahan, 1 and a half years, Presbyterians, from Moyasset to Quebec.

William Mason, 32, Roman Catholic, from Watercloney to Liverpool.

Esther McGonagle, 40, Covenanter, from Cordonaghy to New York.

John Kennedy, 21, Ann Kennedy, 23, Presbyterians, from Moneydolly to New York.

John Magee, 26, Roman Catholic, from Straid to Glasgow.

Daniel McAlister, 22, Roman Catholic, from Straid to Glasgow.

Martha Crosset, 30, Jane Crosset, 10, Elizabeth Crosset, 8, James Crosset, 6, Seceders, from Garvahy to St John's.

Robert Wiley, 26, Presbyterian, from Garvahy to New York.

Daniel McKenny, 50, Established Church, from Mullinasillagh to Sydney.

Robert Loughridge, 18, Presbyterian, from Cullybackey to Quebec.

John Kennedy, 20, Anne Kennedy, 22, Presbyterians, from Moneydolly to Quebec.

Michael Keenan, 35, Sarah Keenan, 22, Jane Keenan, 1, Roman Catholics, from Carmaigraw to Quebec.

David McCahy, 25, Eliza McCahy, 21, Presbyterians, from Killycargan to Quebec.

Robert Arthbutnot, 25, Presbyterian, from Killycargan to Quebec.

Ann Kyle, 30, James Kyle, 32, William Kyle, 12, John Kyle, 10, Robert Kyle, 8, Joseph Kyle, 6, Mary-Ann Kyle, 4, Elizabeth Kyle, 2, Presbyterians, from Killycargan to Quebec.

John Murray, 24, Roman Catholic, from Ballymontenagh to Glasgow.

John Young, 25, Presbyterian, from Ballymontenagh to Philadelphia.

Margaret Sheil, 50, John Sheil, 20, Thomas Sheil, 18, Margaret Sheil Junior, 16, Presbyterians, from Mullinasillagh to Quebec.

Michael Keenan, 36, Ellen Keenan, 25, Rose Keenan, 1, Mary Keenan, 3, Presbyterians, from Largy to Quebec.

Archie Wiseman, 20, Presbyterian, from Ballywatermoy to New York.

Robert Wally, 22, Presbyterian, from Tullgrally to New York.

Emigration in 1836

List of persons who have emigrated from the parish of Ahoghill during the year 1836.

Mary Ann Adair, 22, Ellen Nora Plunkett Adair, 17, Presbyterians, from Brocklamont to New York.

James Ray, 40, Jane Ray, 40, Elizabeth Ray, 10, Sarah Ray, 8, William John Ray, 6, James Ray Junior, 2 (died), Moravians, from Galgorm to Philadelphia.

Margaret Colum, 23, Jane Colum, 30, Robert Colum, 20, Presbyterians, from Galgorm to New York.

Mary-Ann Toole, 20, Roman Catholic, from Galgorm to New York.

Eliza Conwell, 21, Established Church, from Ahoghill village to New York.

Mary Adams, 28, Presbyterian, from Aughanhoy to New York.

Samuel Hammel, 21, Rose Hammel, 40, James Hammel, 28, Presbyterians, from Aughnahoy to New York.

Alexander Maxwell, 22, Presbyterian, from Aughnahoy to New York.

Frank McClernon, 24, James Henry McClernon, 22, Roman Catholics, from Watercloney to New York.

Jane Hunter, 35, Presbyterian, from Moneydolly to New York.

William Eagleson, 30, Moravian, from Ballyminister to Quebec.

James McLaw, 25, Covenanter, from Portglenone to New York.

John McKenny, 22, Established Church, from Mullinasillagh to Sydney.

Daniel McKenny, 20, Established Church, from Mullinasillagh to Quebec.

James McAnally, 26, Roman Catholic, from Watercloney to Glasgow.

Thomas Spencer, 20, Presbyterian, from Tullygrally to New York.

James McCartney, 42, Margaret McCartney, 40, Archie McCartney, 19, Thomas McCartney, 13, James McCartney, 11, Dorothea McCartney, 9, Alexander McCartney, 4, Agnes McCartney, 42, Archie McCartney, 23, Andrew McCartney, 20, Joseph McCartney, 16, Presbyterians, from Gortfad to New York.

Andrew McCartney, 25, Presbyterian, from Gortfad to Glasgow.

Hugh Kyle, 25, James Kyle, 23, Presbyterians, from Lisroddin to Quebec.

James Ray, 40, Roman Catholic, from Bracknamucklagh to Liverpool, returned in 1837.

James McKendry, 25, Peggy-Ann McKendry, 20, Presbyterians, from Mobuoy to St John's.

John McWhinny, 19, Established Church, from Castletown to Quebec.

John McFalls, 30, Roman Catholic, from Finaghy to Philadelphia.

James Murray, 40, Roman Catholic, from Moneydolly to Glasgow.

Mary-Ann Toole, 21, Roman Catholic, from Cardonaghy to New York.

Catherine Duffin, 64, Margaret Duffin, 24, Roman Catholics, from Killeen to Glasgow.

Thomas Hinds, 35, Hesther Hinds, 37, Eliza Hinds, 5, Presbyterians, from Finkiltagh to New York.

James Kennedy, 20, Presbyterian, from Craigs to St John's.

Mary Anne Johnstone, 20, Covenanter, from Craigs to St John's.

Robert Galloway, 20, James Galloway, 22, Covenanters, from Craigs to St John's.

William Machonaghty, 50, Elizabeth Machonaghty, 50, James Machonaghty, 25, Alexander Machonaghty, 21, John Machonaghty, 18, William Machonaghty, 17, Eliza Machonaghty, 13, Catherine Machonaghty, 11, Presbyterians, from Ballyconnolly to Quebec.

Jane Simpson, 50, William Simpson, 12, Margaret Ann Simpson, 22, James Simpson, 14, Presbyterians, from Killyless to St John's.

James McKinney, 21, Presbyterian, from Killyless to St John's.

Charles McCartney, 20, Mary McCartney, 30, Presbyterians, from Bracknamucklagh to Quebec.

David McCahey, 24, Presbyterian, from Billycargan to Quebec.

Anne Wiseman, 22, Presbyterian, from Ballywatermoy to New York.

Eliza Willey, 25, Presbyterian, from Tullygrally to New York.

James Peters, 22, James Wilson, 35, William Peters, 30, James Gregg, 30, Presbyterians, from Crankhill to Philadelphia.

James Madill, 28, Presbyterian, from Crankhill to Philadelphia.

Migration

List of persons who migrate annually from the parish of Ahoghill.

Peter McAnally, 30, Roman Catholic, from Watercloney to Glasgow.

Henry Neeson, 50, John Neeson, 40, Roman Catholics, from Watercloney to Glasgow.

Catherine Henry, 40, Roman Catholic, from Watercloney to Glasgow.

Daniel Mitchell, 30, William Mitchell, 32, Presbyterians, from Carnearney to Glasgow.

Robert Ewart, 28, Presbyterian, from Ballyminister to Glasgow.

Patrick Darragh, 45, James Darragh, 22, William Darragh, 16, Eliza Darragh, 24, Roman Catholics, from Ballyminister to Glasgow.

Ellen Davison, 17, Presbyterian, from Ballymontenagh to Glasgow.

Alexander McKee, 21, Presbyterian, from Ahoghill village to Glasgow.

William Dempsey, 21, Presbyterian, from Ahoghill village to Glasgow.

Daniel Logan, 24, Presbyterian, from Ahoghill village to Glasgow.

Jane Murray, 16, Roman Catholic, from Ahoghill village to Glasgow.

Esther Gillespie, 16, Presbyterian, from Ballymontenagh to Glasgow.

Samuel Witheraw, 24, Presbyterian, from Ballyconnolly to Glasgow.

Henry Blaney, 30, Roman Catholic, from Mullinasillagh to Glasgow.

John Wilson, 30, Presbyterian, from Dreen to Glasgow.

James McClane, 40, Established Church, from Dreen to Glasgow.

Matthew Johnstone, 20, Covenanter, from Dreen to Glasgow.

Edward Gordon, 23, Moravian, from Dreen to Glasgow.

Samuel Caulfield, 25, Presbyterian, from Loane to Glasgow.

William McCracken, 26, Established Church, from Craigs to Liverpool.

Robert Baccus, 46, Established Church, from Craigs to Liverpool.

Joseph Henry, 50, John Henry, 25, Roman Catholics, from Craigs to Glasgow.

Robert Harbeson, 30, Presbyterian, from Craigs to Glasgow.

William McIntyre, 25, John McIntyre, 27, Presbyterians, from Craigs to Glasgow.

William Thompson, 25, Roman Catholic, from Craigs to Glasgow.

Archy Sterling, 18, Presbyterian, from Drumrankin to Glasgow.

James Millar, 26, Presbyterian, from Drumrankin to Glasgow.

John McAleese, 18, Presbyterian, from Drumrankin to Glasgow.

Thomas Sterling, 18, Presbyterian, from Drumrankin to Glasgow.

James Malone, 25, Presbyterian, from Drumrankin to Glasgow.

James McCleary, 55, Roman Catholic, from Drumrankin to Glasgow.

John McMeehan, 38, Presbyterian, from Drumrankin to Glasgow.

Denis [?] McCaheeran, 30, Presbyterian, from Drumrankin to Glasgow.

Hugh [?] McIlornan, 24, Presbyterian, from Loane to Glasgow.

Jane Caulfield, 29, Presbyterian, from Loane to Glasgow.

Nancy Gibson, 35, Presbyterian, from Loane to Glasgow.

John Winnon, 30, Presbyterian, from Loane to Glasgow.

William John Millar, 25, Presbyterian, from Loane to Glasgow.

James Workman, 30, Presbyterian, from Loane to Glasgow.

Robert Doey, 26, Presbyterian, from Loane to Glasgow.

Thomas Kelly, 26, Presbyterian, from Craigs to Glasgow.

Andrew Mooney, 30, Presbyterian, from Craigs to Glasgow.

Hugh Clarke, 26, Presbyterian, from Craigs to Glasgow.

Robert McClane, 28, Presbyterian, from Craigs to Glasgow.

Hugh Holmes, 21, Presbyterian, from Killyless to Glasgow.

Joseph Wright, 26, Presbyterian, from Killyless to Glasgow.

Charles McFalls, 22, Dennis McFalls, 45, Roman Catholics, from Carmaigraw to Liverpool.

John Scullion, 48, Roman Catholic, from Carmaigraw to Liverpool.

James Boorman, 38, Roman Catholic, from Carmaigraw to Liverpool.

John McAlister, 28, Roman Catholic, from Gortgole to Glasgow.

William O'Bryans, 26, James O'Bryans, 24, Roman Catholics, from Gortgole to Glasgow.

John McAntaggart, 30, Roman Catholic, from Gortgole to Glasgow.

Hamish O'Hara, 26, Roman Catholic, from Bracknamucklagh to Glasgow.

Patrick O'Kane, 54, Roman Catholic, from Lisnahuncheon to Glasgow.

Neil Gribbin, 40, Roman Catholic, from Lisnahuncheon to Glasgow.

Henry O'Hara, 30, John O'Hara, 25, Roman Catholics, from Lisnahuncheon to Glasgow.

Robert Whitely, 40, Covenanter, from Lisnahuncheon to Glasgow.

Andrew Boyde, 26, Roman Catholic, from Lisnahuncheon to Glasgow.

John O'Hara, 22, James O'Hara, 34, Roman Catholics, from Lisnahuncheon to Glasgow.

John Henry, 30, Roman Catholic, from Lisnahuncheon to Glasgow.

Bernard O'Neill, 40, Roman Catholic, from Lisnahuncheon to Glasgow.

Henry Maddigan, 35, Roman Catholic, from Lisnahuncheon to Glasgow.

James O'Neill, 35, John O'Neill, 42, Roman Catholics, from Lisnahuncheon to Glasgow.

Neil Mooney, 35, Roman Catholic, from Carmaigraw to Glasgow.

Ennis McFall, 40, Roman Catholic, from Carmaigraw to Glasgow.

William Collins, 30, Roman Catholic, from Killycurry to Glasgow.

David McNeily, 35, Presbyterian, from Killycurry to Glasgow.

Peter Young, 30, Presbyterian, from Loane to Glasgow.

James McCollins, 22, Hugh McCollins, 26, Presbyterians, from Finkiltagh to Glasgow.

Arthur McIntyre, 27, Roman Catholic, from Carmaigraw to Liverpool.

Henry Scullion, 39, Roman Catholic, from Carmaigraw to Liverpool.

Charles O'Neill, 23, Roman Catholic, from Carmaigraw to Liverpool.

Daniel Kielt, 30, Roman Catholic, from Carmaigraw to Liverpool.

William Maxwell, 35, Presbyterian, from Tullygrally to Glasgow.

James Conaghy, 32, Alexander Conaghy, 35, Presbyterians, from Tullygowan to Glasgow.

Daniel Boyle, 25, Roman Catholic, from Broughclone to Glasgow.

Robert McCibbin, 32, Presbyterian, from Broughclone to Glasgow.

Hugh McIlrath, 25, Presbyterian, from Ballycloch to Glasgow.

William Patterson, 40, Presbyterian, from Dunnygarron to Glasgow.

Robert Mays, 32, Established Church, from Portglenone to Glasgow.

Table of Schools

[Table contains the following headings: name, situation and description, when established, income and expenditure, physical, intellectual and moral education, number of pupils subdivided by age, sex and religion, name and religion of master or mistress].

Gracehill Academy, held in a house fitted up for the purpose in the settlement, established 1805; physical education: gymnastics and ball playing, leap frog and cricket; intellectual education: all the classical, English and mercantile authors generally used in academies; moral education: visited by the clergy of settlement daily; number of pupils: males, 8 under 10 years of age, 40 from 10 to 15, 2 above 15, total 50; total number of pupils 50, 37 Protestants, 9 Presbyterians, 1 Roman Catholic, 3 other denominations, Moravian; Revd Christian Frederick Hacker, a Moravian minister, is principal; Mr Theodore Rupper, Mr Joseph Waugh, Mr William Oates, Mr John Leech, teachers.

Gracehill male day school, held in a room fitted up for the purpose in the settlement and is 29 by 18 feet internally; income: from the agent of the settlement per annum 20 pounds, from pupils 25 pounds; intellectual education: books published by the Kildare Place Society and the Hibernian Society, *Thompson's Arithmetic and geography, Jackson's Book-keeping* and *Bonnycastle's Men-*

suration; moral education: visited by the Moravian clergy only, Authorised Version read, catechism on Saturday; number of pupils: 14 under 10 years of age, 4 from 10 to 15, 1 above 15; total number of pupils 19, 1 Protestant, 18 other denominations, Moravians; master Thomas Arnold, Established Church.

Craigs, situated in the townland of Craigs, a good house, thatched, 34 feet by 44 feet inside, established 1822; income from pupils 8 pounds; intellectual education: books published by the Kildare Place Society, *Thompson's Geography and arithmetic, Murray's English grammar*; moral education: visited by the clergy of the Established Church, Authorised Version and catechism on Saturday; number of pupils: males, 18 under 10 years of age, 2 from 10 to 15, total 20; females, 18 under 10 years of age, 2 from 10 to 15, total 20; total number of pupils 40, 4 Protestants, 30 Presbyterians, 3 Roman Catholics, 3 Covenanters; master James Getty, a Presbyterian.

Kildowney, situated on the road leading from Ballymena to Ballymoney, a small thatched house, 14 feet by 14 feet inside, in bad repair, established 1787; income from pupils 12 pounds; intellectual education: *Manson's Spelling book and primer, Gough's Arithmetic* and *Murray's English grammar*; moral education: visited by the Presbyterian clergy only, Authorised Version of Scriptures and catechism is taught by the master; number of pupils: males, 23 under 10 years of age, 5 from 10 to 15, total 28; females, 8 under 10 years of age, 4 from 10 to 15, total 12; total number of pupils 40, 1 Protestant, 20 Presbyterians, 19 other denominations; master William Pollock, a Seceder.

Watercloney national school, situated on the road leading from Randalstown to Portglenone, a good house built of stone and lime, slated, 30 by 17 feet interiorly with 5 windows viz. 3 in front and 2 in the rear, with 1 door on the end, established in 1835; income: from the National Board per annum 8 pounds, from pupils 8 pounds; intellectual education: books published by the National Board only, with *Thompson's Arithmetic*; moral education: visited by the Roman Catholic clergy only, catechism on Saturday by the master; number of pupils: males, 15 under 10 years of age, 25 from 10 to 15, 3 above 15, total 43; females, 11 under 10 years of age, 1 above 15, total 12; total number of pupils 55, 5 Protestants, 9 Presbyterians, 41 Roman Catholics; master Patrick McGolrick, a Roman Catholic.

Whiteshill, situated in the townland of Ballylummin, on the road leading from Crosskeys to Ahoghill, a good house of stone and lime, slated, 24 feet long by 18 feet inside with 4 windows viz. 2 Gothic on front and 2 square in the rear, with a door on the end, established 1831; income: from the London Hibernian Society for the last quarter 10s, from pupils 12 pounds per annum; intellectual education: books published by the London Hibernian Society, with *Thompson's and Gough's Arithmetic* and *Murray's English grammar*; moral education: visited by the clergy of the Established Church and the Presbyterian minister, Authorised Version of Scripture is taught; number of pupils: males, 20 under 10 years of age, 8 from 10 to 15, 5 above 15, total 33; females, 15 under 10 years of age, 4 from 10 to 15, 8 above 15, total 27; total number of pupils 60, 40 Presbyterians, 20 other denominations, Seceders; master John Nelson, a Seceder.

Ballybeg, situated on the road leading from Ahoghill to Portglenone, a good house, thatched, 27 by 15 feet interiorly, boarded floor with 3 windows in front and 2 in the gable, and 1 door in the end, established 1826; income: from Thomas Benjamin Adair Esquire, proprietor, per annum 3 pounds, from pupils 12 pounds; intellectual education: books published by the Kildare Place Society, the London Hibernian Society, with *Thompson's and Gough's Arithmetic*; moral education: visited by the Established Church and the Presbyterian clergy, catechism on Saturday and the Authorised Version of Scripture; number of pupils: males, 20 under 10 years of age, 50 from 10 to 15, total 70; females, 25 under 10 years of age, 5 from 10 to 15, total 30; total number of pupils 100, 10 Protestants, 59 Presbyterians, 11 Roman Catholics, 20 other denominations, Seceders; master Matthew Johnstone, a Presbyterian.

[?] Bridgend, in the townland of Corbilly, near the bridge and stream which divides Galgorm from Corbilly, held in a room attached to a dwelling house, built by subscription, 20 feet by 14 feet inside with 4 windows and 1 door on the side, thatched house, established 1814; income from pupils 20 pounds; intellectual education: books published by the Kildare Place Society, *Thompson and Gough's Arithmetic, Murray's English grammar and geography*, with English history and *Jackson's Book-keeping*; moral education: visited by the clergy of the Established and Presbyterian Church, Authorised Version of Scripture taught and catechism on Saturday by the master; number of pupils: males, 20 under 10 years of age, 39 from 10 to 15, total 59; females, 19 under 10 years of age, 2 from 10 to 15, 2 above 15, total 23;

total number of pupils 82, 4 Protestants, 18 Presbyterians, 12 Roman Catholics, 48 other denominations; master William Beard Martin, Established Church. Report for May 1837.

Moyasset, situated near the leading road from Ballymena and Rasharkin, a good house of stone and lime, slated, and 35 by 16 feet inside with 4 windows on each side and door on the end; income from pupils 16 pounds; intellectual education: books published by the Kildare Place Society, *Thompson and Gough's Arithmetic, Murray's English grammar* and *Thompson's Geography*; moral education: visited by the clergy of the Established Church and Presbyterian clergy, Authorised Version of Scripture is taught and catechism on Saturday; number of pupils: males, 17 under 10 years of age, 5 from 10 to 15, 1 above 15, total 23; females, 14 under 10 years of age, total 14; total number of pupils 37, 2 Protestants, 28 Presbyterians, 1 Roman Catholic, 6 other denominations, Seceders; master James Drummond, Presbyterian.

Ballymontenagh, on the road leading from Randalstown to Ahoghill, a tolerable house, thatched, 16 by 30 feet inside with 3 windows on each side and 1 door at the end, established 1827, re-established 8th May 1837; income from pupils 16 pounds; intellectual education: books published by the Kildare Place Society and the London Hibernian Society, with *Gough's Arithmetic* and *Guy's Geography* and *Murray's English grammar*; moral education: visited by the clergy of the Established and Presbyterian Churches, catechism on Monday and the Authorised Version of Scripture; number of pupils: males, 24 under 10 years of age, total 24; females, 7 under 10 years of age, 1 from 10 to 15, total 8; total number of pupils 32, 2 Protestants, 28 Presbyterians, 1 Roman Catholic, 1 other denomination, Seceder; master David Johnson, Presbyterian.

Galgorm, held in the court house of the seneschal, slated, 19 by 20 feet i.e. the schoolroom, established 1820; income from Lord Mountcashel per annum 5 pounds; intellectual education: books published by the Kildare Place Society, arithmetic published by the National Board and *Gough's, Murray's English grammar, Thompson's Geography* and [?] *Main's Book-keeping*; moral education: visited occasionally by the Revd Frederick Beuick Seceding minister, Authorised Version of Scriptures is taught; number of pupils: males, 21 under 10 years of age, 4 from 10 to 15, total 25; females, 13 under 10 years of age, 5 from 10 to 15, 1 above 15, total 19; total number of pupils 44, 24 Presbyterians, 5 Roman Catholics, 15 other denominations, Seceders; master Hugh Rea, a Presbyterian.

Waterclony evening school, held in the day schoolhouse, established 1836; income from pupils 8 pounds; intellectual education: Kildare and National Board books; moral education: visited by Messrs Edward and Alexander O'Rourke; number of pupils: males, 3 from 10 to 15 years of age, 4 above 15, total 7; females, 5 above 15 years of age, total 5; total number of pupils 12, 2 Protestants, 4 Presbyterians, 6 Roman Catholics; master Patrick McGolrick, Roman Catholic. Report for May 1837.

Garvahey, situated on the road leading from Portglenone to Cullybackey, a good house, slated, with 3 windows on each side and is 20 by 15 feet inside, door on the end; income: from the London Hibernian Society 2 pounds, from the Bishop of Meath 3 pounds, from pupils 4 pounds; intellectual education: books published by the London Hibernian Society with *Gough's Arithmetic* and *Jackson's Book-keeping*; moral education: visited by the Presbyterian clergy, Authorised Version taught; number of pupils: males, 18 under 10 years of age, total 18; females, 7 under 10 years of age, total 7; total number of pupils 25, 21 Presbyterians, 4 other denominations, Seceders; master John Andrews, Presbyterian.

Portglenone, held in the manor court house, established 1822; income: from the London Hibernian Society per annum 2 pounds 10s, from pupils 15 pounds; intellectual education: books published by the London Hibernian Society, *Thompson and Gough's Arithmetic, Johnston's Dictionary* and *Knowles' Elementary English reader*; moral education: visited by the clergy of the Established Church and the Seceding clergy occasionally, Authorised Version is taught; number of pupils: males, 14 under 10 years of age, 12 from 10 to 15, total 26; females, 13 under 10 years of age, 1 from 10 to 15, total 14; total number of pupils 40, 12 Protestants, 25 Presbyterians, 3 Roman Catholics; master Arthur Barns, a Covenanter.

Ahoghill, held in the upper story of the weigh house in the village, slated, 19 by 17 feet inside, with 4 windows, established 1829; income: from Archdeacon Alexander per annum 2 pounds, from pupils 12 pounds; intellectual education: books published by the London Hibernian Society and the Kildare books, *Gough's Arithmetic* and *Murray's English grammar*; moral education: visited by the clergy of the Established Church, catechism on Saturday and Authorised Version; number of pupils: males, 15 under 10 years of age,

9 from 10 to 15, total 24; females, 6 under 10 years of age, total 6; total number of pupils 30, 6 Protestants, 6 Presbyterians, 1 Roman Catholic, 17 other denominations, Seceders; master James O'Herrill, a Moravian.

Tannybrannan, on the road leading from Ballymena to Cullybackey, a good house of stone, thatched, 19 and a half by 14 feet and a half, established 1817; income: from the London Hibernian Society per annum 3 pounds 15s, from pupils 7 pounds; intellectual education: books published by the London Hibernian Society, *Thompson's and Gough's Arithmetic, Murray's English grammar*; moral education: visited by the clergy of the Established Church, catechism on Saturday, Authorised Version of Scripture; number of pupils: males, 44 under 10 years of age, 5 from 10 to 15, 5 over 15, total 54; females, 50 under 10 years of age, 4 from 10 to 15, total 54; total number of pupils 108, 100 Presbyterians, 3 Roman Catholics, 5 other denominations; master William Campbell, Established Church. Report for May 1837.

Cullybackey, situated in the village of Cullybackey, a good house of stone and lime, slated, 36 and a half by 16 feet inside with 4 windows on each side, established 1825; income from pupils 19 pounds; intellectual education: books published by the Kildare Place Society, *Thompson's and Gough's Arithmetic, Murray's English grammar*, with *Thompson's Geography*; moral education: visited by the Revd Clarke Huston, Covenanting minister; number of pupils: males, 21 under 10 years of age, 12 from 10 to 15, total 33; females, 7 under 10 years of age, 6 from 10 to 15, total 13; total number of pupils 46, 42 Presbyterians, 4 other denominations; master Daniel McFall, Presbyterian.

Dreen, near the leading road from Portglenone to Cullybackey, a small house, thatched and in bad repair, 30 by 15 feet inside, established 1822; income: from John McNeill Esquire, proprietor near Belfast, 5 pounds per annum, 12 pounds from pupils; intellectual education: books published by the London Hibernian Society, *Thompson and Gough's Arithmetic, Murray's English grammar* and *Thompson's Geography*; moral education: visited by the clergy of the Established Church, catechism on Wednesday and Saturday, Authorised Version of Scripture; number of pupils: males, 6 under 10 years of age, 14 from 10 to 15, total 20; females, 7 under 10 years of age, 8 from 10 to 15, total 15; total number of pupils 35, 29 Presbyterians, 6 other denominations; master Samuel Sloane, a Covenanter.

Largy national school, situated on the road leading from Toome to Portglenone, a very good house of stone and lime, slated, 30 by 20 feet interiorly, established 1833; income: from the National Board per annum 8 pounds, 8 pounds from pupils; intellectual education: books published by the National Board only; moral education: visited by the Revd John Lynch P.P. of Ahoghill; number of pupils: males, 12 under 10 years of age, 13 from 10 to 15, total 25; females, 15 under 20 years of age, total 15; total number of pupils 40, 2 Protestants, 38 Roman Catholics; master Patrick McLaughlin, a Roman Catholic.

Slavenagh, situated in the townland of Slavenagh, a short distance from the Portglenone road, a good house, 27 by 15 and a half feet inside, established 1817; income: from the London Hibernian Society per annum 2 pounds, from pupils 8 pounds; intellectual education: books published by the London Hibernian Society, Kildare Place Society, *Thompson and Gough's Arithmetic*; moral education: visited by the Presbyterian clergy, Authorised Version and catechism on Saturday by the master; number of pupils: males, 8 under 10 years of age, 6 from 10 to 15, 4 above 15, total 18; females, 6 under 10 years of age, 6 from 10 to 15, total 12; total number of pupils 30, 5 Protestants, 15 Presbyterians, 6 Roman Catholics, 4 other denominations; master David Montgomery, Presbyterian.

Loan evening school, held in the day schoolhouse, established 1836; income from pupils 4s 6d per quarter; intellectual education: day school books are used; number of pupils: males, 7 above 15 years of age, total 7; females, 2 above 15 years of age, total 2; total number of pupils 9, 8 Presbyterians, 1 other denomination, Covenanter; master David Barnes, Presbyterian.

Glenluce, on the leading road from Ballymoney to Ahoghill, a good house, 30 by 13 and a half feet, established 1813; income from pupils 10 pounds; intellectual education: books published by the Kildare Place Society, *Thompson and Gough's Arithmetic*; moral education: visited by the clergy of the Established Church; number of pupils: males, 11 under 10 years of age, 4 from 10 to 15, total 15; females, 5 under 10 years of age, total 5; total number of pupils 20, 1 Protestant, 14 Presbyterians, 2 Roman Catholics, 3 other denominations; master William Grey, Presbyterian. Report for May 1837.

Dreen evening adult school, meets in the lapping room of Hillmount bleach green, established January 1837; income: only the men employed in the bleach green are taught, for which the master receives 2s per week for 2 nights in each week for teaching the whole school; intellectual education: *Thompson's and Gough's Arithmetic, Bonnycastle's Mensuration*, and writing; moral education: none; number of pupils: 11 above 15 years of age, total 11, all male, 9 Presbyterians, 1 Roman Catholic, 1 other denomination; master Samuel Sloane, a Covenanter.

Whitehill evening school, held in the day schoolhouse, established 1832; income 15s per quarter from pupils; intellectual education: writing with *Thompson and Gough's Arithmetic* only; number of pupils: 5 from 10 to 15 years of age, 10 above 15, total 15, all male, 12 Presbyterians, 3 other denominations, Seceders; master John Nelson, Seceder.

Ahoghill, held in the session house of the Presbyterian meeting house in the village; income from pupils 5 pounds 4s; intellectual education: books sent by the parents of the children, chiefly London Hibernian Society books; number of pupils: males, 10 under 10 years of age, 2 from 10 to 15, total 12; females, 6 under 10 years of age, 2 from 10 to 15, total 8; total number of pupils 20, 2 Protestants, 9 Presbyterians, 5 Roman Catholics, 4 other denominations, Seceders; master William Barns, Presbyterian.

Portglenone Classical and English school, held in the vestry room of the Presbyterian meeting house, established 1831; income: paid by committee of 3 Presbyterians per annum 40 pounds 4s; intellectual education: *Virgil Eutrephius, Horace, Juvenal, Cicero, Livy, Homer*, Greek testament, *Xenophon* and *Thompson's Arithmetic and geography, Murray's English grammar* and *Euclid's Elements*; moral education: none; number of pupils: males, 15 from 10 to 15 years of age, 1 above 15, total 16, all male, 1 Protestant, 6 Presbyterians, 2 Roman Catholics, 7 other denominations; master John Alexander Smith, a Covenanter.

Loan, situated on the leading road from Portglenone to Ahoghill, a good house, thatched, 22 by 15 feet inside, established 1832; income: from London Hibernian Society for the last quarter 10s 6d, from pupils 9 pounds; intellectual education: books published by the London Hibernian Society, *Thompson and Gough's Arithmetic, Murray's English grammar*; moral education: visited by the clergy of the Established Church, catechism on Saturday and Authorised Version of Scripture; number of pupils: males, 15 under 10 years of age, total 15; females, 15 under 10 years of age, total 15; total number of pupils 30, 1 Protestant, 23 Presbyterians, 6 other denominations; master David Barns, Presbyterian.

Tullynahunnian, on a road leading from the Ballymena road to Kilrea, a good house, slated, 33 and a half feet by 15 and a half feet inside, established 1820; income: from the London Hibernian Society per annum 5 pounds, 5 pounds from pupils; intellectual education: books published by the London Hibernian Society, *Thompson and Gough's Arithmetic, Murray's English grammar*; moral education: not visited by any of the clergy, catechism on Saturday and Authorised Version of Scripture; number of pupils: males, 15 under 10 years of age, total 15; females, 23 under 10 years of age, 2 from 10 to 15, total 25; total number of pupils 40, 26 Presbyterians, 4 Roman Catholics, 10 other denominations; master John Bickby, a Covenanter.

Tullygrally, on a road leading from Ballymena to Ballymoney, a thatched house in bad repair, 22 feet by 15 feet inside, established 1824; income from pupils 6 pounds; intellectual education: books published by the London Hibernian Society, with *Gough's Arithmetic*; moral education: catechism on Saturday and Authorised Version of Scripture; number of pupils: males, 12 under 10 years of age, 4 from 10 to 15, total 16; females, 9 under 10 years of age, 5 from 10 to 15, total 14; total number of pupils 30, 10 Presbyterians, 20 other denominations; master Samuel Marrs, Covenanter.

Broughdom, on the road leading from Cullybackey to Clough, held in a barn, rented, established 1832; income from pupils 3 pounds; intellectual education: *Manson's Primer and spelling book*, with *Gough's Arithmetic*; moral education: catechism on Saturday and Authorised Version of Scripture; number of pupils: males, 7 under 10 years of age, total 7; females, 8 under 10 years of age, total 8; total number of pupils 15, 8 Presbyterians, 7 other denominations; master Robert Steele, a Seceder.

Ahoghill female school, held in a house in the village rented at [blank] pounds per annum, thatched, 18 by 16 feet inside, in middling repair, established 19th June 1837; income: from London Hibernian Society for 25 pupils at 2s 6d per quarter each; intellectual education: books published by the London Hibernian Society with reading, writing and plain needlework with knitting; moral education: Authorised Version of Scripture is taught; number of pupils: 8 under 10 years of age, 17 from 10 to 15, total 25; total number of pupils 25, 6 Protestants, 8 Presbyterians, 4 Roman Catholics, 7 Seceders; mistress Jane Boyle, Presbyterian.

Laymore national school, on the mail coach road from Ballymena to Ballymoney, 1 and a

quarter miles north west of the former, a good house, slated, 33 by 18 feet inside with 6 windows each 3 feet square, established 1829, connected with the National Board since 1833; income: from the National Board per annum 8 pounds, 12 pounds from pupils; intellectual education: books published by the National Board and the Kildare Place Society, with *Thompson's and Gough's Arithmetic*; moral education: not visited by any of the clergy for the last 6 months, catechism on Saturday by master and Authorised Version of Scripture; number of pupils: males, 20 under 10 years of age, 8 from 10 to 15, total 28; females, 12 under 10 years of age, 2 from 10 to 15, total 14; total number of pupils 42, 41 Presbyterians, 1 Roman Catholic; master James McFadden, Presbyterian.

Carninney, near the road leading from Ballymena to Ballymoney, a small thatched house in bad repair, 24 by 15 feet inside [insert addition: date of establishment of day school anno 1818]; income: from London Hibernian Society per annum 4 pounds, 8 pounds from pupils; intellectual education: books published by the London Hibernian Society, with *Thompson and Gough's Arithmetic*; moral education: visited by the Revd Hugh Smith Cumming, Established Church minister, Authorised Version is taught; number of pupils: males, 14 under 10 years of age, 5 from 10 to 15 years, total 19; females, 19 under 10 years of age, 3 from 10 to 15 years, total 21; total number of pupils 40, all Presbyterians; master George Carter, Established Church. Report for June 1837, 30th June.

Tullygarley, on the mail coach road from Ballymena to Randalstown, a good house, slated, 30 by 18 feet inside and cost 146 pounds, established 1826; income from pupils 15 pounds; intellectual education: books published by the Kildare Place Society, *Thompson's and Gough's Arithmetic, Murray's English grammar, Jackson's Book-keeping*; moral education: not visited by any of the clergy, catechism on Saturday and Authorised Version; number of pupils: males, 15 under 10 years of age, 7 from 10 to 15, total 22; females, 6 under 10 years of age, 2 from 10 to 15, total 8; total number of pupils 30, 28 Presbyterians, 2 Roman Catholics; master James Nicholl, Presbyterian.

Portglenone, Erasmus Smith's school for boys, near the village of Portglenone, an excellent house, 2-storey high, slated, the school room is 16 by 32 feet, established 1814; income: from the board of Erasmus Smith per annum 20 pounds with a gratuity, 6 pounds 10s from pupils; intellectual education: books published by the board of Erasmus Smith and Kildare Place Society, *Thompson's and Gough's Arithmetic, Murray's English grammar* and *Thompson's Geography*; moral education: visited by the clergy of the Established Church, catechism on Saturday and Authorised Version of Scriptures; number of pupils: 16 under 10 years of age, 10 from 10 to 15, 4 above 15, total 30, 10 Protestants, 11 Presbyterians, 9 Roman Catholics; master Edward Patman, Established Church.

Portglenone, Erasmus Smith's school for females, held in a room in the same house, upper storey, 16 by 32 feet inside, established 1814; income from the board of Erasmus Smith 12 pounds per annum with a gratuity; intellectual education: books as in the male [school], with plain and fancy needlework; moral education: visited by the ladies of Archdeacon Alexander's family; total number of pupils 30, 15 Protestants, 7 Presbyterians, 8 Roman Catholics; mistress Rebecca Patman, Established Church.

Gortgole national school, held in a good house, slated, 34 by 22 feet inside, established 1833; income: from National Board per annum 8 pounds, 4 pounds from pupils; intellectual education: books published by the National Board only; moral education: visited by the Revd John Lynch P.P.; number of pupils: males, 10 under 10 years of age, 4 from 10 to 15, total 14; females, 10 under 10 years of age, 1 from 10 to 15, total 11; total number of pupils 25, all Roman Catholics; teacher, Bernard McKenna, Roman Catholic.

Lisroddin, near the leading road from Portglenone to Ballymena, a good house, thatched, 15 by 22 feet, rebuilt 1830; income from pupils 8 pounds; intellectual education: books published by the London Hibernian Society and *Thompson's and Gough's Arithmetic*; moral education: not visited by any, Authorised Version on Saturday; number of pupils: males, 12 under 10 years of age, 6 from 10 to 15, total 18; females, 6 under 10 years of age, 6 from 10 to 15, total 12; total number of pupils 30, 7 Protestants, 23 Presbyerians; master Joseph Hunter, Presbyterian.

Aughnacleagh, on the leading road from Ballymena to Portglenone, good house, slated, 30 by 17 feet, established 1835; income from pupils 10 pounds; intellectual education: books sent by the parents of the children; moral education: visited by the Presbyterian clergy, Authorised Version and catechism on Saturday; number of pupils: males, 16 under 10 years of age, 8 from 10 to 15, 1 over 15, total 25; females, 12 under 10 years of age, 3 from 10 to 15, total 15; total

number of pupils 40, 27 Presbyterians, 3 Roman Catholics, 10 other denominations; master Joseph Scott, Presbyterian.

Milmoy, on the road leading from Ahoghill to Ballymoney, thatched house, in bad repair, 25 by 16 feet, established 1826; income: from London Hibernian Society per annum 15s, 5 pounds from pupils; intellectual education: London Hibernian Society and Hibernian class books, *Thompson and Gough's Arithmetic*; moral education: visited by the Presbyterian clergy, catechism and Authorised Version; number of pupils: males, 6 under 10 years of age, 3 from 10 to 15, total 9; females, 7 under 10 years of age, 2 from 10 to 15, total 9; total number of pupils 18, 6 Presbyterians, 8 Roman Catholics, 4 other denominations; mistress Mary Caulfield, Established Church.

Sunday Schools

[Table contains the following headings: name, situation and description, when established, superintendent, number of teachers, number of scholars, societies with which connected, hours of attendance, observations].

Loane Sunday school, held in the day schoolhouse, established 1832; superintended by a committee alternately; teachers: 4 males, 4 females, total 8; number of scholars: 37 males, 38 females, total 75, 6 Established Church, 49 Presbyterians, 20 other denominations, 55 exclusively Sunday school scholars; Sunday School Society for Ireland give books free, carriage excepted; hours of attendance: from 7.30 a.m. until 9.30 a.m. and from 4.30 p.m. till 7 p.m.; commences with singing and prayer and concludes with the same.

Craigs, held in the day schoolhouse, established 1822; superintendent James Getty, Presbyterian; teachers: 3 males, 3 females, total 6; number of scholars: 22 males, 40 females, total 62, 12 Established Church, 40 Presbyterians, 5 Roman Catholics, 5 other denominations, 40 exclusively Sunday school scholars; Sunday School Society give books free, carriage excepted; hours of attendance: from 7 till 9.30 a.m. and from 5 to 7 p.m.

Ahoghill Roman Catholic Sunday school, held in the Roman Catholic chapel, first held 1837; superintendent Revd John Lynch, P.P. of Ahoghill; teachers: 5 males, 5 females, total 10; number of scholars: 50 males, 30 females, total 80, all Roman Catholics, 50 exclusively Sunday school scholars; books published by the National Board with the Douai Version of Scripture; hours of attendance: alternately from 12 to 1 o'clock and from 2 till 4 p.m. same day, and the following Sunday from 11 till 2 o'clock.

Connaught Ligar, held in the day schoolhouse in the townland of Slavenaght, established 1817; superintendent David Montgomery, a Presbyterian; teachers: 4 males, 4 females, total 8; number of scholars: 24 males, 16 females, total 40, 10 Established Church, 24 Presbyterian, 6 other denominations, 25 exclusively Sunday school scholars; Sunday School Society give books free, carriage excepted; hours of attendance: from 8 till 10 o'clock a.m. and from 5 till 7 p.m.; commences with singing and prayer and concludes with the same. Report for May 1837.

Garvaghey East, held in the day schoolhouse, established 1832; superintendent Arthur Burns, a Covenanter; teachers: 4 males, 4 females, total 8; number of scholars: 30 males, 50 females, total 80, 63 Presbyterians, 2 Roman Catholics, 15 other denominations, Seceders, 68 exclusively Sunday school scholars; Sunday School Society for Ireland give books free, carriage excepted; hours of attendance: from 7 till 9 a.m. and from 6 till 8 p.m.; commences with singing and prayer and concludes with the same.

Gracehill male Sunday school, held in the day schoolhouse, established 1826; superintendent Revd Benjamin Beck, the Moravian minister, and a committee; teachers: 9 males, total 9; number of scholars: 40 males, total 40, 1 Established Church, 19 Presbyterians, 12 Roman Catholics, 8 Moravians, 34 exclusively Sunday school scholars; Sunday School Society for Ireland give books free, carriage excepted; hours of attendance: from 9 till 11 o'clock a.m.; commences with singing and prayer and concludes with the same.

Gracehill female Sunday school, superintendent Miss [blank]; teachers: 4 females, total 4; number of scholars: 30 females, total 30, all exclusively Sunday school scholars; Sunday School Society give books free, carriage excepted; hours of attendance: from 8 till 11 o'clock a.m. in summer and from 9 till 11 o'clock a.m. in winter; commences with singing and prayer and concludes with the same.

Tannybrannon, held in the day schoolhouse, established 1830; superintendent William Campbell, Established Church; teachers: 4 males, total 4; number of scholars: 10 males, 15 females, total 25, 18 Presbyterians, 3 Roman Catholics, 4 other denominations, 6 exclusively Sunday school scholars; Sunday School Society for Ireland give books free, carriage excepted; hours of attendance: from 8 till 10 o'clock a.m.; commences with singing and prayer and concludes with the same.

Dreen Sunday school, held in the day schoolhouse, established 1825; superintendent Samuel

Sloane, Covenanter; teachers: 3 males, 3 females, total 6; number of scholars: 30 males, 20 females, total 50, 38 Presbyterians, 12 other denominations, 25 exclusively Sunday school scholars; Sunday School Society give books free, carriage excepted; hours of attendance: from 8 till 10 a.m. and from 4 till 6 p.m.

Ballylummin Sunday school, held in the day schoolhouse, established 1832; superintendent James Nelson, a Presbyterian, the Revd George Kirkpatrick, patron; teachers: 3 males, 3 females, total 6; number of scholars: 60 males, 50 females, total 110, 5 Established Church, 70 Presbyterians, 2 Roman Catholics, 23 Seceders, 80 exclusively Sunday school scholars; the Sunday School Society for Ireland give books free, carriage excepted; hours of attendance: from 8 till 10 a.m. during the year; commences with singing and prayer and concludes with the same.

Ballybeg Sunday school, held in the day schoolhouse, established 1826; superintendent Matthew Johnston, a Presbyterian, Revd George Kirkpatrick patron; teachers: 9 males, 8 females, total 17; number of scholars: 51 males, 73 females, total 124, 10 Established Church, 62 Presbyterians, 42 other denominations, 114 exclusively Sunday school scholars; Sunday School Society give books free, carriage excepted; hours of attendance: from 8 till 10.30 a.m.; commences with singing and prayer and concludes with the same.

Bridge End Sunday school, held in the day schoolhouse, established 1817; superintendent Robert Gault, a Seceder; teachers: 8 males, 3 females, total 11; number of scholars: 20 males, 15 females, total 35, 10 Presbyterians, 9 Roman Catholics, 16 other denominations, 20 exclusively Sunday school scholars; Sunday School Society give books free, carriage excepted; hours of attendance: from 8 till 10 o'clock a.m; commences with singing and prayer and concludes with the same.

Straid Sunday school, held in the day schoolhouse, established 1831; superintendent William McConnell, a Baptist; teachers: 7 males, 1 female, total 8; number of scholars: 35 males, 35 females, total 70, 40 Presbyterians, 15 Roman Catholics, 15 Moravians, 15 Seceders, all exclusively Sunday school scholars; Sunday School Society give books free, carriage excepted; hours of attendance: from 8 till 10 a.m. and from 5 till 7 p.m.; commences with singing and prayer and concludes with the same.

Garvahey Sunday school, held in the day schoolhouse, established 1830; superintended by 8 of a committee alternately and the Revd James Knox,

Seceding minister; teachers: 6 males, total 6; number of scholars: 25 males, 25 females, total 50, 44 Presbyterians, 6 Seceders, all exclusively Sunday school scholars; Sunday School Society give books free, carriage excepted, and bibles at a reduced price; hours of attendance: from 8 till 10 a.m. and from 5 till 7 p.m.; commences with singing and prayer and concludes with the same.

Galgorm Sunday school, held in the manor court house where the day school is held, established 1819; superintendent William Raphael, Seceder, and patronised by George Joy Esq.; teachers: 4 males, 8 females, total 12; number of scholars: 40 males, 54 females, total 94, 4 Established Church, 52 Presbyterians, 12 Roman Catholics, 26 other denominations, 30 exclusively Sunday school scholars; the Sunday School Society for Ireland give books free, carriage excepted: hours of attendance: from 5 till 7 o'clock p.m. and from 8 till 10 o'clock p.m.; commences with singing and prayer and concludes with the same.

Ballymontena, held in the day schoolhouse, established 1822; superintendent James Hogg; teachers: 5 males, 5 females, total 10; number of scholars: 65 males, 65 females, total 130, 10 Established Church, 100 Presbyterians, 20 other denominations, 100 exclusively Sunday school scholars; Sunday School Society for Ireland give books free, carriage excepted; hours of attendance: from 7 till 10 a.m. and from 5 till 8 o'clock p.m.; commences with singing and prayer and concludes with the same.

Ahoghill Sunday school, held in the church, established 1834; superintendent Revd George Kirkpatrick, minister; teachers: 6 males, 5 females, total 11; number of scholars: 40 males, 41 females, total 81, 27 Established Church, 39 Presbyterians, 15 other denominations, 50 exclusively Sunday school scholars; Sunday School Society for Ireland give books free, carriage excepted, and bibles at a reduced price; hours of attendance: from 9.45 a.m. till 11.45 a.m.; commences with prayer and concludes with an address and singing.

Watercloney, held in the day schoolhouse, established 1835; superintendents Messrs Ambrose and Edward O'Roarke; teachers: 7 males, 3 females, total 10; number of scholars: 90 males, 80 females, total 170, 5 Established Church, 30 Presbyterians, 135 Roman Catholics; Sunday School Society give books free, carriage excepted; hours of attendance: from 9 till 11 a.m. and from 1 till 5 o'clock p.m.

Glenhue, held in the day schoolhouse, established 1823; superintended by a committee;

teachers: 6 males, total 6; number of scholars: 25 males, 15 females, total 40, 6 Established Church, 31 Presbyterians, 3 other denominations, 36 exclusively Sunday school scholars; Sunday School Society for Ireland give books free, carriage excepted; hours of attendance: from 8 till 11 o'clock a.m. and from 4 till 7 p.m.

Largy Sunday school, held in the day schoolhouse, established 1833; superintendent Robert McLaughlin, a Roman Catholic; 1 male teacher, total 1; number of scholars: 30 males, 10 females, total 40, all Roman Catholics, 20 exclusively Sunday school scholars; the day school books are used; hours of attendance: from 9 till 11 o'clock a.m. on one Sunday and from 3 till 5 p.m. on the following Sunday.

Portglenone Sunday school no.1, held in the endowed schoolhouse of Erasmus Smith, established 1819; superintendent John Smith, a classical teacher; teachers: 1 male, 4 females, total 5; number of scholars: 6 Established Church, 21 Presbyterians, 3 Seceders, 15 exclusively Sunday school scholars; Sunday School Society for Ireland give books free, carriage excepted; hours of attendance: from 9 till 11 a.m.; commences with singing and prayer and concludes with singing only.

Portglenone Sunday school no.2, held in the Presbyterian meeting house, established 1835; superintended by a committee of 5, viz. 3 men and 2 women; teachers: 6 males, 4 females, total 10; number of scholars: 35 males, 25 females, total 60, 8 Established Church, 46 Presbyterians, 6 other denominations, 25 exclusively Sunday school scholars; Sunday School Society give books free, carriage excepted; hours of attendance from 9 till 11.30 a.m.; commences with singing and prayer and concludes with the same. Report for May 1837.

Tullynahunnion, held in the day schoolhouse, established 1820; superintendent John Birkby, a Covenanter; teachers: 5 males, 3 females, total 8; number of scholars: 40 males, 50 females, total 90, 1 Established Church, 56 Presbyterians, 15 Roman Catholics, 18 other denominations, 50 exclusively Sunday school scholars; hours of attendance: from 7 till 10 o'clock a.m. and from 4 till 7 p.m.; Sunday School Society give books free, carriage excepted; commences with singing and prayer and concludes with the same.

Laymore, held in the day schoolhouse, established 1830; superintendent John Wilson, Presbyterian; teachers: 3 males, 2 females, total 5; number of scholars: 26 males, 24 females, total 50, 48 Presbyterians, 2 Roman Catholics, 40 exclusively Sunday school scholars; hours of attendance: from 7 till 9 o'clock a.m. in winter and from 5 till 8 o'clock p.m. in summer; Sunday School Society for Ireland give books free and bibles at half price; commences with prayer only.

Carninney, held in the day schoolhouse, established 1821; superintendent Matthew Kyle, Presbyterian; teachers: 2 males, 2 females, total 4; number of scholars: 26 males, 39 females, total 65, 60 Presbyterians, 5 other denominations, 48 exclusively Sunday school scholars; hours of attendance: from 6 till 10 o'clock a.m.; Sunday School Society give books free and bibles at half price; commences with singing and prayer and concludes with the same. Report for June 1837.

Gortgole Sunday school, held in the day schoolhouse, established 1832; superintendent Bernard McKenna, Roman Catholic; teachers: 8 males, total 8; number of scholars: 40 males, 20 females, total 60, all Roman Catholics, 20 exclusively Sunday school scholars; held on every second Sunday from 1 till 4 o'clock p.m. and from 9 till 12 a.m. on the other Sunday; the day school books are used i.e. national school books.

Tullygurley Sunday school, held in the day schoolhouse, established 1837; superintendent James Nicholl, Presbyterian; teachers: 4 males, 2 females, total 6; number of scholars: 44 males, 56 females, total 100, 90 Presbyterians, 10 Roman Catholics, 85 exclusively Sunday school scholars; hours of attendance: from 7 till 9 p.m. and from 5 till 7 p.m.; Sunday School Society give books free, carriage excepted; commences with reading a chapter in the Bible and concludes with the same.

Lisroddin Sunday school, held in the day schoolhouse, established 1819; superintendent John McCaw, a Presbyterian; teachers: 6 males, 6 females, total 12; number of scholars: 30 males, 30 females, total 60, 10 Established Church, 46 Presbyterians, 4 Roman Catholics, 50 exclusively Sunday school scholars; hours of attendance: from 8 till 10.30 a.m. and from 4 till 6.30 p.m.; Sunday School Society give books free, carriage excepted; commences with singing and prayer and concludes with the same.

Aughnacleagh Sunday school, held in the day schoolhouse, established 1835; superintendent Joseph Scott, a Presbyterian; teachers: 8 males, total 8; number of scholars: 20 males, 20 females, total 40, 1 Established Church, 23 Presbyterians, 16 other denominations, 29 exclusively Sunday school scholars; hours of attendance: from 7 till 10 a.m. and from 3 till 6 p.m.; Sunday School Society give books free, carriage excepted;

commences with singing and prayer and concludes with the same.

Molvay Sunday school, held in the day schoolhouse, established 1826; superintendent Mary Caulfield, Established Church; teachers: 3 males, 2 females, total 5; number of scholars: 15 males, 15 females, total 30, 4 Established Church, 5 Presbyterians, 8 Roman Catholics, 13 other denominations, 18 exclusively Sunday school scholars; hours of attendance: from 8 till 10 a.m. and from 4 till 6 p.m.; Sunday School Society give books free, carriage excepted.

School Statistics

Social Economy

Table of Schools

[Table contains the following headings: name of townland where held, name and religion of master and mistress, free or pay school, annual income of master or mistress, description and cost of schoolhouse, number of pupils subdivided by religion, sex and the Protestant and Roman Catholic returns, societies with which connected. All are pay schools].

Bridgend, townland Corbally, master Richard Gilpin, Protestant; income about 23 pounds; schoolhouse stone and lime, thatched, built by subscriptions and donations from Kildare Place Society, 30 to 40 pounds; number of pupils by the Protestant return: 50 Presbyterians, 1 other denomination, 10 Roman Catholics, 31 males, 30 females; by the Roman Catholic return: 50 Presbyterians, 1 other denomination, 10 Roman Catholics, 31 males, 30 females; connected with the Kildare Place Society, the schoolhouse built partly by subscription.

Ballylummin, master Daniel Shaw, Presbyterian; income about 12 pounds; a temporary schoolhouse, unfurnished; number of pupils by the Protestant return: 27 Presbyterians, 6 Roman Catholics, 19 males, 14 females; by the Roman Catholic return: 27 Presbyterians, 6 Roman Catholics, 20 males, 13 females; associations none.

Laymore, master John Houston, Presbyterian; income about 17 pounds; schoolhouse stone and lime, cost 18 pounds, a grant from Kildare Place Society of 5 pounds for repairs; number of pupils by the Protestant return: 30 Presbyterians, 1 Roman Catholic, 16 males, 15 females; by the Roman Catholic return: 29 Presbyterians, 1 Roman Catholic, 16 males, 14 females; connected with the Kildare Place Society.

Tullygrawley, master James Livingston, Presbyterian; income about 12 pounds; schoolhouse stone and lime, thatched, built by subscription and a grant from Kildare Place Society, 20 to 30 pounds; number of pupils by the Protestant return: 48 Presbyterians, 2 Roman Catholics, 25 males, 25 females; connected with Kildare Place Society, the schoolhouse built partly by subscription.

Gracehill, Ballykennedy, master Revd William Essex, mistress Miss Brunswick (boarding school), Moravians; rates of payment: 25 guineas a year for boys and 24 guineas for girls; schoolhouse a large commodious house built by the Moravian Society; number of pupils by the Protestant return: 40 males, 20 females; connected with the Moravian Society.

Gracehill, Ballykennedy, master Thomas Courtney, mistress Elizabeth Brownlees, Moravians; income: master 20 guineas, mistress 15 guineas; schoolhouse a large commodious house built by the Moravian Society; number of pupils by the Roman Catholic return: 40 Established Church, 20 males, 20 females.

Ballymontenagh, master Robert Davison, Presbyterian; income 22 pounds; schoolhouse a good house of stone and lime, built partly by subscription, partly by donations from the lord lieutenant's fund and partly from Kildare Place Society; number of pupils by the Protestant return: 40 Presbyterians, 4 Roman Catholics, 24 males, 16 females; by the Roman Catholic return: 36 Presbyterians, 4 Roman Catholics, 24 males, 16 females; connected with Kildare Place Society, the schoolhouse built partly by subscription.

Lisnafillen, master John Wilson, Presbyterian; income 20 pounds and a house, rent free, given by Mr McClelland; schoolhouse stone and lime, probable cost 40 pounds; number of pupils by the Protestant return: 19 Presbyterians, 6 Roman Catholics, 11 males, 14 females; by the Roman Catholic return: 19 Presbyterians, 6 Roman Catholics, 15 male, 10 females; the Revd G. McClelland built the schoolhouse.

Straid, master David Johnston, Protestant; income from 15 to 17 pounds; a schoolhouse building, to cost about 60 pounds; number of pupils by the Protestant return: 47 Presbyterians, 26 males, 21 females; by the Roman Catholic return: 47 Presbyterians, 26 males, 21 females; associations none.

Cullybackey, master John Kenney, Protestant; income from 12 to 15 pounds; a schoolhouse now building by private subscription and assistance from Kildare Place Society; number of pupils by the Protestant return: 30 Presbyterians, 13 males, 17 females; by the Roman Catholic return: 30 Presbyterians, 20 males, 10 females; connected with Kildare Place Society, a new schoolhouse is building, partly by subscription.

Kilcurry, master Andrew McClure, Presbyterian; income about 20 pounds; no permanent schoolhouse, at present a room in an outhouse serves the purpose; number of pupils by the Protestant return: 13 Established Church, 24 Presbyterians, 11 Roman Catholics, 30 males, 18 females; by the Roman Catholic return: 13 Established Church, 25 Presbyterians, 10 Roman Catholics, 30 males, 18 females; connected with the Kildare Place Society.

Ballybeg, master James Glover, Presbyterian; income about 9 pounds 10s; schoolhouse a small building of stone and lime, cost 12 pounds; number of pupils by the Protestant return: 1 Established Church, 46 Presbyterians, 5 Roman Catholics, 30 males, 20 females; by the Roman Catholic return: 1 Established Church, 43 Presbyterians, 8 Roman Catholics, 31 males, 21 females; associations none.

Glenhue, master Gilbert McKee, Presbyterian; income about 13 pounds; schoolhouse stone and lime, thatched, cost 15 pounds; number of pupils by the Protestant return: 4 Established Church, 24 Presbyterians, 2 Roman Catholics, 20 males, 10 females; associations none.

Dreen, master James McFadden, Presbyterian; income from 8 to 10 pounds; schoolhouse in a state of dilapidation, a new schoolhouse is in progress; number of pupils by the Protestant return: 28 Presbyterians, 2 other denominations, 2 Roman Catholics, 17 males, 15 females; by the Roman Catholic return: 31 Presbyterians, 1 other denomination, 2 Roman Catholics, 19 males, 15 females; associations none.

Dysertstown, Garvaghy, master Charles Connor, Protestant; income about 13 pounds; a temporary schoolhouse; number of pupils by the Protestant return: 5 Established Church, 29 Presbyterians, 6 Roman Catholics, 28 males, 12 females; associations none.

Connaught Liggar, Slavinagh, master Alexander Dunlop, Presbyterian; income 9 pounds 10s; schoolhouse stone and lime, cost 12 pounds; number of pupils by the Protestant return: 29 Presbyterians, 1 Roman Catholic, 14 males, 16 females; by the Roman Catholic return: 2 Established Church, 32 Presbyterians, 3 Roman Catholics, 20 males, 17 females; connected with Kildare Place Society.

Moyasset, master John Peters, Presbyterian;

income from 18 to 20 pounds; schoolhouse a very good house, stone and lime, slated, built by subscription, aided by a grant of 40 pounds from Kildare Place Society; number of pupils by the Protestant return: 42 Presbyterians, 23 males, 19 females; by the Roman Catholic return: 42 Presbyterians, 23 males, 19 females; connected with Kildare Place Society; the schoolhouse built partly by subscription.

Ballyconnelly, master John Davison, Presbyterian; income 8 pounds; schoolhouse a thatched barn; number of pupils by the Protestant return: 3 Established Church, 28 Presbyterians, 22 males, 9 females; by the Roman Catholic return: 3 Established Church, 27 Roman Catholics, 20 males, 10 females; associations none.

The Craigs or Aughnakeely, master Robert Thompson, Presbyterian; income 25 pounds; schoolhouse stone and lime, built by local subscription, aided by a grant of 15 pounds from the lord lieutenant's fund and 17 pounds from the Kildare Place Society; probable cost 65 pounds; number of pupils by the Protestant return: 8 Established Church, 38 Roman Catholics, 33 males, 13 females; by the Roman Catholic return: 6 Established Church, 30 Roman Catholic, 20 males, 16 females; connected with Kildare Place Society, the schoolhouse built partly by subscription.

Swanstown Carnmegrum, master William Campbell, Presbyterian; income about 5 pounds; schoolhouse a small temporary building between the gables of 2 farm offices; number of pupils by the Protestant return: 2 Established Church, 16 Presbyterians, 4 Roman Catholics, 17 males, 5 females; by the Roman Catholic return: 3 Established Church, 13 Presbyterians, 5 Roman Catholics, 15 males, 5 females; associations none.

Lisrodden, master Bristow Miniss, Presbyterian; income 20 pounds 13s 4d; schoolhouse stone and lime, built by subscription and a grant of 10 pounds from the lord lieutenant's fund, 17 pounds 10s from the Kildare Place Society and [?] 6 pounds from the patron, the Revd William Stewart, value 60 pounds; number of pupils by the Protestant return: 4 Established Church, 45 Presbyterians, 12 Roman Catholics, 35 males, 26 females; by the Roman Catholic return: 4 Established Church, 45 Presbyterians, 12 Roman Catholics, 35 males, 26 females; connected with Kildare Place Society; the schoolhouse was built partly by subscription, the Revd William Stewart gave 16 pounds 16s.

Tullynahinnion, master John Birkby, Protestant; income 7 pounds 10s; schoolhouse stone and lime, built by subscription, aided by grants of 23 pounds from lord lieutenant's fund and 16 pounds from Kildare Place Society; number of pupils by the Protestant return: 3 Established Church, 33 Presbyterians, 4 Roman Catholics, 23 males, 17 females; connected with Kildare Place Society, the schoolhouse built partly by subscription.

Portglenone, Garvaghy, master Robert Kane (classical school), Roman Catholic; income 40 pounds, allotted by committee of subscribers, rates of payment 5s to 15s a quarter, school at present held in a hired room; number of pupils by the Protestant return: 3 Established Church, 10 Presbyterians, 14 Roman Catholics, 14 males, 13 females; by the Roman Catholic return: 3 Established Church, 10 Presbyterians, 17 Roman Catholics, 21 males, 9 females; the school supported by subscription.

Portglenone Garvaghy, master Arthur Barnes, Presbyterian; income 13 pounds; school held in the court house; number of pupils by the Protestant return: 1 Established Church, 21 Presbyterians, 3 Roman Catholics, 19 males, 6 females; by the Roman Catholic return: 1 Established Church, 21 Presbyterians, 2 Roman Catholics, 18 males, 6 females.

Portglenone Garvaghy, mistress Margaret McGregor, Presbyterian; income from 5 to 8 pounds; schoolhouse a hired room in a slated house; number of pupils by the Protestant return: 4 Established Church, 15 Presbyterians, 2 Roman Catholics, 9 males, 12 females; by the Roman Catholic return: 4 Established Church, 18 Presbyterians, 2 Roman Catholics, 24 males.

Mount Stafford, Gortfad, master John Orr, Presbyterian; income not yet ascertained, rates 2s 6d a quarter; schoolhouse a temporary and ill-suited room (but recently opened); number of pupils by the Protestant return: 9 Presbyterians, 14 Roman Catholics, 15 males, 8 females; by the Roman Catholic return: 17 Presbyterians, 10 Roman Catholics, 17 males, 10 females.

Aughnacleagh, master William Arbuthnot, Presbyterian; income from 12 to 15 pounds; schoolhouse an outhouse built of lime and stone; number of pupils by the Protestant return: 2 Established Church, 36 Presbyterians, 8 Roman Catholics, 30 males, 16 females; by the Roman Catholic return: 2 Established Church, 40 Presbyterian, 8 Roman Catholics, 50 males.

Mullinsallagh (male school), master Edward Patman, Protestant; income 40 pounds 8s 3d, viz. 30 pounds from Erasmus Smith's fund, 3 pounds 8s 3d from land allotted to the school and about 7 pounds from scholars; schoolhouse an excellent house with accommodation for master and mistress, built of stone and lime and slated, cost 600 pounds, built by a grant from Erasmus Smith's fund, donations from Bishop Alexander and others; number of pupils by the Protestant return: 7 Established Church, 12 Presbyterians, 21 Roman Catholics, 40 males; by the Roman Catholic return: 7 Established Church, 12 Presbyterians, 21 Roman Catholics, 40 males; connected with board of Erasmus Smith, Bishop Alexander and others.

Portglannon Mullinsallagh (female school), mistress Rebecca Patman, Protestant; income 25 pounds, of which 20 pounds is derived from the funds of Erasmus Smith, a division of the above described (see male school); number of pupils by the Protestant return: 13 Established Church, 4 Presbyterians, 12 Roman Catholics, 29 females; by the Roman Catholic return: 16 Established Church, 4 Presbyterians, 17 Roman Catholics, 37 females; connected with the Board of Erasmus Smith's fund.

Ahoghill, master James Glover, Protestant; income 16 pounds; schoolhouse a slated house built of stone and lime, in good repair, cost 80 or 100 pounds; number of pupils by the Protestant return: 3 Established Church, 50 Presbyterians, 13 Roman Catholics, 38 males, 28 females; by the Roman Catholic return: 3 Established Church, 30 Presbyterians, 27 Roman Catholics, 40 males, 20 females; connected with Kildare Place Society, the parish school, the incumbent pays 40 pounds a year; Alexander McManus Esquire gave the schoolhouse.

Cullybackey Creggan, master Samuel Aiton Lockhart, Presbyterian; income 20 pounds; temporary schoolhouse; number of pupils by the Roman Catholic return: 20 Presbyterians, 11 males, 9 females.

Parish of Ballyclug, County Antrim

Statistical Report by Lieutenant Edward
Durnford, November 1832

NATURAL STATE

Name and Situation

The name of Ballyclug is supposed to be derived
from the words baile clug *Baile-clog* "bell town or
the town of bells." It is situated in the barony of
Lower Antrim, in the county of Antrim and lies
south east by east of the town of Ballymena, being
separated from it by the River Braid.

It was until lately a part of the archdeaconry of
Connor, the archdeacon being rector and receiving two-thirds of the tithes, the vicar receiving
one-third only. The present Lord Bishop of Down
and Connor, the Right Reverend Dr Mant, has,
with the consent of the legislature, disunited the
rectorial tithes from the archdeaconry so that on
the death of the archdeacon in 1831, the vicar, the
Reverend H.J. Cumming, became the rector of
the parish and entitled to the entire tithes, the
usual amount of which is 130 pounds, a settlement having been made under the Composition
Act for that sum. It is in the diocese of Connor and
province of Armagh, and is episcopally united
pro hac vice to the perpetual curacy of Kirkinriola,
the adjoining parish.

Boundaries, Extent and Divisions

It is bounded on the north west by the parishes of
Kirkinriola and Racavan <Rathcavan>, on the
north east by Racavan, on the east by Glenwhirry,
on the south and south west by Connor, and on the
west by Ahoghill. Its greatest extent north and
south is about 4 British statute miles and from east
to west about 4 and three-quarter miles. The
parish contains 8,268 British statute acres.

It is divided into 11 townlands, 10 of which are
in the manor of Karte, the property of Henry
Hutchinson Hamilton O'Hara Esquire. The remaining townland, Cross, was also in the manor
of Karte but was sold some years ago by a decree
of the court of chancery to Henry Joy Tomb
Esquire of Belfast.

NATURAL FEATURES

Surface, Soil and Produce

There is nothing remarkable in the features of
ground in this parish. [A] great part of it is high but
of easy ascent. Cross hill, which is the highest

ground, is very good pasture. The soil generally is
light and gravelly.

The general crops are potatoes, flax and oats.
Potatoes yield from 15 to 20 boles per acre (the
bole is 10 bushels) and oats from 8 to 12 boles.
When there was a brewery at Ballymena, barley
was a good deal cultivated, but that crop has been
much neglected lately. Wheat has been tried but
the soil is considered too light for that crop.
Agriculture in general is depressed; rent is considered to be still kept at too high a rate. The leases
are usually for 21 or 31 years with lives.

The only rocks in the parish are basalt.

MODERN TOPOGRAPHY

Towns and Villages: Harryville

There is no town within this parish. The only
village is that of Harryville, which is situated at
the north west extremity of the parish, contiguous
to the town of Ballymena, with which it is connected by a stone bridge across the Braid river. It
is very small, containing only 2 or 3 good houses
and a few cottages. [Insert marginal note: By the
census of 1831 the population amounted to 252].

Crebilly

Crebilly hill is the principal place in this parish,
having 2 fairs held annually on 26th June and 21st
August. Here also is the mansion house of the
proprietor, Henry Hutchinson Hamilton O'Hara
Esquire, a minor and ward of the court of chancery. It was built within the last century and is one
of 3 residences which this family have had in the
parish. The first was in Crebilly, of which some
remains appear behind the present house. Afterwards the ruin at Liminary appears to have been
the principal residence of the family, and upon its
falling into decay, the present mansion was built
and occupied by the great-grandfather of the
present proprietor.

Tradition states that the manor of Karte, called
in the old writings the "tuaghe of Karte", situate
in Lower Clandeboy <Clandebuay> in the province of Ulster, has been in the family of O'Hara
from time immemorial. It was held by them as a
fief or tributary under the ancient family of O'Neill,
formerly Kings of Ulster. They were in rebellion
frequently and their estates forfeited, the manor
of Karte included. The manor was afterwards

restored by letters patent in the 4th year of King James I to Cahil O'Hara, the ancestor of the present proprietor.

SOCIAL ECONOMY AND MODERN TOPOGRAPHY

Manor Court

A court leet and court baron is held within the manor for recovery of small debts under 2 pounds late currency.

Chapel

The Roman Catholic chapel is also at Crebilly. It was built by general subscription in 1807, on a lease made by the then proprietor of the estate for 3 lives, at a rent of 1s if demanded.

Charitable Bequest

The only charity existing in the parish is the sum of 20 pounds per annum bequeathed to the poor of the parish by one of the late landlords, H.H. O'Hara Esquire.

PRODUCTIVE ECONOMY

Manufactures

The manufacture of brown linen and spinning of flax is carried on to a considerable extent by the inhabitants of this parish, at their own houses, which they sell in Ballymena market. There is but 1 small bleach green in the parish, which is situated at the south east extremity of it, on the bank of the Glenwhirry river.

MODERN TOPOGRAPHY

Roads

The principal roads in this parish are: the mail coach road from Belfast to Derry, which crosses a very small portion of the parish at its west extremity; one from Ballymena to Kells, which passes through the south west of the parish; another from Ballymena to Larne (by Crebilly), which traverses the parish from west to east nearly; and another from Belfast to Broughshane (by Doagh and Crebilly), which traverses the parish from south to north nearly. These roads are all in good repair, as well as several crossroads running from these to other parts of the parish.

NATURAL FEATURES

Rivers

The River Braid forms a part of the north western boundary of the parish, dividing it from the parishes of Kirkinriola and Ahoghill; and the Glenwhirry river forms a small part of the boundary between it and Connor parish at the south east extremity.

Bogs and Woods

There are several good bogs which are used for fuel by the inhabitants.

There is a district of underwood on the north west side of Crebilly hill, which is said to be the last remaining portion of the woods in the county. It is now only underwood with grazing between it. There are some fine trees around the mansion at Crebilly, and some young plantations have been recently laid down near it.

SOCIAL ECONOMY

Population

By the census of 1831 the population of the whole parish was 3,692, and was by townlands as follows.

Ballykeel: males 118, females 142, total 260.

Ballycraigy: males 107, females 110, total 217.

Ballymarlogh: males 117, females 114, total 231.

Ballylesson: males 144, females 155, total 299.

Crebilly: males 151, females 161, total 311 [sic].

Caherty: males 233, females 220, total 453.

Cross: males 174, females 152, total 326.

Deerfin: males 119, females 135, total 254.

Dunnivaddin: males 144, females 159, total 303.

Liminary: males 227, females 240, total 468 [sic].

Tully: males 150, females 168, total 318.

Village of Harryville: males 109, females 143, total 252.

There are a few descendants of the Scotch immigrants among the population of this parish, but they are by no means so large a portion as in some of the neighbouring parishes.

ANCIENT TOPOGRAPHY

Antiquities

In the graveyard in Ballylesson townland, which is close to the road from Ballymena to Kells, there is a ruin of a building, but when it ceased to be used or by whom it was used is not known among the inhabitants. The oldest headstone at present in the graveyard is dated 1727. It is now used almost exclusively by the Roman Catholics.

There is in Ballykeel townland a very large moat which is now thickly planted over. [Signed] Edward W. Durnford, Lieutenant Royal Engineers, 12 November 1832.

Memoir by James Boyle, November 1835, with insertions from Office Copy with additions by J.R. Ward

MEMOIR WRITING

Memoir Writing

Refer to Mr Boyle to complete this Memoir. Social Economy to be written etc. [initialled] RKD, 18 September 1835. Forwarded to Lieutenant Larcom, 19 December 1835.

NATURAL FEATURES

Hills

This parish occupies a portion of the ridge extending south westward from Slemish <Slemmish> mountain in the adjoining parish of Racavan and which, passing through this parish, terminates at the Kells water in that of Connor, near the southern boundary of this parish. Cross, 870 feet above the sea, at the eastern side of the parish, is the highest point in it. From this it declines gently westward to an average elevation of 170 feet above the sea. The descent northward is rapid and regular, and terminates at an average elevation of 160 feet above the sea. Towards the south the descent is rather irregular. On this side its average elevation above the sea is 320 feet. The principal points in this parish are Cross, 870 feet and Dunnyvaden [insert addition: 1 and a half miles east of Cross], 632 feet above the level of the sea].

Lakes and Rivers

There are no lakes in this parish.

The principal river is the Braid, which flows south west for 1 and a half miles along the north west boundary of this parish. This river takes its rise in the parish of Tickmacrevan, at an elevation of 650 feet above the sea. After flowing south west for 10 miles between the parishes of Kirkinriola and Skerry on the north and that of Racavan on the south, it enters the parish, at which point it is 140 feet above the sea. From this it declines to an average elevation of 126 feet above the sea, being an average fall of 1 foot in 565 feet. After quitting this parish it continues its south west course for 1 and three-quarter miles

and discharges itself into the Main river 1 and three-quarter miles south west of the town of Ballymena. Its average breadth in this parish is 70 feet and average depth 3 feet. Its bed is gravelly and its banks high and beautifully wooded. It does not overflow them. It is usefully situated for machinery, drainage and irrigation.

The Kells water or Glenwhirry river, which takes its rise in the mountains in Glenwhirry and the adjoining parishes at an elevation of above 1,200 feet above the level of the sea: it flows westerly for 7 and a quarter miles and enters the south east extremity of this parish, at which point [it] is 414 feet above the sea. From this it descends to an elevation of 370 feet and, continuing a westerly course for 8 miles through the parish of Connor, it discharges itself into the Main river at a distance of 7 and a half miles from its mouth and at an elevation of 101 feet above the sea. Its average fall (in this parish) is 1 foot in 90 feet, average breadth 30 feet and average depth 2 feet. It is usefully situated for machinery, drainage and irrigation. It is subject to floods which sometimes do considerable mischief to the crops and cultivated ground along it. The meadows alone are benefitted by its inundations, which soon subside. Its bed is stony and gravelly but its banks generally low.

The Devenagh stream rises in Racavan parish at an elevation of 728 feet above the sea and, flowing westerly, enters on the northern boundary of this parish, along which it flows for 2 and a half miles and discharges itself into the Braid river at an elevation of 140 feet above the sea. Its average fall is 1 foot in 66 feet, average breadth 5 feet and average depth 9 inches. It is applicable to machinery, drainage and irrigation. Its bed is gravelly and banks low.

A stream which rises in the townland of Kilgad at an elevation of 500 feet above the sea flows for [blank] miles along the south west boundary of this parish and, descending to a level of [blank] feet, enters the parish of Connor, through which it flows for 2 and three-quarter miles in a north westerly direction and discharges itself into the Braid river at an elevation of 106 feet above the sea. Its average fall is 1 foot in 58 feet, average breadth 8 feet, but is very shallow. It might be applied to machinery drainage and irrigation.

This parish is amply supplied with spring water and also with soft water by the numerous streams flowing down its sides.

Bogs

There is no large tract of bog in this parish, but

patches of it are to be found in every townland. [Insert addition: Those of Deerfin, Dunfadden and Crossa contain the largest portions]. Its elevation varies from 200 to 697 feet above the sea and from 30 to 499 feet above the Kells water. These bogs vary in depth from 3 to 10 feet. Their subsoil is mostly a sort of reddish clay. There [is] nothing deserving of notice in their formation or position. Timber, principally fir and a little birch and sallow, is found lying indiscriminately in them. Oak stumps and a few trunks are found on the subsoil and along the edges of the bogs.

Woods

[Insert addition: There are no woods of natural growth in the parish].

It is said that an extensive forest covered the townland of Crebilly and also some of the adjacent townlands. The only evidence of this, or the former existence of woods in this parish, is a tract of underwood extending over 85 acres 2 roods in the townland of Crebilly, and the timber found in the bog. There is some very fine old timber, principally beech, sycamore, ash and fir, about the mansion house at Crebilly [insert addition: and some young plantations, chiefly fir, have been lately made in its vicinity. In the neighbourhood of the bleach green in Cross townland, on the southern bank of the Glenwhirry water, is a small extent of plantation consisting of ash, fir and beech].

Climate

There is very little difference between the climate of this parish and that of Connor parish, and it may be quoted much the same. Of the two, it is a little later and is more exposed to the winds, which are injurious to the heavy grain.

MODERN TOPOGRAPHY

Village of Harryville

There is no town in this parish and the only village is Harryville, which is situated at the north western extremity and contiguous to the town of Ballymena, with which it is connected by the bridge across the River Braid, which flows by the north western side of the village. It is in fact the suburb of Ballymena and merely consists of 2 little streets at right angles to each other, and containing 55 1-storey and 7 2-storey houses.

[Insert addition: It contains 2 or 3 comparatively good houses and a few cottages. The population in 1831 was 252 persons. [J.R. Ward: There

are 10 houses of 2-storeys and upwards, and about 30 of 1-storey]. [Insert query by R.K. Dawson: The number of houses in Harryville: it should appear that there must be more than the report would lead one to expect? [Answer] I got this information from the person who collects the cess for the parish. The village is in Mr Hannyngton's district].

These streets are rather narrow and that on the road to Belfast particularly dirty and the houses small and filthy. The other street is not quite so dirty and the houses are of a better description. The population, which amounts to 270 persons, are almost all either tradesmen or labourers, those inhabiting the street on the Belfast road being of the poorer class and those in the other street of a more independent description of persons.

The only public building is the bridge over the Braid. It consists of 9 small semicircular arches and is 146 feet long and 28 feet wide. It is a perfectly plain structure.

The gentlemen's residences are those of James Young Esquire, Mrs Casement and Peter Aicken Esquire, J.P. These houses are plain, comfortable 2-storey residences, without anything worthy of description.

There is neither fair nor markets in Harryville.

Crebilly

There are a couple of wretched 2-storey houses in the townland of Crebilly. Their situation is on the summit of the high bank extending along the north side of the parish. This village, if it may be so termed, takes its name from the townland in which it is situated. The only public building is the Roman Catholic chapel, which was rebuilt in the year 1834. The old materials were used, and the other expenses amounted to 150 pounds. This sum was defrayed by subscription among the Roman Catholic inhabitants. It is perfectly plain in its structure. Its dimensions are [blank] feet long and [blank] feet wide, and it would accommodate 400 persons.

[Insert addition: The Roman Catholic chapel is the only public building in the parish. The building is stone but nothing remarkable in appearance, and contains accommodation for 700 persons, and the average attendance is 600. The chapel was rebuilt in 1834, when the old materials were used for the present building. The cost was 150 pounds, which was paid by subscription from the congregation. Persons were appointed in each townland to gather a certain sum, which they levied on the people who paid it without demure].

Fairs at Crebilly

There are 2 very large annual fairs held at Crebilly, one on the 26th June and the other on the 1st August. The latter fair is the larger. At this fair from 300 to 400 head of black cattle, 400 horses (averaging about 16 pounds value each), 200 to 300 sheep and 400 pigs are sold at it. At the June fair the numbers are less, not more than 200 sheep being sold at it and the other descriptions of cattle less in proportion. The horses are brought from the counties of Derry and Antrim, the black cattle from the county Fermanagh and the western counties of Mayo, Sligo and Roscommon, pigs from the country, sheep from the Highlands (they land at Cushendun) and the mountains in this county. The pigs and black cattle are bought up in considerable quantities by dealers for exportation.

The tolls on cattle amount to about 20 pounds on an annual average. They are 3d for horses, 2d for cows, 1d for sheep and pigs. The tolls on tents are 7s 6d each in the large fair and 2s 6d each in the small fair. At the large fair there are usually from 40 to 50 of these tents and at the lesser fair 25 of them. Refreshments, whiskey etc. are sold in them. There are from 10 to 12 large broth pots, which are kept boiling on the ground. This broth is sold in quart noggins for a ha'penny each.

These fairs used to be the scene of dreadful party riots, which were tending much to their injury, dealers being afraid to attend them. They have, however, from the exertions of the police [insert marginal query]. The fights generally commenced from 3 to 5 o'clock in the evening, their plans of attack and engaging at close quarters being regularly and systematically preconcerted. The attack usually commenced with a volley of stones from the party which considered itself strongest, and an immediate rush on their enemies to take them before they could recover the shock. The engagement was then carried on with the "colts" which have been elsewhere described, and continued until the rout of one party, who in their retreat never met with any mercy.

Gentlemen's Seats

The only gentleman's residence is Crebilly House, the ancient residence of the ancient family of O'Hara, the proprietors of the estate, which is situated in the townland of Crebilly. The house is plain [in] its exterior. It presents a large front and has 2 extensive wings. The rooms are numerous and spacious but, as the family now occupying it is but small, many of them are unoccupied. The house is therefore sadly out of order, as are also the offices which are also very extensive.

[Insert addition: The building may be described as an old-fashioned mansion house. It is proposed to pull it down and to rebuild].

There are many very fine full-length portraits of several ancestors of the present family of O'Hara, as also of several eminent individuals, among whom is Bishop Hutchinson, who was tried in the reign of James II and whose daughter was married to Colonel Henry O'Hara, who, with the fortune he got with her from the bishop, built the present house in 1704. These portraits are said to be, and evidently are, the productions of masters of eminence, whose names are forgotten by the family.

The former residence (on the ruins of which the present house is partly erected) was built by the O'Haras when they came from Sligo in 1156. There is but little of the foundations of the castle now discernible.

In front of the present house are several parallel rows of venerable old beech trees, extending from the house to the road. There is also a considerable quantity of timber and planting about it. [Insert addition: The demesne has some fine timber on it but is at present in a very neglected state].

Bleach Greens and Mills

There is 1 small bleach green extending over 4 acres 2 roods in this parish. The machinery of the beetling and washing mill attached to it is propelled by a breast water wheel 25 feet in diameter and 7 feet broad. There is a second beetling mill attached to it; the machinery is propelled by a breast water wheel 14 feet in diameter and 8 feet broad.

There is a beetling mill in the townland of Crebilly. The machinery is propelled by a breast water wheel 30 feet in diameter by 6 feet broad.

The corn mill in the same townland is propelled by a breast water wheel 24 feet in diameter and 6 feet broad.

The flax mill in the same townland is propelled by a breast water wheel 14 feet in diameter and 2 feet 6 inches broad.

Communications

The roads in this parish are sufficiently numerous and in tolerable order but, owing to the nature of the ground, many of them are very hilly. The principal roads are: the mail coach road from Ballymena to Belfast, which crosses the western extremity of the parish for half a mile. It is 28 feet broad, level but very wet and dirty.

The road from Ballymena to Kells traverses the south western side of the parish for 3 miles. It is a good hard road but hilly; its average breadth is 24 feet.

A road from Ballymena to Larne, which traverses the parish from east to west for 4 miles. [It] is hilly but in pretty good order. Its breadth is 22 feet.

And a road from Broughshane to Belfast by Crebilly. [It] is also very hilly but a hard and pretty good road.

Except the mail coach road, which is kept in repair by the county at large, these roads are kept by the barony. The by-roads are also sufficient.

The principal bridge is the one over the Braid at Harryville. It is perfectly plain, 146 feet long, 28 feet wide, and consists of 9 semicircular arches.

General Appearance and Scenery

There is nothing interesting in the scenery or appearance of this parish. On the contrary, it is deficient in any natural or artificial beauty. Its more remote parts are particularly bleak and cheerless, being but partially cultivated and destitute of trees, hedgerows or anything that could tend to vary or relieve the scenery. Though the lower grounds are better cultivated and more fertile, there is still a cheerless and bare appearance over its entire surface, except immediately about Crebilly.

[Insert addition: The parish in general has a well cultivated appearance, but is very tame and wants wood to relieve the sameness which occurs throughout it].

SOCIAL ECONOMY

Early Improvements

The greater number of the inhabitants of this parish are descended from the Scottish settlers of the 17th century, whose habits manners and customs, as also their dialect, they still in a great measure retain. There are still in the remote and uncultivated parts of the parish many Roman Catholics of Irish descent. They are among the poorer inhabitants.

The first migration to this parish took place when Henry II invaded Ireland. He, having received the assistance of Loughlin Connaght O'Hara (an Irish prince in Sligo) in subduing this kingdom, gave him, as a reward for his services, 12 townlands in this parish. O'Hara and his followers then settled in this parish and he then built Crebilly Castle, a small portion of the foundations of which still remain near the present house of

Crebilly. The O'Hara family still possess the estate and some of them inhabit Crebilly House. The heir being a minor, the property is under the court of chancery.

The march of improvements in this parish, particularly in the more remote districts, seems to have been but slow, as the inhabitants are far inferior to those of the adjoining parishes. They are much less comfortable in their circumstances, habitations and manner of living, and more irregular in their habits, than their neighbours. Of later years they have improved a little, but chiefly owing to the introduction of Sunday and other schools.

Obstructions to Improvement

There is no legal obstruction to improvement. There is, however, a great barrier to it in the numerous unlicensed whiskey houses, better known by the name of "sheeban houses", of which there are fully 30 in this parish. These are the resort of the idle and dissolute of both sexes, and afford every encouragement and incitement to immorality. Within a short period the harmful effects of such nuisances have been exhibited in 2 instances, one person having died of drunkenness and a woman (in the same house) being burned to death while drunk. They are also the harbour for all the bad characters of the country.

Local Government

The only magistrate is Peter Aicken, who resides in the village of Harryville at the western extremity of the parish. He is rather old and wants both firmness and decision. There are not any police. The nearest petty sessions are those held in Ballymena on every alternate Monday. A manor court is held monthly and a court leet twice a year, in a house near Crebilly, for the manor of Carte, in which this parish is situated, Michael Harrison of Ballymena, Esquire, seneschal. Sums not exceeding 2 pounds (late Irish currency) are recoverable at these courts, and at the courts leet the incidental expenses of the manor, such as the repairs of pound, the salaries of bailiffs etc., are applotted on the tenants.

Party Fights

No outrages have lately occurred. Crebilly was, until the last 3 years, the scene of many a bloody party fight. Previous to the last 8 years these fights were as regular as the fairs, and though lives were but seldom lost on the ground, still many never recovered [from] the beatings they received.

Latterly these riots have ceased. The last that took place was a year ago and it was but trifling. Had they continued the fair must have been ruined, as the respectable dealers were afraid to come to it, but the presence of the constabulary has put an end to them. Both parties are equally disposed to riot. Their fights [began] by a volley or two of stones and an immediate rush to close quarters. They have but few firearms, and even these they do not use, but they have much more dangerous weapons called "colts", which are made of osiers or woodbine plaited <platted> to the thickness of an inch, and loaded with a heavy knob of lead at one or both ends. They are about 18 inches long and are generally concealed under the sleeve. A stick will not throw off a blow from one of these as, from its elasticity, it will bend over it.

Illicit Distillation

Illicit distillation was formerly carried on extensively in the more mountainous parts of this parish. It is now, however, seldom attempted. Its being given up is chiefly owing to the reduction in the duty in whiskey and the greater facility afforded for the sale of grain, together with the good prices that article now brings.

There are few, if any, fire or life insurances.

Dispensary

There is no dispensary in this parish. Its want is not much felt as the people are considered healthy and comparatively free from contagious or infectious diseases.

Schools

Schools are not numerous in this parish, there being 2 schoolhouses at present unoccupied and only 2 open. There is still, however, a greater facility afforded for education than formerly and the schools of the present day are of an improved description. The people do not so gladly avail themselves of the advantages they afford as readily as might be expected, and besides, they take their children from them on the merest pretence and for the most trifling purposes. They all seem to wish to know how to read, but possess very little taste for useful or religious knowledge.

Sunday schools have tended more to the improvement of the people and caused a stricter observance of the sabbath.

Poor

There is no regular provision for the poor of this parish. The sum of 20 pounds was bequeathed in 1770 by the will of Henry Hutchinson O'Hara (then proprietor), to be paid annually from the estate and distributed annually by the rector among the poor of this parish.

Religion

By the revised census of 1834 there are in this parish 150 Episcopalians, 1,349 Roman Catholics, 1,982 Presbyterians and 61 other Dissenters. This parish is episcopally united to that of Kirkinriola. The tithes, which amount to 140 pounds per annum, are paid to the Reverend Hugh Smyth Cumming, the rector, who resides at the parsonage contiguous to the town of Ballymena and in the parish of Kirkinriola.

There being no meeting house in this parish, the Presbyterians worship in those in the neighbouring ones and pay their stipend to the ministers of these.

The priest has the usual variety of emoluments from his flock, but these cannot be discovered.

Habits of the People

The people of this parish are inferior in their general dispositions as to industry, cleanliness, comfort etc. to the inhabitants of the adjacent parishes. They are not industrious nor proverbial for sobriety. In their houses they are untidy and rather comfortless. Except on Sundays and at fairs, they are careless and negligent in their persons. In their circumstances they are not comfortable, arising principally from their farms, however small, being divided by the father among his sons, each perhaps not obtaining more than 1 acre. When they have got this they imagine they are called on to marry, which they invariably do, when they have erected a small cabin on their "farm", as they term it. Poverty is of course entailed on them and their family by this step, as the land, instead of assisting the payment of the rent, does not afford sufficient provision for them.

Their circumstances have certainly improved within the last 2 years, owing to the constant employment and good wages they receive for the manufacture of linen, and in this the majority of them is engaged. They seem, however, to have but little idea of management or economy, and are slovenly in their houses and persons. This, however, is more the case in the higher and more remote parts of the parish than in the lower and more cultivated, where there are some busy farmers and residences, and the people partake more of the habits of those in Kirkinriola.

[Insert addition: No appearance of prosperity to be met with amongst thèm. On the contrary, many of the farms are deserted and the houses remain unoccupied].

Houses and Diet

Their houses are all 1-storey, thatched, and consist generally of 2 apartments, but frequently of only 1. They are lit by tolerable glazed windows but are untidy internally and externally; but little regard is paid to neatness. Turf, which is their only fuel, is convenient and abundant, and the fir timber found in the bogs, from its resinous nature, affords when split excellent light and sometimes serves instead of candles.

Potatoes and milk constitute the principal food of the poorer class, particularly in winter. At other seasons meal is used, but not so much as formerly. Salt herrings are much used. Flesh meat is but seldom, except by the richer, made use of. On Sundays and at fairs and markets they dress very well, nearly so much so as the people of Kirkinriola.

Family Size and Marriage

The usual number in a family is 6. They are considered very long lived, there being few townlands in which there are not persons of 80 years of age. They marry early, a sure sign of a backward state of civilisation: within a year a girl of 14 having been married to a boy 3 years older. It may be remarked that the Irish marry much earlier than the Scots.

Amusements and Traditions

The 12th of July is observed by the Orangemen and the 24th of June by the Freemasons walking in procession. There are no patrons nor patron's days, ancient music nor anything peculiar in their dress, manners or appearance.

The only ancient custom is that of 12 pounds being paid annually to the Bishop of Down and Connor from the estate. It is said this was desired by the will of one of the O'Haras of old, who, for some evil deed which he had committed, left this sum to this bishop to pray his soul out of purgatory. This, however, though currently reported, is not accurately known.

Traditions are very common among them, and therefore old persons: one, a poor woman named O'Hara, who has enabled the agent to the estate under the court of chancery to trace back the genealogy of the O'Hara family to Noah, and he has accordingly drawn out a genealogical tree from that person to the present O'Hara.

Remarkable events: none.

Emigration

About 10 on average annually emigrate in spring to Canada. They are of the working class, and such as take no capital out of the country; few return.

About 50 young men (unmarried) go annually to the Scottish or English harvest and return when they are over. This practice is decreasing.

Table of Schools

[Table contains the following headings: name, situation and description, when established, income and expenditure, physical, intellectual and moral education, number of pupils subdivided by sex, age and religion, name and religion of master and mistress].

Under the Board of National Education, in a very good house built for the purpose by the National Board in the townland of Craigbilly, established 1833; income: bequest of the Revd Mr Fitsimmons 6 pounds, from the Board of National Education 10 pounds, from pupils 11 pounds; intellectual education: books of the National Board, the Latin and Greek works usually taught, trigonometry, algebra, mensuration; moral education: Sunday school, occasional visits of the clergy, Douai and Authorised Version at stated hours, catechisms (all kinds) on Saturdays; number of pupils: males, 14 under 10 years of age, 28 from 10 to 15, 12 above 15, 54 total males; females, 6 under 10 years of age, 17 from 10 to 15, 3 above 15, 26 total females; total number of pupils 80, 3 Protestants, 20 Presbyterians, 57 Roman Catholics; master Roger McArt, Roman Catholic.

Under the London Hibernian Society, in a very good house built for the purpose by subscription in the townland of Ballyclug, established 1835; income from pupils 14 pounds; intellectual education: books of the London Hibernian Society, trigonometry, book-keeping; moral education: Sunday school, occasional visits from the clergy, Scriptures (Authorised Version) daily; number of pupils: males, 15 under 10 years of age, 2 from 10 to 15, 2 above 15, 19 total males; females, 5 under 10 years of age, 6 from 10 to 15, 11 total females; total number of pupils 30, 20 Presbyterians, 10 Roman Catholics; master Hugh Dorsay, Roman Catholic.

Private school, in a house built for the purpose by subscription in the townland of Leminary, established more than 30 years; income from pupils 27 pounds; intellectual education: books from the Sunday School Society, *Gough's Arithmetic*; moral education: occasional visits from the minister, Sunday school, Authorised and Douai Version daily; number of pupils: males, 6 under 10 years of age, 3 from 10 to 15, 2 above 15, 11 total males; females, 4 under 10 years of age, 46 from 10 to 15, 9 above 15, 59 total females; total number of pupils 70, 41 Presbyterians, 23 Roman Catholics, 6 other denominations; master John Brady, Roman Catholic.

[Totals]: income from individuals 16 pounds, 52 pounds from pupils; number of pupils: males, 35 under 10 years of age, 33 from 10 to 15, 16 above 15, 84 total males; females, 15 under 10 years of age, 69 from 10 to 15, 12 above 15, 96 total females; total number of pupils 180, 3 Protestants, 81 Presbyterians, 90 Roman Catholics, 6 other denominations.

Benevolence: Establishments for the Indigent

[Table contains the following headings: name, object, management, number relieved, funds, annual expense of management, relief afforded, when founded].

2 schools, supported partly by the public; object: the removal of ignorance; management: sundry societies; number relieved: 110 pupils receiving instruction; funds: from the National Board annually 10 pounds, from private individuals 6 pounds; relief afforded: 110 children instructed daily; when founded: at sundry times.

Bequest, object: 20 pounds to be annually distributed among the poor; management: distributed by the rector of the parish; number relieved: uncertain; funds: 20 pounds bequeathed by Henry Hutchinson O'Hara, to be paid annually from the estate; relief afforded: 20 pounds annually distributed among the poor; when founded: 1770.

Memoir on Ancient Topography of Ballyclug and Ballyscullion by J. Stokes, August 1837

ANCIENT TOPOGRAPHY

Map

Map showing the relative position of the standing stones and other monuments of Ballyclug, scale 3 miles to 1 inch.

Ecclesiastical: Ballyclug Graveyard and Ancient Church

The ancient graveyard of Ballyclug stands on the northern side of a gently sloping hill and at the distance of five-eighths of a mile statute south east from the town of Ballymena. It contains about half an acre Cunningham measure and is surrounded by a modern wall built 13 years ago, i.e. in 1824, the old one having completely fallen down. The dimensions of the yard were at the same time a little enlarged and the entrance changed from the north west corner (its ancient position) to the south east. At the eastern side the foundations of a church still appear, 58 feet in length and 28 in breadth. None of the masonry is standing, the only part left being what is sunk in the earth. The stones were taken to build an adjacent schoolhouse. It was ruined since the time of the Reformation.

From the old gate at the north west corner there formerly extended an ancient paved road, said to have led from Kells via Ballyclug to the neighbourhood of Gracehill, in the parish of Ahoghill. It was altogether destroyed at the changing of the gate. Some of the paving stones with which it was constructed are said to have been 3 feet broad. The length to which it extended at the period of its destruction is not exactly remembered. [Insert note: It is believed that this church was founded by St Patrick].

Burials in Graveyard

The following families are interred here: Montgomery, Ker, Maxwell, Sutler, Dill, Johnston, Haslet, Gilmor, Robison, McKeen, Kennedy, Kissock, Walkinshaw, Doel, Millar, Barkley, Wilson, O'Hara (1708), the oldest. The name Walkinshaw is that of the Walkinshaw family of Forthill, parish of Connor, who came from a place called by their name in Renfrewshire, Scotland. The laird of Walkinshaw left that country after the battle of Killycrankie, he being of the defeated party. The name O'Hara abounds in this part of the country. The head of the clan, as it may be so called, is Mr O'Hara of Crebilly, but the lineal descendant is Mr O'Hara of Portstewart.

Military: Crebilly Castle

Immediately at the back of Crebilly House, the seat of Henry O'Hara Esquire, there are the remains of all that can be called a castle in this parish. It is known by the name of the Old Castle at Crebilly. The front line is all that is visible. It can be traced through the grass to the distance of 40 yards, each end being terminated by a small lump of masonry overgrown with weeds. These had been the corners. It is situated on high ground which falls off gradually on all sides towards Broughshane and Ballymena.

It was erected immediately after the destruction of the original castle of the O'Haras which stood at Slaght in the parish of Connor and was destroyed in 1641. See Ancient Topography of the parish of Connor. It is said to have been pulled down in 1735, being not large enough for a commodious dwelling house.

Pagan: Giant's Graves

In the townland of Caherty, at the foot of a rocky ledge, there is a remarkable giant's grave, composed of very large stones. See drawing[s] for plans and dimensions. Nothing remarkable has been ever found in or about it. Immediately adjacent to it, and on the top of that ledge, there was formerly a standing stone 7 feet high which, from its being in so a conspicuous a situation, served as a landmark to travellers. It was overthrown about 18 years ago by a drunken party and broken to pieces.

[Insert marginal note: Circumstance showing the long continuance of the belief that a certain class of monuments are the graves of giants]. In the townland of Ballymarlow, and on a small piece of ground that appears to have been long uncultivated, there is a rude imitation of a giant's grave. Each side of it is set with large stones; see drawing[s].

The tradition about it is to the following effect: "It is the grave of John Todd, a man of gigantic stature, who, immediately after the rebellion of 1641, came from some distant country for the sole purpose of killing one Carson, who had distinguished himself in the massacre that then took place by sundry cruelties, especially by decoying certain ladies of rank by promises of his protection from their enemies, into corn kilns, where he burned them to death by setting fire to the buildings. Todd therefore called at his house and challenged him to come out and fight him. They both accordingly went out, but as Todd was in the act of stooping down to tie his shoe, Carson struck him from behind with an axe on the back of the neck and killed him. The axe he had concealed under a blue cloak, and from his constantly carrying it about with him, he earned the title of Powaxe Carson, by which he is still remembered. Todd he then buried, and in honour of his stature made an imitation of an ancient giant's grave, not very exact indeed, but sufficient to show his intention. The hill upon which it is situated is known by the name of Todd's Knowe to this day."

Moat

In the townland of Ballylessan there is, at the top of a precipice sloping into the Braid river and close to the road from Ballymena to Connor, from the former of which place it is distant but one-eighth of a mile, a remarkable moat made in the same form as Drumfane moat in the adjacent parish of Kirkinriola, only that this one is larger and more perfect. It is composed of earth and stones. There is no appearance of any cove entering into the heart of it, but there is one in a field about 100 perches westward, now choked up. There is no appearance of any ridge proceeding from the bottom of the trenches to the top, as there is in the moat at Drumfane. The top is very sharp and is composed of a small flat platform 15 feet across. There is a very good view from it, extensive and commanding. See drawing[s] for plans and dimensions.

It appears in nature to be exactly similar to the partially destroyed monument found in the parish of Aghadowey in the county of Londonderry, which consisted of a tumulus having at one side the remains of a square superstructure and being also encompassed by a ditch. Those remains belonged to something similar to the square platform in drawing.

The bodies of 2 men hung in the rebellion of 1798 are buried in the ditch.

Forts

In the townland of Deerfin there is a fort of remarkable form situated in low ground at the head of a small valley. It is commanded on every side by sloping hills. See drawing[s] for plan and dimensions. The foundations, represented in the interior by double lines, are never elevated above the general level of the fort more than 18 inches and appear to be composed of small stones and clay. In all probability they were made for supporting the sticks of wooden huts. As for the small cairns of stones and the hearth situated in the parapet, it is uncertain whether they may not have been made by the people who fled to this fort for refuge in great numbers in the rebellion of 1798. It was then an uncultivated lonely place and the fort itself was covered with a natural growth of trees since cut down. It was also used by the Roman Catholic priests as a place for divine service during the existence of the Penal Laws. They built an altar in it for that purpose.

The form is remarkable. From its defenceless situation and great extent, it seems probable that it was anciently used for the reception of cattle. There is no cove adjacent to it. No antique of any kind was ever found at or within it. A large flock of cattle would require a large space within the ramparts, in which place only would they be safe from the attacks of wolves at night. The average depth of the ditch is 7 feet. The principal entrance is at the south. It is the original one, the others are modern, i.e. the entrance.

The other forts of the parish are quite uninteresting. In the townland of Ballylessan there is a fort, now converted into a garden, in the centre of which there is a cove containing 5 separate apartments arranged in a remarkable way. See drawing[s] for plans. There are 2 entrances. The fort itself is constructed in the usual manner with clay and stones. The ditch is greatly filled up and very torn away. It is about 5 feet deep.

Coves

In the townland of Crebilly there is a cove of unusual form. It is in the form of a cross, but with no doors or separating partitions of any kind at the intersections; see drawing[s]. At the corners the stones are built up in a careful and workmanlike manner, the heaviest and squarest being always placed at the angle. The part marked "a-a" in the plan was once an outer room, now torn away, it

being the intention of the owner to render the whole available as a pigsty.

In a cove in the townland of Caherty, now choked up, the bottom was found paved with small stones. Rooms opened off from each side and from the floor of one of them a "peh pipe" was picked up. In another in the same townland a smooth spherical stone and a "thunderbolt" or small stone-cutting instrument were found. The former was apparently intended as a weight. It weighed three-quarters of a pound Irish measure.

Silver Coins

In 1831 42 silver coins, from the size of a shilling to that of a 2s 6d, were found in a field near the giant's grave in that townland. They were not contained in any vessel. They were immediately sold to a Ballymena watchmaker and it is not known what reign they were of.

Miscellaneous Discoveries

In drawings there are delineated some remarkable stone rings, some of them curiously ornamented.

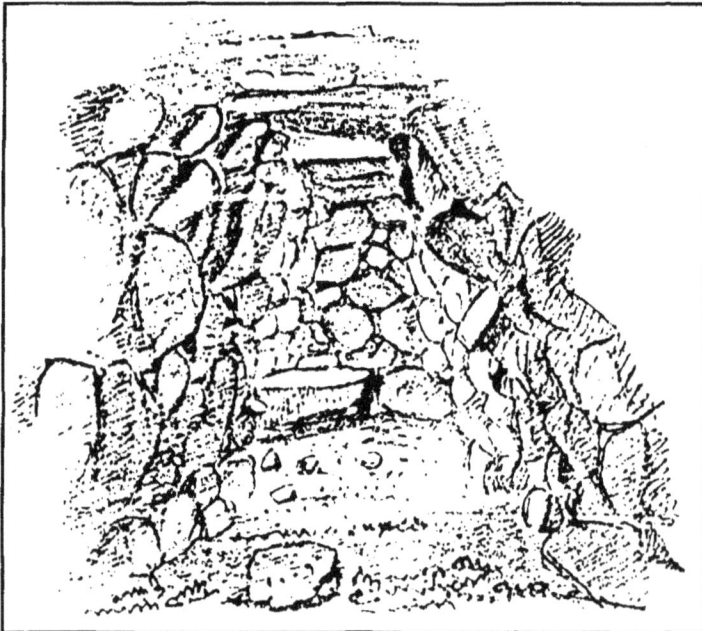

Cove from Crebilly

They are copied from a private collection. They had been obtained from a fool who was in the habit of going through all parts of the country with an ass and cart, collecting specimens of antiquity from the people by bartering little insignificant articles for them, and then retailing them to others at a very low price. They seem to have been intended for ornaments, especially the one marked [blank], which has a continued hole passing laterally through the 2 sides, evidently intended for the passage of a string. They are made some of limestone and others of freestone. It is impossible to ascertain to what parish or district they properly belong, or have been found in.

Salt-cellars

In a drawing there is a relic of 1641, found near the fort delineated in the drawing[s] and buried about 2 feet beneath the surface. The top has a hemispherical cavity. It is called by the people an "ancient salt-cellar." It is evidently of the same date as a glass salt-cellar that was found in the parish of Bovevagh, county Londonderry, as well as numerous decayed keys, padlocks and hammers etc., all evidently modern but all found from time to time in such places and situations as plainly showed <shewed> that they had been brought there by a civil commotion of unusual extent and severity. Nothing else could have brought them to places never known to have been cultivated and there is no other modern convulsion that could have done so but the great and sudden rebellion of 1641. For that cause, therefore, this antique or rather this illustration of history has been here designated "a relic of 1641." It is made of red baked clay and glazed.

Other Discoveries

In drawing[s] there are shown some remarkable flint arrowheads obtained from the same source as the stone rings.

Few miscellaneous articles of antiquity appear to have been picked up in this district. Near the fort of Deerfin an ancient wooden mether was found, filled with "ancient butter", in a bog. No remarkable spearheads or hatchets have been heard of among the parishioners.

Tradition

It may be mentioned in conclusion that there is here a remarkable tradition corroborating one which was reported some years ago from the neighbourhood of Coleraine. It is that there was once a tribe or clan in possession of Dunluce

Castle, who treacherously killed some hundreds of the O'Cathans by stabbing (at a feast in which both clans met) each man, his right-hand neighbour; that as a providential retaliation for such a deed, it happened that the English soon after got possession of that castle, slaying to a man the whole tribe in one night and casting their bodies into the sea. The name has been since that night utterly extinguished.

Templemoyle Church and Graveyard

The old graveyard of Templemoyle in Kilvillis is situated on one of the gentle ridges so frequent in an undulating country and is not far from the centre of the grange of Ballyscullion (see map attached). It contains half an acre Cunningham measure of ground. There are some traces of the foundations of a church in the interior, extending to 75 feet in length by 25 in breadth. The only person of respectability buried in the yard is George Charlton, a man of property who lived in the neighbourhood prior to 1790 and died at that date. Nothing particular is remembered about him.

The other names are Courtney, Rainey, Carmichael, Speers, Nicholl, McMaster, McCool, Boyd, Patterson, Lindsay, Granan, Dickey, McClenaghan (1749). It is preserved with decency and care. The wall is in good order but is not ancient. The Presbyterian and Catholic families of the neighbourhood continue to bury in it, but not so frequently as formerly. There is no stone older than 1700.

According to the tradition of the place, the unfinished church which stood here, and which gave the name Templemoyle to part of the townland, was begun by a St Bridget who, being prevented from her undertaking by the supernatural obstructions usual to a "templemoyle", desisted and left the walls undone. The masonry executed by day fell down by night etc.

There is also a tradition that there once stood adjacent to it a priory of the Knights of St John. Not a trace of it now remains.

There is no cross or holy well adjacent to this graveyard, or in any other part of the grange.

Remarks on Antiquities

This district appears to be singularly deficient in antiquities. No coves, cromlechs, giant's graves or standing stones can be reported. There is a natural rock protruding from the surface of a hill a couple of fields distant from this graveyard but it has no real claim to the title of standing stone, though it is called so by the country people. There are a few Danish forts but they are without any interesting peculiarities. They [are] all of the ordinary size and of the usual mixture of clay and stones, and in excellent repair. Almost all the ditches possess their original depth and dimensions.

It is more than probable that the people have destroyed great numbers of ancient places, from a wish to save all the land they possibly could, a higher rent than usual being laid on them on account of the district being tithe free. No antiques or coins can be obtained among them at present.

Drawings of Antiquities

Giant's grave in Caherty, with human figure for proportion; view with dimensions, height 5 feet; ground plan with dimensions.

Todd's Grave, 1641, view and ground plan, dimensions 10 feet long by 2 feet wide.

Moat in the townland of Ballykeel, ground plan and section with dimensions, scale half an inch to a chain.

Fort in Deerfin, plan and section with dimensions and orientation; drawings of fire hearth, scale half an inch to a chain.

A series of coves in a fort in townland of Ballylessan, scale 16 feet to an inch; enlarged plan of coves and sections with annotations; fort and cove, ground plan, scale half an inch to a chain.

View of the interior of Thomas McKeen's Cove, Crebilly, with plan, scale 16 feet to an inch, with dimensions.

2 stone rings from a private collection, overhead and side views of each, one with dimensions; 3 stone rings, 2 views, full size.

3 decorated stone rings from a private collection, one with both sides and edge, others with overhead and side views, all full size.

Salt-cellar of baked clay, a relic of 1641, with dimensions.

4 flint arrowheads, full size views.

Fair Sheets on Ancient Topography by J. Bleakly, June and July 1837

Ancient Graveyard

The old graveyard of this parish is situated 1 and a half miles south east of Ballymena, on the leading road from Ballymena to Belfast, in the townland of Ballylesson, on the farm of John Kerr. The oldest gravestone is near the gate, dated 1708, to the memory of Richard O'Hara, and another of the same date to the memory of Michael O'Hara.

Fort in Ballylesson

The fort on William Duffin's farm in the same townland is dug up and taken away. About 8 years ago John Keeran dreamed of money being deposited in this fort and, accompanied by Michael McDevit, went by night to the fort and commenced digging, in the act of which he was taken by the fairies a considerable distance into the bog, but was pursued by his companion, at whom he made several attempts to grasp but had not power, until his companion had the presence of mind to take a small bottle of holy water from his pocket and cast some of it into his face, when instantly he fell into his arms, but remained speechless and quite deformed about the mouth and face and struck blind. [He] remains a travelling pauper until this day through the country, who was formerly a farmer in the above neighbourhood. The hole remains in which he was digging in the undisturbed part of the fort until this day. Information obtained from William Duffin, farmer, and Michael McDevit, labourer. 22 June 1837.

Forts and Caves

There is a fort on John Duffin's farm in the townland of Ballyleeson which is his garden but planted. There is an artificial cove in this fort in which there are 5 rooms, all open for inspection and well worth drawing.

There was a fort of earth on the farm of Patrick O'Hara in same townland, but dug up, and one on the farm of Lawrence O'Lone in same townland but laboured. There is a fort of earth in Ballycraggy townland, on the farm of Hugh Wasson.

There is also a cave in the same townland but closed up, on the farm of James Wilson.

There is also a cave on the farm of James Blaney in Lamonerry, but closed up.

Ancient Coins, Querns and Fort

A quantity of silver coins of sixpenny magnitude found by John O'Hara in digging a field in the townland of Caherty, but all sold; also a pair of querns [found] by Peter Walsh of Caherty and on his farm in same townland.

Fort on the farm of Charles O'Hara in same townland.

Caves and Forts

Cave on the farm of Patrick O'Hara in a meadow below the moat in the townland of Ballykeel; the mouth nearly closed up but can easily be opened and is said to be worth drawing.

There is a fort on the farm of Samuel Armstrong in Ballykeel, very small and very low.

Cave on the farm of James Walkinshaw near his house in same townland, but long since closed up; also a cave on the farm of Robert Johnstone in the townland of Ballymarlow but closed up; and one on the farm of James Robinson, same townland; and one on the farm of James Wilson. 23 June 1837.

A quantity of ancient silver coins of sixpenny magnitude of Edward II found by Henry O'Hara and on his farm about 20 years ago, but sold for old silver, in same townland. 26 June 1837.

Chapel and Fort in Dunnavaddin

The ruins of a Roman Catholic chapel in the farm of Thomas Walsh in the townland of Dunnavaddin. The walls are still in a good state of preservation, although the roof was taken off about 20 years ago, of [ground plan, "T"] form and well worth roofing again.

There is also a fort on the farm of Thomas Walsh in same townland, but laboured.

Forts

The fort on the farm of Henry O'Hara in Deerfin is of stone and earth, very large and undisturbed, with smaller forts inside and on very low ground, and is worth drawing.

The fort on Neil Granny's farm in same townland is dug up.

Fort in Tully, on the farm of William Neely, but dug up; and one on the farm of Hugh Cushnahan, but laboured, in same townland. 27 June 1837.

Giant's Grave

In Boydstown Rock, townland of Caherty, on the farm of Hugh O'Hara, about 10 perches south east of the leading road from Craigbilly to Broughshane <Broshane>, under the rock on which mass was celebrated before the Craigbilly chapel was built, and about three-quarters of a mile north east of Craigbilly; total length of the grave is 10 feet with 4 stones, viz. 2 standing at each side. At the head of the grave is a space between the 2 side stones 2 feet wide. The 2 side stones are each 4 feet high. The 2 stones at the foot are each 4 feet high.

Another grave near the engine house of Mr Sayers in the townland of Ballymarlow, on the farm of Robert Johnstone. The grave is 11 feet long by 2 feet wide, composed of stone but nearly level with the ground.

Craigbilly Castle

For the particulars of Craigbilly Castle and the ancient history of the O'Hara family, see Mr Michael Harrisson, Ballymena, agent for the estate, or Margaret O'Hara, Caherty. From Mr James Walkinshaw and Mr Sayers, 29 June 1837.

Fort in Owen O'Hara's farm, Caherty townland.

Cave

The cave in the townland of Craigbilly, at the back of Thomas McKeen's house, is open at both ends with 2 rooms turning off at right angles, the one 20 feet long and the other 16 feet long by 3 feet wide and 4 and a half feet high [crossed out: was much longer but the stones of part have been taken away for building]; worth drawing.

Giant's Grave

The giant's grave near the engine house in the townland of Ballymarlow is said to be the grave of John Todd, a man of gigantic stature, who came to fight a little man called Powaxe Carson and whom Carson [killed] by coming behind him and treacherously cutting off his head. Carson resided in the townland of Ballee, parish of Connor and was commonly called Powaxe Carson, from carrying an axe at all times about him, concealed under a blue cloak, for the purpose of treacherously cutting off the heads of all those who injured him. He was of a very spiteful disposition and is said to have killed a number of ladies by putting them into a corn kiln under the pretence of saving them from their enemies during the '41 war, but having a former dispute with some of their friends, revenged it on the ladies by setting the kiln on fire and consuming the ladies, in the townland of Slaght.

Carson lived until his chin made a hole in his breast. His friends boast of him in Carsonstown, townland of Ballee, until this day. The small hill above the grave is called Todd's Now until this day. From Rodger McCart, Ballykeel and Patrick O'Hara, 3 July 1837.

Forts

The fort on the farm of James Blackley in the townland of Caherty is on low ground and undisturbed, but not remarkable.

Meddar and Pikehead

An ancient meddar <meadder> found in Deerfin moss, full of butter about 8 years ago by James Blackley, but destroyed.

A pikehead was found by Samuel Bones in Ballycraggy, of iron.

Ancient Pillars

The 2 pillars below Craigbilly hill called the Rosslim Pillars, on the road leading from Craigbilly to Broughshane, are very ancient but have been repaired lately by William Sayers Esquire. [Signed] J. Bleakly, 6 July 1837.

School Statistics

SOCIAL ECONOMY

Table of Schools

[Table contains the following headings: name of townland where held, name and religion of master or mistress, free or pay school, annual income of master or mistress, description and cost of schoolhouse, number of pupils subdivided by religion, sex and the Protestant and Roman Catholic returns, societies with which connected].

Rankinstown, master William Hamilton, Presbyterian; pay school, annual income 10 pounds; schoolhouse very bad, cost 20 pounds; number of pupils by the Protestant return: 23 Presbyterians, 1 Roman Catholic, 17 males, 7 females; by the Roman Catholic return: 22 Presbyterians, 4 Roman Catholics, 19 males, 7 females; associations none.

Ballymarlow, master Hugh Dowey, Roman Catholic; pay school, annual income 13 pounds; schoolhouse in good repair, cost 25 pounds; number of pupils by the Protestant return: 2 Established Church, 15 Presbyterians, 11 Roman Catholics, 16 males, 12 females; by the Roman Catholic return: 2 Established Church, 14 Presbyterians, 14 Roman Catholics, 20 males, 10 females; associations none.

Scottstown, master John Brady, Roman Catholic; pay school, annual income 5 pounds; schoolhouse a barn; number of pupils by the Protestant return: 13 Presbyterians, 7 Roman Catholics, 10 males, 10 females; by the Roman Catholic return: 2 Established Church, 15 Presbyterians, 7 Roman Catholics, 12 males, 12 females; associations none.

Deertin, master Pat Magill, Roman Catholic; pay school, annual income 12 pounds; school-

house his own house; number of pupils by the Protestant return: 8 Presbyterians, 16 Roman Catholics, 12 males, 12 females; by the Roman Catholic return: 8 Presbyterians, 24 Roman Catholics; associations none.

Crebilly, mistress Eliza Magill, Roman Catholic; pay school, annual income 8 pounds; schoolhouse her own house; number of pupils by the Protestant return: 18 Presbyterians, 2 Roman Catholics, 13 males, 7 females; associations none.

Parish of Finvoy, County Antrim

Officer's Statistical Account by Lieutenant
R. Alexander, September 1831

NATURAL STATE

Name and Situation

The name of Finvoy is supposed to be derived
from fin "fair" and ouch "a grave", or from fin
"fair" and voy "a place for cows." By others it is
supposed to mean "Fin's victory", a place where
Fin McCool (Fingal) gained a great battle; or from
Finn-mhagh "beautiful plain", planities amona.

Boundaries and Extent

It is situated in the barony of Kilconway and in the
western part of the county of Antrim. It forms a
principal part of the prebend of Rasharkin in the
diocese of Connor.

It is bounded on the north by the parish of
Ballymoney, on the east by the parishes of
Kilraghts and Killagan, on the south by the parish
of Rasharkin and on the west by the River Bann.
It extends from north to south about 5 British
statute miles and from east to west about 8. It
contains 16,383 British statute acres. It is divided
into 39 townlands.

NATURAL FEATURES

Surface and Soil

The parish is divided into 3 parts by 2 large bogs
which run through it, and adjacent to these, and in
the same direction of nearly north and south, are
2 ridges of basaltic cliffs. That one which faces
the west and is the most precipitous, rising to the
height of 639 feet above the level of the sea, is
called Craigs from its rough and craggy heights;
and the eastern one, Killymurris, from chiltia
"woods" and mora "great", probably from the
woods once abounding there. About a third of the
parish is bog or heathy ground and in no part is the
soil considered good. It is not well cultivated and
the want of hedgerows and planting is everywhere apparent.

PRODUCTIVE ECONOMY

Farms

A few of the farms are so large as to contain 100
acres, but most of them are from 20 to 30 acres.
There are 2 or 3 considerable grazing or stock
farms, as they are called, the summer grass of
which, to fatten a cow, is let at about 2 guineas.

NATURAL HISTORY

Turbary and Geology

There is a considerable extent of good turbary.
The only rock is the basalt, of which 2 remarkable
cliffs have already been mentioned. There are 2
singular lines of gravel hills, the one extending
more than a mile along the Main water, the other,
near the River Bann, has the high road running
along its top from the Vow to Ballinagarvy. They
are composed of rolled masses of basalt of all
sizes and of various degrees of inclination, containing zeolites. They are called drumkeels, i.e.
"little hills", and their contents are made use of in
the repairs of the roads. Along the shores of the
River Bann is a stiff clay of which bricks are
made.

PRODUCTIVE ECONOMY

Manufactures

There is no manufacture of any consequence
except linen, the staple one of the province of
Ulster.

MODERN TOPOGRAPHY

Roads

The mail coach road from Belfast to Coleraine
traverses the eastern part of the parish running
nearly north and south. Another road from
Rasharkin to Ballymoney runs in the same direction and nearly through the middle of the parish,
and a third runs along the River Bann, leading
from Kilrea to Ballymoney. Several crossroads
connect the 2 latter, one road only communicat-
ing with the mail coach road. There are none of
them in good order except the coach road.

Hamlets

The only hamlet of any extent is Dunloy, situated
in the townland of the same name and through
which the mail coach road passes. There are 4
fairs held here quarterly, on the 15th February,
May, August and November.

Plantations

There are no plantations of any size with the
exception of those around Moore Lodge, the seat

of William Moore Esquire. At the Glebe, in the Mullans and in Caroreagh are some plantations, and Mr Hutcheson of Ballymoney has planted a little near Dunloy.

SOCIAL ECONOMY

Population

From a return made in the year 1813 by the high constable, the parish contained about 868 houses and 4,720 people, of whom 2,286 were males and 2,434 females. In the parish are a church, a Presbyterian meeting house and a Roman Catholic chapel. There is no established school for the education of the poor.

ANCIENT TOPOGRAPHY

Antiquities

Near to the Glebe House is a large circular fort which gives name to the barony Kilconway, "Con's burying place." By Con is here meant Conway McQuillan, whose family and fortunes were ruined by Sourleboy in the famous battle of Aura, fought on the 13th July 1569. A fort of an elliptical form, and called Drumaboichan or "the hill of enchantments", is situated east of the Bannside road and near to the Vow ferry.

In the Craigs is a large square fort surrounded by a deep ditch and near to it is a large cromlech or druid's altar, as it is called. It is a large stone 10 feet long and 8 broad, set up in an inclined position upon 2 other stones. It is emphatically termed by the country people the Broad Stone.

Within a few hundred yards of the hamlet of Dunloy is a circle of large stones called the Giant's Bed. [Signed] R. Alexander, Lieutenant Royal Engineers, 26 September 1831.

Memoir by James Boyle, September 1835, with additions from Draft Memoir

NATURAL STATE

Locality

[Insert addition: It is situated in the west of the county Antrim and the north west of the barony of Kilconway. It contains 16,474 acres 1 rood 9 perches, including 94 acres 1 rood 11 perches of water.

Divisions

The chain of mountains on the west side of the parish, and the bog which runs in a parallel direction nearly through, divides the parish into 3 natural divisions, which are known in the county by the following names: the Bannside, which lies between the bog and the river; Between-the-mosses is the space between the bog and the mountains; and Killymorris is that west of the mountains adjoining the parish of Killyglen and the grange of Dundermot].

NATURAL FEATURES

Hills

The Killymurrys range of hills, which extend from the adjoining parish of Ballymoney along the western side of this county, traverse the centre of this parish from north to south. There is nothing striking in the appearance of this ridge, either as to its formation or altitude, its extreme elevation in this parish not exceeding 707 feet above the level of the sea. The descent eastward is at first, though rapid, rather gradual and finally terminates in a variety of undulating features at the eastern boundary of the parish. The descent westward is irregular and broken, and towards the summit (which is nearly flat) consists of several successive abrupt steps caused by outbreaking of the strata. At the base of the western side is a large tract of nearly level country, averaging about 200 feet above the sea, and this is succeeded by a broken and diversified strip extending along the River Bann from the northern to the southern extremity of the parish.

The average elevation of the ridge above the sea is 675 feet and the principal points on it are Ballymacaldrack, 707 feet, Craigs, 689 feet and Tullaghans, 551 feet above the level of the sea.

Lakes

The southern boundary of the parish intersects a small lake extending over 5 acres 3 roods 28 perches, of which 3 acres 1 rood 12 perches are in the townland of Ballymacaldrack at the south side of the parish. Its extreme depth does not exceed 5 feet.

Rivers: Bann

The Bann flows in a northerly direction along the western boundary of the parish for 4 and a half miles and also forms the boundary between the counties of Antrim and Londonderry. It takes its rise from Lough Beg near the north south west extremity of the county and at an elevation of 47 feet above the level of the sea at low water. From this it flows north between the counties of Antrim and Derry for 24 miles and enters on the boundary of this parish, and finally, after an entire course of [blank] miles, it discharges itself into the sea within the tideway. Its elevation above the sea on entering this parish is 26 feet and on quitting it 16 feet, being an average fall of 1 foot in 380 feet. Its extreme breadth is 620 feet, least breadth 59 feet and average breadth 258 feet. Its depth varies from 18 inches to 8 feet and might probably average (in its channel) 4 feet. Its bed is for the most part gravelly.

It is not navigable nor usefully situated for irrigation or machinery, though it might be applied to these purposes. It is subject to high and frequent floods, which do not commit any mischief nor make any injurious or beneficial deposit. They soon naturally subside. Its banks are sufficiently high (except in a few places) to confine it and the scenery along them in the neighbourhood of Moore Lodge is very pleasing, the ground being thickly clothed with wood to the water's edge.

There are several fords in the river which are easily passable in ordinary seasons: that near Moore Lodge does not exceed 18 inches in depth in dry seasons. The others are not quite so shallow.

The only ferry is that at the Vow townland, where the river is 113 and a third yards broad and averaging 8 feet deep. This river cannot be said to facilitate or impede communication.

There are several little rivulets which flow down the sides of the hills in this parish and, being collected in dams, are rendered applicable to machinery. The parish abounds with springs and there is an ample supply of soft water for domestic purposes. There are not any hot or mineral springs.

Bogs

The summit of the ridge which intersects this parish is covered with a deep coat of bog, some of which is swampy and marshy. The bogs on the hills are deep, varying from 5 to 20 feet and probably averaging 10 feet. The substratum is most commonly basalt, but in some places it is blue clay. Immense quantities of timber have been taken out of these bogs and still remain in them. Fir is the principal kind and there is but little oak, any there is, being on the substratum or soil. The fir is at some distance from the surface and rarely rests on the bottom, though instances of fir roots being entwined in and grasping the rocks sometimes occur.

Few fir sticks or trunks are found. Many have been carried off. Some of them are said to have been 4 feet across the face. Many of the stumps are of enormous size. They all stand upright and seem broken or burnt at the same height and very little of the trunk attached to the stump. There is seldom more than one layer found in the mountains. A little birch is occasionally found in them.

There are numerous tracts of bog in the lower grounds. One of these is of considerable extent, occupying a greater portion of Knockans, Drumlee, Dirran, Marrola wood and the adjoining townlands, and averaging 180 feet [insert addition: 170 feet] above the level of the sea and 162 feet above the River Bann at its nearest point. This bog is nearly level. Little or no oak but immense quantities of fir timber or rather stumps are, and have been, taken out of it, and a great deal still remains. The roots are contiguous and almost interwoven. They are about 3 and a half above the subsoil, which is blue clay, and 6 feet below the surface of the bog as it now is, but it has been greatly cut.

Many fine fir trunks have been taken out of it: few are now in it. They were frequently found under the stumps lying transversely. The stumps are standing. They seem to have been broken at the same height and very little of the trunk is attached to them. The trees might have been on an average 14 inches square. There is now only one layer of timber, but there was another which has been carried off within memory.

Causeway

A very remarkable causeway or road exists in this bog, at a depth of about 4 feet from the surface and probably 8 from the bottom of the bog. It is 3 feet broad and half a mile in length, and is formed by laying oak sticks transversely, upon which clay and then a pavement of large stones is placed. Hazel and alder stakes from 3 to 4 feet long and 2 and a half inches in diameter are driven perpendicularly into the bog along the sides of the causeway and about 3 feet from each other, to confine and keep it together.

This causeway extends in almost a right line across the bog and between a fort on a little gravel hill (only 3 feet higher than the bog) in the townland of Drumlee (and where, it is said, there was also a celebrated bowling green) and the townland of Killymaddy, where there are several forts and where there formerly was a racecourse on the opposite side of the bog. It was accidentally discovered in cutting turf and only a small portion of the causeway has been removed.

In the townland of Vow there are numerous little patches of bog, many of them the bottoms of lakes which evidently at one time existed there. They are mostly cut to, or nearly to, the bottom. The subsoil is a tough white clay, similar to the bed of the Bann.

Large quantities of enormous fir trees and stumps have been taken out of these bogs. One stump when cut into billets for burning (without the roots) filled 7 gages (a gage is a cubic yard). There is still a great deal of oak stumps and trunks lying indiscriminately on the subsoil. The trunks do not exceed 1 foot diameter.

Woods

There is a great deal of oak, hazel, birch, ash, holly and alder brushwood in this parish. The 2 former kinds prevail. There is scarce a townland in which it is not to be met with, but there is most in those on the western side of the parish. It is rapidly disappearing, partly owing to the cultivation of the ground and partly to cattle being let on it. This, with the timber found in the bogs, are the only remains of natural wood in the parish, though within a century "a man could walk on the trees from Coleraine to Portglenone."

[Insert addition: There is a tradition amongst the inhabitants that the low grounds in this parish were formerly well wooded, which account is partially supported by the fact that the lower division of the parish pays a much less proportion of the county cess than its present population would authorize. Of the county cess, it pays only a third, while of the parish cess it pays seven-fifteenths, because the latter was settled at the vestry since the woods were cut down].

Climate

The climate of this parish is tolerably healthy, though cold and subject to fogs and rain, owing to its exposure to the south west, west and north west winds (the former of which prevails and is generally followed by rain and the last by storms) and the quantity of bog and uncultivated ground in it and its vicinity. The seasons for sowing are a little later than those in Rasharkin and the crops, particularly in the higher ground, do not ripen for fully 3 weeks after them.

MODERN TOPOGRAPHY

Villages: Dunloy

There is no town in this parish and the only village is Dunloy, in the townland of the same name, on the east side of the parish and on the mail coach road from Ballymena to Ballymoney, from the latter of which towns it is 6 miles in a south east direction.

It consists of 16 houses built of stone; 6 are 2-storey and slated. There are 3 spirit and 1 grocery shops, 1 blacksmith and 4 police. The rest of the inhabitants are engaged in agriculture. There is 1 post-car for hire. The fare is 8d per mile.

There is nothing interesting in the appearance of Dunloy. It is situated in a bleak and bare part of the country, on the east side of the Killymurrys range of hills.

There are 4 annual fairs held in Dunloy, on the following days: 15th February, 15th May, 15th August and 15th November. Cattle of all kinds are exposed for sale, but not in any great quantity. No tolls are levied but, on the contrary, the following premiums are offered by the proprietor, George Hutchinson of Ballymoney, Esquire, viz. 5s for the best horse, cow, sheep or pig, 2s 6d for the second and 1s 3d for the third quality of each. Still, the fair is not thriving.

The mail coach from Derry to Belfast changes horses here, as does also the Champion stage-coach from Coleraine to Belfast. [Insert addition: It has a good inn at which the mail coach stops and changes horses. Several of the houses are slated, which is rather a rare covering for a roof in this part of the countryside. The business formerly transacted in the court house of Clogh under the jurisdiction of the manor of Oldstone was transfered to this village by the seneschal, George Hutchinson Esquire, in the year [blank] (Shaw Mason, Dunaghy parish)].

Public Buildings

The church, which stands in the townland of Knockans and near the centre of the parish, is a plain building in good order and has a small square tower at its western end. It is 60 feet long and 30 feet wide, and would accommodate about 180 persons. It was rebuilt about the year 1816.

The Presbyterian meeting house, which stands in the townland of Mullans, about three-quarters of a mile south of the church, is a plain old house, originally built about the year 1698. It has been lately roofed at the expense of the congregation and is in good order. It is 70 feet long and 38 feet wide, and has a spacious gallery extending all round it. It could accommodate 900 persons.

The Roman Catholic chapel stands in the townland of Ballymacaldrack, a little to the south of the village of Dunloy. It is 80 feet long and 24 feet wide, and might accommodate 400 persons.

It is, however, very ruinous and comfortless, being without seats and the roof leaky. It is said to be a place of great antiquity but nothing is known as to its date of erection.

Gentlemen's Seats

Moore Lodge, the seat of George Moore Esquire: the house, which is 2-storey and in very nice order, is situated in the townland of the same name and near the edge of the River Bann. It commands a fine view of the river, the banks of which are ornamented for considerable distance by thriving plantations of ash, fir and larch. The house, though rather modern in its appearance, has been built some time.

Cullytrummin, the seat of Mrs Moore, is situated in the townland of Rosnashane, about half a mile north east of Moore Lodge. The house is 1-storey and almost hidden by wood.

Culmore, in the townland of the same name, the residence of James William Armstrong Esquire: it is a plain modern house with nothing about it worthy of notice.

The Glebe, the residence of the Reverend Richard Waddy, perpetual curate of the parish, is situated in the Glebe townland, about 1 and a half mile south of the church. The house is plain and 2-storey high, and was erected in 1809 by the Board of First Fruits at a cost of 760 pounds.

Mills and Manufactories

There are 2 corn mills, 2 flax mills and 4 brickfields in this parish. The corn mill in the Vow townland is propelled by a breast water wheel 13 feet diameter and 1 foot 10 inches broad. The flax mill in the same townland is propelled by a breast water wheel 12 feet diameter and 2 feet 4 inches broad.

The corn mill in Slievenaghy townland is propelled by a breast water wheel 12 feet in diameter and 2 feet broad. The flax mill in the same townland is propelled by a breast water wheel 13 feet diameter and 2 feet broad.

The brickfields are very inconsiderable and are along the edge of the River Bann.

Communications

The main roads in this parish are: the mail coach road from Derry to Belfast through Ballymoney, which traverses the eastern side of this parish for 3 miles. Its average breadth is 24 feet. It is hilly but in tolerable repair. It is kept in order at the expense of the county at large.

The road from Portglenone to Ballymoney traverses the centre of the parish. There are 4 and a half miles of it and its average breadth is 21 feet. It is hilly and its direction might be improved. It is in but middling repair. It is kept in order by the barony.

There are 5 miles of the road from Ballymoney to Kilrea running along the Bann. The direction of this road might be much improved as it is hilly. In some places it is in but middling repair. Its average breadth is 19 feet. This road is kept up at the expense of the barony.

The by and crossroads are pretty good and well laid and sufficiently numerous.

The materials used in making and repairing these roads is chiefly whinstone or greenstone. A soft sort of basalt almost totally decomposed is too frequently used. It does very well for a short time in dry weather, but in wet weather very soon turns into mud. A great fault with the roads through the bogs is that they are frequently overflown, owing to the water tables not being kept clear and deep, and that instead of being convex, these roads are more frequently concave.

There are no bridges and only a few pipes in this parish. They are, however, sufficient for their purposes in every respect.

Ferry

There is a ferry over the Bann at the townland of Vow. The distance between the landing places is 450 feet and the breadth of the river 340 feet. Its average ordinary depth is about 8 feet. The fare for each passenger is a ha'penny. A nominal rent is paid by the ferryman to the Mercers' Company, who possess the lands along the county Derry side of the river and also the royalties of the river.

The parish is amply supplied with communications of every kind.

General Appearance and Scenery

Except immediately along its eastern and western borders, where cottages and farmhouses are comfortable and neat looking, and the ground more highly cultivated, the scenery and appearance of the parish itself is bare and rather bleak. The immense tracts of uncultivated bog and rocky mountain are not at all relieved by the appearance of the houses or farms of the peasantry and the want of planting is sadly exhibited. But the prospect of the surrounding country is exceedingly beautiful and extensive: the view from the higher grounds being bounded by the splendid chain of mountains in the counties of Derry and Tyrone on the west, by the lofty chain in Antrim on the east, and extending from the Scottish islands and the headlands on the northern coast of the county to Lough Neagh and the far distant mountains of Mourne towards the south. The sides of the 2 great valleys watered by the Bann and the Main, sloping gently from the base of neighbouring mountains, studded with their numerous villages, cottages and clumps of planting and varied with all the tints of autumn, present a rich and cheering prospect and form a beautiful contrast to their wild and impending boundaries.

ANCIENT TOPOGRAPHY

Antiquities

[Insert addition: Many of the forts throughout this parish have been levelled; 3 remarkable ones still remain.

Kilconway Fort is situated about the centre of the parish, immediately south of the Glebe farm. It is circular and has an artificial cave round its extent on the inside. It is supposed that the name of the barony is taken from this fort.

Drumalorchan is of an elliptical form and commands the pass called the Vow ferry.

The fort of Craigs is a square of 150 feet with a very deep trench].

SOCIAL ECONOMY

Early Improvements

The Scots settled in this parish in considerable numbers during the 16th and 17th centuries, and the greater number of the present inhabitants are their descendants. A Presbyterian congregation was established here in 1698 and this was probably the first step towards improvement and civilisation. Of later years the introduction of schools, particularly sabbath schools, which are nowhere more general than in this parish, has tended mainly towards the civilisation and improvement of the morals of the people. They are sober, honest, industrious and peaceable, and all classes live on the best terms. They are generally of the lower class, who principally subsist by weaving or labouring in the fields, but chiefly the former, and considering their station, they are comparatively comfortable in their circumstances. There are several comfortable farmers throughout the parish who have snug residences and seem independent in their circumstances.

Obstructions to improvement: none.

Local Government

There are no magistrates, 4 constabulary in the village of Dunloy, no petty sessions. The manor courts and courts leet for the barony are held in the village of Clogh in the parish of Dunaghy.

No outrages of any kind have recently occurred. There formerly was a good deal of illicit distillation but now there is scarcely any. There are few, if any, insurances of any kind.

Dispensary

There is not a dispensary in the parish. There is one, however, in the neighbouring parishes of Ballymoney and Kilrea, to which patients from this parish are admissible. The comforts of the poor have certainly been much increased by their establishment and the prevalence of disease or infection checked by the ready aid they afford. There has not, however, been any prevalent contagious or infectious disease in this parish for many years.

Schools

The introduction of schools, particularly Sunday schools, has been an incalculable benefit to this parish and has caused a very perceptible change in the morals of the people. There are few parishes where their introduction has been more general, though almost totally unaided by charitable grants or societies. The people are anxious for information and gladly avail themselves of their advantages.

[Insert addition: As to the state of learning, it must be acknowledged that it stands very low. There is no endowed school in the parish. There are generally 3 schoolmasters, whose only source of income is the pay received from the scholars. The following are the customary charges for education per quarter: reading 3s 4d, writing 4s 2d and arithmetic 5s].

Poor

Except the usual collections on Sundays, there is not any regular provision for the poor of this parish.

Religion

By the revised census of 1834 there are 267 Episcopalians, 3,754 Presbyterians and 2,482 Roman Catholics. The perpetual curate has a glebe house (which was built by the Board of First Fruits in 1809 at an expense of 760 pounds), a glebe containing 12 acres 3 roods 16 perches and the tithes of 5 townlands containing 3,427 acres. The Presbyterian clergyman is supported by his regium donum (100 pounds) and his stipend. The priest is supported in the usual way by his flock.

[Insert addition: The inhabitants consist of Protestants, Presbyterians and Roman Catholics. This parish forms a principal part of the prebend of Rasharkin. It was erected into a perpetual cure in 1808, to which the Reverend Mr Dickson apportioned the following townlands: Moneycannon, Drumlee, Carrowreagh, Dirraw and Mullans, containing in all 3,427 acres].

Habits of the People

The houses of the lower class are all 1-storey, some built of brick, but mostly of stone. They are thatched, well lit and generally consist of 2 apartments, though many cannot boast of more than 1. They do not generally present a very clean or comfortable appearance and almost all have manure pits or heaps close to the door. The cottages along the Bann are more untidy and comfortless than those in the interior of the parish.

Turf is their only fuel and is very abundant. Meal, potatoes, milk and a little fish constitute their food. Scarcely any animal food is used by them.

They are not in general long-lived, though there [are] a few of about 90 years of age living in the parish. They marry rather early, that is to say from 18 upwards. They dress pretty well and comfortably.

Amusements and Traditions

They have almost quite given up the amusements of which they were at one time very fond, such as dancing, cammon playing (a sort of hurling) at Christmas, assembling round the Broad Stone or cromlech in the townland of Craigs at certain seasons, particularly at Easter; and there was formerly a bowling green in Killymaddy townland. All these are now totally given up, chiefly by the advice of their clergy. They have not any patrons nor patrons' days, peculiar games, legends nor ancient music, nor funeral cries.

There is a tradition that the parish was at one time so well wooded "that a bird could hop from bough to bough from Coleraine to Portglenone along the Bann." This is in a great measure supported by the fact of the lower division of the parish paying a much less proportion of the county cess than its present population would authorize. Of the county, it only pays one-third, while of the parish cess it pays seven-fifteenths, because the latter was settled at a vestry since the woods were cut down.

There is not anything peculiar in their costume.

Emigration

Emigration used formerly [to] prevail in this parish: not more than 9 on an annual average now emigrate. They embark in spring and go to Canada.

About 12 Roman Catholics go annually to the English and Scots' harvests, and return when they are over. They are generally single young men.

PRODUCTIVE ECONOMY

Manufacturing

[Insert addition: A considerable quantity of bricks are made of the clay found on the banks of the River Bann. The best are sold at 16s 8d per thousand, second quality 11s 4d ha'penny, third quality 8s 1d ha'penny. Linen is also manufactured in the farmhouses.

Rural Economy

The general size of the farms is from 10 to 20 acres, a few contain 100. The general tenures are for lives and years. The highest rent is 2 guineas per acre. There are many farmers in this parish who enjoy all the comforts of life and exhibit a considerable degree of civilisation and hospitality. Although this parish has been opened by roads, yet it is not well cultivated. The want of hedgerows and planting is everywhere apparent. The soil in general is not considered good.

Labourers receive from 6d ha'penny to 8d per day and their food, and 10d a day in winter and 1s 1d in summer, without food.

There are 2 or 3 large farms devoted exclusively to grazing, the summer grass of which is let at about 2 guineas].

SOCIAL ECONOMY

Tradition: Mary Kerr's Island

The following tradition concerning a little island in the River Bann is current among the Roman Catholic inhabitants of the parish. The island is about 2 miles north of the bridge over the Bann near Kilrea. It is commonly called Mary Kerr's Island. Mary McGeary's Island, however, is its proper name, as it will be seen below.

A nun of exemplary piety named Mary McGeary, belonging to the convent of Bonamargy <Bonamarga>, while at her devotions had a visit from St Bridget, who came to instruct her how to execute 2 very important tasks which she had assigned her. The first of these was the conversion of the inhabitants in the neighbourhood of the island from the sinful life which they were then leading, as they had eaten flesh-meat during Lent and had got drunk and quarrelled at a midnight mass held at Cloyn Lynn on Christmas <Christmass> Eve.

The second task she had to perform was the reformation of a young man of the sept of O'Cahan, who, having been disappointed in love, had given himself up to a profligate course of life and was going rapidly to perdition. The first of these tasks was quickly accomplished, but not so with the latter, as many obstacles were thrown in her way by the common enemy, who so often assumed the appearance of O'Cahan and committed so many horrible actions in his name for the purpose of frustrating her object, that she grew almost hopeless of success. For when she charged O'Cahan with what he was supposed to have committed, he of course denied it, which made her doubly unhappy. The deception was at last found out, for one day when the Devil (having personified O'Cahan) and his associates were carrying on all manner of debauchery in the island, she chanced to see them from her dwelling and immediately hastened down to the river.

She commenced wading, but, the water proving deeper than usual, she was forced to put her cloak over her head. The Devil and his friends, seeing her awkward plight, fell into a violent fit of laughter and commenced ridiculing her in a very indecent manner, and were so much entertained at her appearance that they forgot their usual trick of vanishing before she could reach the island. They were now clearly detected, as she soon spied the cloven foot, and she instantly bound the Devil under a heavy penalty never again to personate O'Cahan. She afterwards chose the island for her residence, and her residence, a house of twigs and clay, was built on it for her. She lived in it for 52 years and gave many prophecies as to the spread and punishment of heresy (Protestantism), but these the Roman Catholics are unwilling to relate.

No vestiges of the house now remain. It is said that in the year 1702 part of it was standing, or rather the sods etc. were, on the island. The cause of its destruction is said to have been as follows: a man named Dempsey had a cot in which he used to convey his mother to the island. On one occasion a man named Gillespie, when the old woman and her son were on the island, pushed off the cot and left them to return as they could. This bred a fight in which the Gillespies were defeated. They nevertheless returned to the island and totally destroyed the house, throwing the greater part of

it into the Bann. Picked up at a wake by James Boyle, September 21st 1835.

Schools

[Table contains the following headings: name, situation and description, when established, income and expenditure, physical, intellectual and moral education, number of pupils subdivided by age, sex and religion, name and religion of master and mistress].

Under the Kildare Place Society, in a house built for the purpose by Sampson Moore Esquire, townland of Galdanagh, established 1830; income: from Sampson Moore Esquire annually 4 pounds, from pupils 8 pounds; intellectual education: books of the Kildare Place Society, spelling, reading, writing and arithmetic; moral education: Sunday school and occasional visits from the clergy, Authorised Version of Scriptures daily and Shorter Catechism on Saturday; number of pupils: males, 14 under 10 years of age, 7 from 10 to 15, 21 total males; females, 13 under 10 years of age, 6 from 10 to 15, 19 total females; total number of pupils 40, 7 Protestants, 18 Presbyterians, 15 Roman Catholics; master Robert Patten, Presbyterian.

Under the London Hibernian Society, in a house built by subscription in the townland of Ballinagarvey, established 1820; income: from the London Hibernian Society on an average 5 pounds per annum, from pupils 16 pounds; intellectual education: Hibernian Society reading and spelling books, *Murray's Grammar, Thompson's Arithmetic, Jackson's Book-keeping, Heney's Mensuration*; moral education: Sunday school, occasional visits from the clergy, Authorised Version of the Scriptures daily; number of pupils: males, 26 under 10 years of age, 13 from 10 to 15, 1 above 15, 40 total males; females, 31 under 10 years of age, 9 from 10 to 15, 40 total females; total number of pupils 80, 2 Protestants, 51 Presbyterians, 27 Roman Catholics; master William Dinsmore, Presbyterian.

Under the London Hibernian Society, in a house built by subscription in the townland of Killins, established 1832; income: from the London Hibernian Society annually 5 pounds, from pupils 18 pounds; intellectual education: books of the Hibernian Society, spelling, reading, writing, *Gough's Arithmetic*; moral education: Sunday school, occasional visits from the clergy, Authorised Versions of the Scriptures daily; number of pupils: males, 28 under 10 years of age, 13 from 10 to 15, 41 total males; females, 24 under 10 years of age, 10 from 10 to 15, 34 total females;

total number of pupils 75, 4 Protestants, 46 Presbyterians, 25 Roman Catholics; master John Dalhouse, Presbyterian.

Private school, in a house built by subscription in the townland of Eden, established 1825; income from pupils 25 pounds; intellectual education: *Dublin, Manson's and Universal spelling and reading books, Gough's Arithmetic, Murray's Grammar*, writing; moral education: Sunday school, occasional visits from the clergy, Authorised Version of the Scriptures and Shorter Catechism daily; number of pupils: males, 29 under 10 years of age, 15 from 10 to 15, 44 total males; females, 43 under 10 years of age, 8 from 10 to 15, 51 total females; total number of pupils 95, 2 Protestants, 93 Presbyterians.

Private school, in a wretched cabin given gratis for the purpose in the townland of Vow, established 1834; income: from the London Hibernian Society annually 5 pounds, from pupils 3 pounds 15s; intellectual education: spelling and reading; moral education: Shorter Catechism and Authorised Version of Scriptures daily; number of pupils: males, 3 under 10 years of age, 3 total males; females, 9 under 10 years of age, 9 total females; total number of pupils 12, all Presbyterians; master John Crawford, Presbyterian.

In a good house built by subscription in the townland of Ballytun, established 1834; income from pupils 12 pounds; intellectual education: *Manson's and Universal spelling and reading books, Gough's Arithmetic*, and writing; moral education: Authorised and Douai Version of the Scriptures daily; number of pupils: males, 12 under 10 years of age, 3 from 10 to 15, 15 total males; females, 15 under 10 years of age, 15 total females; total number of pupils 30, 2 Protestants, 12 Presbyterians, 16 Roman Catholics; master John Robinson, Roman Catholic.

[Totals] income: from public societies and individuals 14 pounds, from pupils 81 pounds 15s; number of pupils: males, 112 under 10 years of age, 51 from 10 to 15, 1 above 15, 164 total males; females, 135 under 10 years of age, 33 from 10 to 15, 168 total females; total number of pupils 332, 17 Protestants, 232 Presbyterians, 83 Roman Catholics.

Schools

[Table contains the following headings: name of townland where held, name and religion of master or mistress, free or pay school, annual income of master or mistress, description and cost of schoolhouse, number of pupils subdivided by

religion, sex and the Protestant and Roman Catholic returns, societies with which connected].

[Insert addition: Finvoy church, master Andrew Moore, Protestant; pay school, annual income 10 pounds 10s; schoolhouse stone and lime, bad repair; number of pupils: about 35, neither sex nor religion distinguished.

Craigs, master Daniel McDonnell, Roman Catholic; pay school, annual income 2s 6d per quarter; schoolhouse: room 18 feet by 13 feet, built by vestry; number of pupils by the Protestant return: 2 Established Church, 23 Presbyterians, 17 Roman Catholics, 22 males, 20 females; associations none.

Dunloy, master Patrick McCambridge, Roman Catholic; pay school, annual income 15 pounds; schoolhouse: his own house; number of pupils by the Protestant return: 1 Established Church, 3 Presbyterians, 29 Roman Catholics, 19 males, 14 females; associations none.

Kilhans, master William Stewart, Established Church; pay school, annual income 8 pounds; schoolhouse: newly built, stone and lime; number of pupils by the Protestant return: 12 Established Church, 27 Presbyterians, 5 Roman Catholics; associations: Reverend Mr Olpherts and the parish built the schoolhouse.

Galdanagh, master Hugh Dinsmore, Dissenter; pay school, income not stated; schoolhouse under repair; number of pupils by the Protestant return: 8 Presbyterians, 19 Roman Catholics, 10 males, 17 females; connected with Sampson Moore Esquire.

Ballinagarvey, master Alexander McDonnel, Roman Catholic; pay school, annual income 2s 1d per quarter; schoolhouse: held in the room of an Orange lodge; number of pupils by the Protestant return: 32 Presbyterians, 3 Roman Catholics, 16 males, 19 females; associations none].

Memoir by J. Stokes

ANCIENT TOPOGRAPHY

Ecclesiastical: Graveyard

In the townland of Ballymacaldrack there is, upon the sloping sides of Dunloy hill, an old graveyard. It at present contains about half an acre Irish measure, and is enclosed by a quickset hedge and loose stone wall. It was formerly surrounded by an ancient ditch or fosse in the form of a circle, that circle containing within its circumference a full acre. 40 yards of the ditch are still nearly as it originally was. It runs through a multitude of small fields and is at present 15 feet wide at an average, by 6 feet in depth at the middle.

Formerly the space between the spot now occupied as a graveyard and the circumference of the area enclosed and formed by the ditch above described was covered with ancient fences from 2 to 4 yards broad and overgrown with moss. They were of earth and stone. They divided the grounds into plots at an average 20 perches in area. They are almost wholly destroyed. They are said to have stood untouched about 100 years ago, but have been gradually removed since as the country became more inhabited. The people can give no explanation of them further than a supposition that they had belonged to a monastery.

At the northern and southern ends or sides of this circle there formerly existed 2 coves, but which are now destroyed. The graveyard is at the north eastern side. At each side of the old entrance it is said that there had been a large standing stone. Burials of adults only began here within the memory of the oldest inhabitant. Formerly it was children only that were interred. Roman Catholics are the chief subjects.

The names on the stones are O'Neill, Mulloy, Deane, McGuckla, Scullion, O'Kane, Carnachan. The last, Carnachan, is the oldest. Its date is 1778.

There are no crosses or holy wells in the neighbourhood. It is called Caldernagh and seems to have given a designation to the next townland, which goes by the same name.

Knockans and Finvoy Graveyards

The graveyard in the townland of Knockans is believed to be of equal age with the one at the Vow ferry which shall presently be noticed. It stands near the parish church, at the distance of about 150 yards to the westward. It is but 6 perches square and contains but 1 tombstone, and that but a few years old. There are, however, many graves. None but Presbyterians at present bury in it. No remains of a building of any kind have ever been seen near it. An ancient paved road formerly ran between it and the church in a direction from north to south. It was finally destroyed about 12 years ago.

The graveyard near the Vow ferry, commonly called Finvoy graveyard, is situated on the top of a little hill near the River Bann. It contains half an acre and is used as a place of interment by the following families: Keers, Hannah, Thompson, Steen, Ferrier, McAlary. The oldest in the yard are 3 stones of the Kennedys, inscribed with the dates of 1767, 1713 and 1723 respectively.

Burials are not so frequent here of late years, the Roman Catholics having begun to use the yards of their respective chapels. No remains of a building of any kind have ever been seen near it, nor can any tradition of such a building be discovered either here or at the Knockans.

Church

No remains of an ancient church can be found. The parish church was first built in 1720. There are the foundations of a building called the Bloody Church situated a few townlands off, but it is merely what was built previous to the erection of the parish church, at the date above mentioned. There was a great deal of dispute and bad feeling in the parish about the propriety of the site chosen, which at length was to such pitch that in a fight that took place, on the subject a man was killed. This was the origin of the name. The church was then erected on the present site.

Military Remains

There are no castles.

Pagan: Broad Stone

The most remarkable of the pagan remains is a cromlech called the Broad Stone, situated in a bleak wild valley in the townland of the Craigs. There are appearances as if a cairn had once covered the whole monument, see drawing. The great stone itself had been once supported on 4 pillars. 2 of them have been destroyed by treasure seekers and the stone has in consequence sunk down on 1 side. Still, it is a very remarkable and striking object.

There are, in the valley and on the hills on each side, traces of ancient fences. These at first sight appear to be very ancient and are said by the people to have been considered so by some of the gentlemen (from the neighbouring counties perhaps) who have occasionally visited the place. But they have by no means the look or construction of the Danish fences of Tamnybrack in the parish of Cumber, county Londonderry, and in all probability are about 200 years old. Their foundations only appear, being in many parts entirely concealed from view by a thick covering of heath.

This monument appears to have consisted of 3 great receptacles for urns, each circular in form, see the plan, see drawing[s]. At "a" and "b" many small stones appear that must have once formed part of the cairn. The ring was probably the circumference of it. No ancient articles of any

The "Broad Stane"

Broad Stone in Craigs

kind have been found at it or about it. The stones are from 1 to 5 feet high.

Giant's Graves

In the townland of Dunloy, and at a short distance to the east of the high road from Ballymoney to Ballymena, there are the remains of a giant's grave, now much dilapidated as many of the houses in the hamlets of Dunloy have been built from it. No ancient articles were found at it; see drawing[s], upper part. At the part marked "a" there was formerly an ancient building made of 6 standing stones, situated 3 on each side in 2 parallel lines and covered at the top by 3 flagstones laid close to each other.

In the townland of Ballymacaldrack, and in the immediate neighbourhood of the above monument, there is another of the same character and having a remarkable resemblance to it in form. It is situated in a rocky field close to the old Roman Catholic chapel; see drawing[s] for a plan and for a view of it.

Between both these and the Teecloy or Stone House described in the parish of Racavan there is a great similarity. They have the same rectangular platform or the remains of it, the same amphitheatre of standing stones at one end and the same small building at the centre of that amphitheatre or semicircle.

At the distance of a few fields there was formerly another of them, but now destroyed. Several others with small cairns also stood in their immediate neighbourhood, but all are now destroyed, no traces of them being left behind.

Forts and Coves

[Insert footnote: There are no remarkable forts of circular form].

There is a large square fort 220 feet long by 220 broad standing near the Broad Stone. It is in the same townland. It is surrounded by an ancient ditch 20 feet broad and from 10 to 20 feet deep. It is bearing crops, which circumstance is rapidly filling up the ditch and otherwise destroying it. There was once a rampart and also a cove under it, passing from east to west, but it is now choked up. It is made of earth and stones.

At the distance of 300 yards to the south west

there is another, but of a much smaller size. It is four-cornered and is 100 feet long by 90 wide. There is a cove under it, also in a direction from east to west, but choked up and rendered impassable. This is also earthen. It has borne crops and accordingly the ditch has been effaced, but there are still the traces of a rampart along its edge. It rises to the height of 5 feet above the field.

At the distance of 600 yards to the south there was once another square earthen fort about 100 feet along each side, having a cove near it. All, however, has been destroyed by the tenants.

In the townland of Moneycanon, at the distance of half a mile to the north, there is another. It is in good preservation, having been planted with trees. It is about 60 feet square. The sides rise 6 feet above the field. It is surrounded by a shallow ditch. There is a cove under it but entirely choked up.

In the townland of Knockans there is a cove 420 feet long. 46 feet only is accessible, but the remainder can be traced along the surface of the fields. Within, it is 5 feet high and 3 broad, and divided at regular intervals of 18 feet by a door generally two-thirds the height of the passage. The tops of them are formed according to the manner represented in the above longitudinal section [drawing]. It runs from east to west.

Near the eastern end, and partly extending over its top, there was found by the tenant a paved hearth of 20 feet in diameter. Many pieces of charcoal and much ashes were found among them.

In the same townland, and at the distance of a quarter of a mile, another cove was found with a similar hearth at its mouth. The former was smaller but the latter was of the same size. Both of these are destroyed.

At the distance of about 2 stones' throw from the first and largest cove there was found, by the tenant, an iron instrument 14 lbs in weight and of the form of the number 4. It was much decayed. From the verbal description given of it by the people, it seems to have been very like the peculiar instrument near a cove in Racavan. See the Memoir of that parish.

Other Coves

With respect to the other coves of Finvoy, it may be generally remarked that there seems to have been at an average one to each townland. Most are choked up. There is one in Carvadoon Fort in the townland of Dunloy. It is 28 feet long, 3 and a half feet wide and 5 feet high, but very badly built. It has an ante-chamber 12 feet long attached to it

like the letter L. The fort is not remarkable. It is of earth, of ordinary form and with a ditch 20 feet deep. In the rampart about 12 years ago some silver coins of different sizes were found.

Coins and Stone Article

In a natural island in the bog of Dunloy called Culnavey Island, there was found in 1831 a collection of coins hid under a flagstone. A bush near at hand appears to have served the purpose of a mark to those who originally buried it. They were of different sizes and were immediately sold.

A curious stone article was found in the townland of the Craigs; see drawing[s].

Drawings of Antiquities

Giant's grave in Ballymacaldrack, 2 views with dimensions.

Giant's grave in Ballymacaldrack, plan and view of cromlech, scale 1 inch to a chain with dimensions.

Stone monuments, including Broad Stone, plan, scale 20 feet to an inch.

The Broad Stone, with human figure for scale, front-on view.

The Broad Stone, view with annotations and dimensions; detailed plan of monument with fences.

Stone article [axehead]: overhead view, side view and section with dimensions.

Map of standing stones etc. of Finvoy, scale 3 miles to 1 inch.

Parish of Killagan, County Antrim

Statistical Account by Lieutenant J. Greatorex, September 1832

NATURAL STATE

Name and Situation

The name of Killagan is perhaps derived from *Cill-Aedagain* "Aegan's church." *Aedagan* was a man's name, the ancestor of the McEgans.

It is situated in the baronies of Upper Dunluce and Kilconway (the barony boundary dividing it nearly into 2 equal parts), and in the county of Antrim. It is 2 miles north west from Clogh and 7 south east from Ballymoney. Killagan is a rectory attached to the vicarage of Connor. It was until lately (about 5 years) a grange and extra-parochial, paying no tithe. It is in the diocese of Connor, patron the bishop.

Boundaries, Extent and Divisions

It is bounded on the north and north east by the parishes of Kilraghts and Loughguile <Loughgule>, on the east by Loughguile and Dunaghy, on the south by the grange of Dundermot and on the west by the parishes of Finvoy and Rasharkin. It extends from north to south about 4 and a half statute miles, its greatest width being about 2 miles. It contains 3,837 statute acres. It is divided into 12 townlands, 2 of which, Ballynalube and Drumaduragh, are in the barony of Upper Dunluce, the rest being in that of Kilconway.

NATURAL FEATURES AND PRODUCTIVE ECONOMY

Surface and Soil

This parish, being situated in the lowland, presents no remarkable rising ground. Broghanore hill, which is the highest in the parish, is 492 feet in height. The rest of the surface gradually falls from east to west throughout its length, until it becomes a marsh extending the whole course of the River Main, which forms the western boundary. This marsh occupies a considerable portion of the parish and is always flooded over during the winter and wet summers. The inhabitants cut the long grass and rushes it furnishes from cots. The soil is generally of a light stony nature, formed chiefly of the decomposed basalt. In the lowlands clay is found, producing good crops.

Produce

The general crops are potatoes, barley, flax and oats, potatoes, oats, flax and oats, or potatoes followed by 2 crops of oats. It is usual to sow clover and grass seed with the oats for winter use for the cattle, and with the last crop of oats, grass seed is sown to lay the land down in meadow the following year. The culture of wheat is not attempted here, the soil not being adapted for it.

Great quantities of pork, butter, flax, linen and yarn are yearly raised, which find a ready sale at the weekly markets at Ballymena or the monthly ones at Ballymoney. The prices vary almost every year. During the last season pork averaged 40s per cwt, first butter [blank], second butter [blank], third butter [blank] per cwt.

Turbary is very abundant and very good.

NATURAL HISTORY

Limestone

There is none: whatever limestone is used for manure is brought from the parish of Loughguile, where chalk is found in great abundance at Corky.

Basalt

Abounds all over the parish and is found in all the quarries that have been opened for building or other purposes, and in the beds of the streams. There is no other geological features in the parish. The basalt nowhere (where it has been exposed) assumes the crystallized form and is very poor in mineralogical productions. It is very useful for building and making roads, making the latter good and durable.

MODERN TOPOGRAPHY AND PRODUCTIVE ECONOMY

Towns and Villages

Each townland takes its name from a few houses situated in it, but which are all too insignificant to be denominated towns. The only village of any size is Cloghmills <Cloughmills>, containing about 20 houses. It is situated in the townland of that name, on a small mountain stream which bounds the parish on the south. There are neither fairs or markets held here. Cloghmills is about 2 English miles north east from Clogh <Clough>.

Manufactures

The only manufacture is that of brown linen,

which, however, has much decreased of late years owing to the great depression of the trade. The same is to be observed of the spinning. An active spinner at work all day barely earns what keeps her alive. It is much to be lamented that more encouragement is not given to the linen manufacture in this part of the country, as the prosperity of the north of Ireland evidently rose with the progress of its manufactures which, unfortunately, are now on the decrease.

There is 1 bleach green (not of any extent) situated in the townland of Drumadaragh, near the bridge over the barony boundary.

Roads

This parish is well supplied with roads and in very good repair. They are, however, very hilly (as is usual with old Irish roads). The road from Clogh to Dervock (through part of Loughguile parish and Stranocum) traverses the parish from south to north. From this are 2 roads running east to meet the mail road from Belfast to Coleraine, and 1 into the parish of Kilraghts, and to the east 4 roads into the parishes of Loughguile and Dunaghy. These roads are kept in repair by the county and are all metalled with basalt.

Natural Features

Rivers

The River Main rises at the extreme north west extremity of the parish and, running in a south east direction through a morass, forms the western boundary. This river subjects its banks to frequent inundations, flooding the banks a considerable distance on each side [of] the bed of the river. The Main is plentifully supplied with trout and sometimes salmon. The preservation of the fish is, however, little attended to.

There are 2 other streams, both of which fall into the Main. One, called the Altakeeragh river, rises in the parish of Loughguile, in the mountain of Carnbuck, and becomes the parish boundary between Dunaghy and Killagan and Killagan and the grange of Dundermot, and falls into the River Main about a mile and a half below the village of Cloghmills. The other river rises also in the parish of Loughguile and, after forming part of the parish boundary between Killagan and Loughguile, takes a direction nearly south through the middle of the parish and falls into the Main about a mile above the bridge on the road from Cloghmills to Dunloy. This river is also the barony boundary.

Bogs and Woods

The bogs in this parish are numerous and scattered, afford good fuel and bog fir for firing. The only appearance of wood is about the hill of Broghanore, and that very trifling.

Social Economy

Population

The inhabitants are chiefly descendants of the English and Scots emigrants, especially the latter as the dialect they make use of seems to imply that, being full of remarkable Scotch words and sayings. Although there are not wanting instances of great poverty and distress, yet generally the peasantry appear better off than is usually the case in other parts of the country. The cabins are neat and the occupiers have some idea of comfort. When not busy with their agricultural pursuits they employ themselves in weaving brown linen which, if it obtains them but small gain, at any rate prevents idleness, the source of too much of Irish misery.

Ancient Topography

Antiquities

In the townland of Broghanore, at the north extremity and close to the barony bridge, are the remains of an old place of worship and burying ground. There is nothing interesting about it except its antiquity. There are several forts or mounds, of which those in Ballynalube and Mount Hamilton are very large. There is nothing, however, in the construction to warrant any particular description, as they are similar to the greater part of those that are scattered so plentifully all over the country.

Productive and Social Economy

Manures

Those of the inhabitants who have not the advantage of stable manure are accustomed to clean turf out of the bog into their manure pits in the summer, upon which is thrown what vegetable matter and ashes the home supplies. This compost is usually covered with water during the winter, and when required in the spring, is soured and forms tolerable manure for potatoes. Others dig down their field banks and turn the earth over with a portion of slaked lime and then let it lie during the winter. Others draw the lime into the field and lay it in small heaps all over it, to be afterwards spread, and others again content themselves with merely turning up sods and burning them. The last method is chiefly used in reclaiming boggy ground, and it very often happens that ground so prepared produces both more abundant crops of potatoes and oats than any other description of soil.

Religion

The religion of the inhabitants of this parish is principally that of the Scotch church and its various branches. There are a few Protestants and Catholics, but although the population may be estimated at 1,500, there is no place of worship whatever and the peasantry are obliged to go into the neighbouring parishes of Kilraghts and Dunaghy to attend divine service.

Fairs

There are 2 fairs for cattle held during the year in Drumadune townland, in a field about half a mile from Cloghmills. [Signed] J. Greatorex, Lieutenant Royal Engineers, 28 September 1832.

Memoir by J. Boyle, with Office Copy

MEMOIR WRITING

Memoir Writing

Time employed 27 hours, [signed] James Boyle, September 1835. Forwarded to Lieutenant Larcom, 26th September 1835, [signed] R.K. Dawson, Lieutenant Royal Engineers.

NATURAL STATE

Locality

[Insert addition: It is situated in the north of the county Antrim and in the baronies of Upper Dunluce and Kilconway. It is bounded on the north by Kilraghts and Loughguile, on the east by Loughguile and Dunaghy, on the south by the grange of Dundermot, and on the south west and west by Rasharkin and Finvoy. It contains 3,837 acres 2 roods 33 perches: in the barony of Upper Dunluce there are 1,406 acres 24 perches of this parish and in Kilconway 2,431 acres 2 roods 9 perches].

NATURAL FEATURES

Hills

One large feature or ridge extends from the southern to near the northern extremity of the parish, where it is separated from the southern extremity

of another feature, extending into this parish from that of Kilraghts, by the Killagan river. Broughanore hill, near the northern end of the former feature, is its highest point and also of the parish. It is 494 feet above the level of the sea. From the summit of this ridge there is a gradual fall east and west. The lowest level in the parish is 271 feet (on the west side) and its average level may be estimated at 370 feet. The principal points are Broughanore, 494 feet and Drumadoon, 389 feet above the level of the sea.

Lakes and Rivers

There are no lakes in the parish.

The principal rivers are: the Main river, which takes its rise in a bog in the adjoining parish of Kilraghts, at an elevation of about 290 feet above the level of the sea. After flowing about half a mile, it enters on the western boundary of this parish, along which it flows for 3 miles, and descends to a level of 268 feet, being an average fall of 1 foot in 792 feet. In its course it is joined by the Killagan river, by which it is considerably augmented. This latter river, from being the larger body of water and from its source being the more distant from the mouth of Main river, might with more propriety be termed the Main river. The height of the source of the Killagan water is upwards of 900 feet above the sea.

The Altakeeragh river, which passes through the village of Cloghmills, is also a tributary of the Main river and joins that river 1 mile west of that village. Owing to its trifling fall, its low banks and the impetuosity of the floods from the mountains in its tributary streams, this river is subject to frequent and very injurious inundations, which in rainy seasons and after heavy rains lay all the level plains through which it flows under water and, as there is not sufficient fall from either side towards the river to drain it off, the water remains on the ground until it is absorbed by it. These tracts, which would be otherwise exceedingly fertile and valuable, are from constant immersion and soakage rendered perfectly marshy and comparatively unprofitable, the hay being destroyed and the grass so soured that cattle will not taste it. There is besides, a very injurious deposit thrown up by it which also tends to sour the grass.

It is neither applicable to machinery, drainage nor irrigation. Its bed is soft and its course choked by a variety of water plants. Its banks in no place exceed 3 feet high and seldom reach that height. Its extreme breadth is 12 feet and average breadth 7 and a half feet. Its extreme summer depth is about 4 and a half feet. This river, after a southerly course of 21 miles from the southern extremity of the parish, discharges itself into Lough Neagh 1 and a half miles south of the village of Randalstown.

Killagan River

The Killagan river takes its rise in the south of Slievenahanagan mountain in the adjoining parish of Loughguile and at an elevation of about 930 feet above the level of the sea. From this it flows south westerly in a very irregular manner for 5 miles, crossing the parish of Killagan, and discharges itself into the Main river, at which point it is 268 feet above the level of the sea. Its average fall is 1 foot in 39 feet, its average breadth 6 feet and its average summer depth 13 inches. It is applicable to machinery, drainage and irrigation. Owing to the height of its source, this river is in heavy rain subject to violent and sudden floods which sometimes do mischief to the crops along its banks, which are in general very low. Its bed is in some places soft, but mostly stony. It does not make any deposit. This river receives the tributes of numerous small streams in its course.

Altakeeragh River

The Altakeeragh river takes its rise in Carnbuck mountain in Loughguile parish, at an elevation of about 1,000 feet above the level of the sea. From this it flows south west in a very irregular and circuitous manner for 6 and a quarter miles, passing through the village of Cloghmills, and discharges itself into the Main river about 1 mile west of that village and at an elevation of 268 feet above the level of the sea, its average fall being 1 foot in 44 feet. This river is subject to frequent and sudden floods which, from the height of its source, rise rapidly and subside equally so. Except towards its mouth, these floods are seldom attended with injurious results. No deposit is made by it except a very little gravel. On one or 2 occasions some stones have been washed over the adjacent lands and mischief done, but this seldom occurs.

In some places this river flows over a rocky bed, but for the most part in the low grounds its bed is soft and consists of fine gravel. Except in the mountains, where it has worn a channel, its banks are low. Its average breadth is 10 feet and its average depth 1 foot. It is applicable to machinery, drainage and irrigation.

There are no mineral springs. There is no parish better supplied with spring and river water than this.

Bogs

There is a considerable quantity of bog in this parish, though there are not any very large tracts of it. The principal is that at the south west side of the parish, in the townland of Mounthamilton. It forms part of a large tract of bog in Loughguile parish. It is nearly level, falling a little from its centre towards its sides. Its average height above the sea is 363 feet and above the Altakeeragh and Killagan rivers about 25 feet. This bog is very soft, spongy and deep, and is very little cut. It is said to contain but little timber.

Towards the northern side of the same townland is a portion of bog containing about 50 acres. It now is in meadow, but was formerly the bed of an artificial lake which was drained. This lake contained 2 artificial islands raised on stones which had been thrown in, but they have been totally removed. This lake was formed by the family of Hamilton, who formerly resided here. They had a handsome residence in this townland to which they gave their own name, having changed that of the townland from Lochardvernish to its present name. The bogs in this meadow is said to be very deep and to contain some timber. However, but little is known of it.

There is nothing worthy of notice in the other bogs in the parish.

Woods

There is a little stunted hazel brushwood in Culcrum townland. This, with the timber found in the bogs, is the only evidence of the former existence of woods in the parish.

Climate

The climate of this parish is rather dry and healthy and the air pure. The south west, west and north west winds are generally followed by rain. Seedtime begins early in March and potato digging about the middle of April. Harvest sets in regularly and generally about the middle of September, and potato digging is nearly over by the beginning of November.

MODERN TOPOGRAPHY

Villages: Cloghmills

There is no town in this parish and the only village is that of Cloghmills, which is prettily situated at its southern extremity and on the Altakeeragh river, which flows through the village forming the boundary between this parish and the grange of

Dundermot. Nearly half the village is in the grange, but the patent for the fairs specifies that they are to be held in the townland of Drumadoan, which is in the parish of Killagan and within half a mile of the village of Cloghmills. The main road from Ballymena to Ballycastle passes through the village. It is 9 and a half miles north of Ballymena (which is its post and market town) and 16 miles south of Ballycastle.

It is said that this village was built soon after the landing of King William III in this country, but nothing is known as to what determined its site. It does not seem as if it had ever been of greater importance than at present but, on the contrary, is rather increasing in size, population and business. It now consists of 42 houses, of which 3 are 2-storey. They are generally small, thatched and, except about 6 or 7, are of an inferior description and not very neat or cleanly in their appearance. They are occupied by labourers and tradesmen, and a few persons in business (see Table of Trades and Occupations). The people are industrious and well conducted, but there are not many who seem to be in comfortable circumstances. There is no gentleman's residence or public building in the town, except the bridge over the Altakeeragh river, which is a rude old structure 90 feet long and 18 feet wide, and consists of 3 semicircular arches.

There is no market in Cloghmills. 2 annual fairs are held in it, one on the 9th June and the other on the 22nd November. About 200 head of black cattle, 100 horses (principally Highland ponies), besides a considerable number of pigs and sheep, are sold at these fairs, and both pigs and black cattle are bought up by dealers for exportation. These, with a little meal, yarn and pedlars' goods, comprise nearly all the articles sold. The tolls are 2d for each horse and cow, and 1d for each sheep and pig. They amount to 6 pounds annually and are paid to Sampson Moore Esquire, the proprietor of the town.

2 cars with passengers leave Cloghmills every Saturday morning at 8 o'clock for Ballymena market and return the same evening. The fare for going and coming is 1s 6d for each person. There are 4 post cars and 1 tax[ed] cart for hire. The fare by these varies from 7d to 8d per mile for each passenger.

There are not any new houses building. Cloghmills is improving in business, owing principally to the industry of its inhabitants. Being on the main road between Ballycastle and many of the inland towns of the country, there is a considerable thoroughfare of driving through it, particularly in summer.

There is neither public buildings nor gentleman's seat in the parish.

Bleach Greens and Mills

There is a small bleach green, the property of Mr Warren, in the townland of Drumadaragh. The spread field extends over about 8 acres. The wheel of the beetling engine is 14 feet in diameter and 4 feet broad and is driven by breast water. The wheel of the wash mill is 12 feet in diameter, 3 feet 2 inches broad and is driven by breast water.

The corn mill in the same townland is propelled by a breast water wheel 15 feet in diameter by 3 feet broad.

The corn mill in Cloghmills townland is propelled by a breast water wheel 14 feet diameter and 2 feet 5 inches broad. This is a double-gear mill, that is, it can shell and grind at the same time.

The flax mill in Loughhill townland is propelled by a breast water wheel 12 feet in diameter and 2 feet broad.

Communications

There are 3 and a quarter miles of the main road from Cloghmills to Dervock in this parish. It is a good road 22 feet broad and kept in order at the expense of the barony. It is, however, hilly and its direction might be much improved.

One and a quarter miles of the road from Cloghmills to Ballycastle: this is also a tolerable road 22 feet broad and kept in order at the expense of the barony. It is rather level.

The by-roads are sufficiently numerous but hilly and in bad order.

Bridges

The principal bridges are: that over the Altakeeragh river in the village of Cloghmills. It is a rude old structure 90 feet long and 18 feet wide, and consists of 3 semicircular arches.

The bridge over the Killagan water, on the road from Cloghmills to Ballymoney, is 29 feet long and 20 feet wide and consists of 3 small circular-segment arches.

The bridge on a road from Portglenone to Ballycastle, over the Main, is 18 feet wide and 36 feet long, and consists of 3 small semicircular arches.

All these bridges are in sufficient repair.

General Appearance and Scenery

The surface of this parish has rather a bare appearance and wants planting very much. There is, however, considerable diversity in the ground which, with the snug appearance of the cottages, in some degree makes up for it. The neighbouring scenery is, however, very fine and the view from the higher parts of this parish, of the cultivated ridge of the Killymurrys hills on the west and the wild and lofty chain of mountains extending north and south from the adjoining parish of Loughguile on the east, is very beautiful and extensive.

ANCIENT TOPOGRAPHY

Antiquities

[Insert addition: In the townland of Broughanore in the north of the parish are the ruins of [an] old place of worship with a graveyard attached. It is still used as a place of interment].

SOCIAL ECONOMY

Early Improvements

The first migration to and settlement which took place in this parish was in the reign of King John and about the middle of the 12th century, when some of the English came over to this parish and that of Loughguile. Subsequent settlements of Scots took place in the 16th and 17th centuries. The last settlement took place in the commencement of the 17th century and soon after the year 1610, when some Presbyterians, who had fled from Scotland to avoid the persecutions then existing against them, landed at Carrickfergus and along the coast of this county, and soon after proceeded into the more interior parts of it and finally settled in its lower and more fertile districts.

This last settlement may probably be looked on as the first step towards civilisation and improvement, as previous to that time, this and the neighbouring districts had been greatly distracted by the bloody feuds between the rival families of McDonnell and McQuillan and the wars between the native Irish and the Scotch and English emigrants, and these wars seem to have only terminated with the extermination of the former, as none of them are now to be found in this parish, or indeed in the lower or more fertile parts of the country.

The present inhabitants are mostly all Presbyterians of different sects and their names denote their being of English or Scottish descent. No name is particularly prevalent, but the names of Thompson, Smith, Richards, Ford, Huey, Brown, Stewart, McCollum and Heney (all of which are Protestants or Presbyterians) are those usually met with. There are some McKeavers, but they are Roman Catholics.

Progress of Improvement

The more general introduction of schools and diffusion of knowledge have combined towards their improvements in every respect and they are generally a moral and well-conducted people. Crime is unknown among them. They are industrious and well disposed, and very obliging and intelligent. They are in general comfortable in their circumstances and manner of living and there is but little poverty or distress in the parish. They possess much of the Scottish customs and dialect, and are independent in their notions and opinions. They, like all their neighbours, were engaged in the rebellion of 1798 and, like them, suffered enough of its fruits to learn then never again to meddle in political events; and it also produced a total change in their political sentiments.

Obstructions to improvement: none.

Local Government

There are no magistrates, no constabulary and no troops. There are not any petty sessions. The manor courts and courts leet of the barony are held in the village of Clogh. The only outrage of any kind that has happened for a number of years occurred at a fair at Cloghmills in June 1835, when a man was killed returning from it at night. It has not been ascertained whether this arose from a private or party quarrel. One person was tried for it, but acquitted.

There has not been any illicit distillation for some years, no smuggling, nor are there any insurances.

Dispensary

There is not a dispensary in the parish. Patients from it are admissible to the dispensary in Loughguile parish, but no separate list of them is kept. As there is but little poverty or distress and the people are healthy, the effects of the dispensary are not so manifested in this parish as they would otherwise be.

Schools

The introduction of day schools into this parish is not of a recent date; that of Sunday schools is rather so, and their effects have proved very beneficial. The people are very desirous of having their children instructed and of obtaining knowledge and information (see Table of Schools).

Poor

There are very few, indeed scarcely any, resident poor. There is no regular provision for them, but the inhabitants possess sufficient voluntary charity to relieve all objects who call on their assistance and few instances occur of charity being refused.

Religion

By the revised census of 1835 there are [blank]. [Insert note: The enumerator has not kept a copy of the census. I am therefore unable to ascertain it [signed] J. Boyle]. The inhabitants are almost all Presbyterians of various sects. They have not any place of worship in the parish, but pay tithe and contribute in the usual manner to the support of the ministers of the congregations to which they belong.

Habits of the People

There are many comfortable farmers' houses in the parish, and the general description of the houses is comfortable, substantial and cleanly, built of stone, thatched, well lit and consisting of 2 apartments. The furniture is in general old-fashioned and substantial. Meal, potatoes, milk, some bacon, salt herrings, with tea and a little baker's bread, constitute their food. Turf is their only fuel and it is abundant.

They dress very neatly and respectably. They are rather long-lived and do not marry early. The usual number in a family is 6. They are not very prone to amusement, and going to fairs and a little dancing seem to be their only recreations.

The Orangemen celebrate the 12th July and the Freemasons the 24th June, but there are no such things as patrons or patrons' days, those being only found among the Roman Catholics. There are not any traditions, local customs, peculiar games or legendary tales among them, nor is there any peculiarity of costume.

Emigration

There is less emigration than formerly from this parish, owing to there not being such encouraging accounts from America. About 10 persons still annually emigrate in spring to Canada; few, if any, return.

Not more than 3 on an average go to the English or Scottish harvests, and they return when they are over. This may be accounted for by the parish not being too thickly peopled, by there being few actual labourers or persons who do not possess a little land of their own, and by their being of a settled disposition and sufficiently comfortable at home.

Remarkable events: none.

Table of Schools

Druamadoon townland, Protestants 57, Catholics 13, males 39, females 31, total 70; this school is under the London Hibernian Society; the teacher has a free house and plot of ground from the landlord Sampson Moore Esquire, and 2 pounds; established 1830.

PRODUCTIVE ECONOMY

Cloghmills: Table of Trades and Occupations

Apothecaries and surgeons 2, blacksmiths 3, coopers 1, carpenters 2, coopers and carpenters 4, grocers and spirit dealers 4, hecklers 1, masons 1, police 4, shoemakers 3, tailors 2, total 24.

Manufacturing

[Insert addition: The inhabitants, when not engaged in agricultural pursuits, employ themselves weaving linen and spinning flax. These are the only manufactures in the parish.

Manures

Backs of old ditches mixed with lime form a good manure and are eagerly sought for. Land is sometimes manured by spreading lime over the surface. Reclaiming bog is often effected by burning the surface.

SOCIAL ECONOMY

Table of Schools

[Table contains the following headings: name, situation and description, when established, income and expenditure, physical, intellectual and moral education, number of pupils subdivided by sex, age and religion, name and religion of master and mistress].

Ballynalube, master Archibald McCallum, Presbyterian; pay school, annual income 3s 4d per quarter; schoolhouse built by subscription, cost 20 pounds; number of pupils by the Roman Catholic return: 19 Presbyterians, 4 other denominations, 7 Roman Catholics, 20 males, 10 females; the schoolhouse was built by subscription.

Drumadoan, master Henry McGaughan, Roman Catholic; pay school, annual income 2s 2d and 3s 3d per quarter; schoolhouse a hired room;

number of pupils by the Roman Catholic return: 17 Presbyterians, 1 other denomination, 7 Roman Catholics, 18 males, 7 females].

Memoir by J. Stokes

Ecclesiastical: Graveyard

At the side of a stream in the townland of Broughanore there is an old graveyard. It is called Killeagan. Its surface is entirely cultivated and it contains but a rood of ground. It can still be recognised in the field, but merely by its edges rising a little above the rest of its surface. It was once larger and surrounded by an ancient circular ditch like the fosse of a fort, all traces of which have, however, long since disappeared. 2 blocks of stone were found that were, apparently, once gateposts. The part which has been dug away is said by the present tenant, who is the person who did so, to have contained no bones whatever. He thinks that the remaining patch is the graveyard properly so called. Children are still occasionally interred in it. There are no remains of a church.

Kilmandil Graveyard and Discoveries

In the townland of Kilmandil, and on a bank rising from the side of the same stream, there had been until very lately another graveyard called Kilmandil. This was much smaller, containing, as it is said, but 8 square perches. It was surrounded also by a circular ditch like the fosse of a fort. A few bones were found. No burials are recollected to have taken place in it excepting that of a child 80 years ago. A paved causeway once ran from north to south along its western side. This was also destroyed about 3 years ago, but there are some portions of it still below the surface of the field.

At the distance of about 40 yards west of the graveyard a great quantity of loose stones, ashes and pieces of burnt timber were found, as if of the remains of a building destroyed by fire. There was found 4 feet in depth of them and they extended over a space equal to 2 square perches. They were found by the present tenant in digging up the field after he came into possession of the farm.

On the steep slope of the hill on the north east side of the field are found a flight of steps apparently leading from the stream up to this ruined building. All were made of undressed stones. There were 30 in number of them and they ex-

tended over a line 60 feet in length. Along the top of the field 5 or 6 round water-worn stones were found with curious holes drilled in them; also a great number of small white pebbles evidently from the shore of the sea. For representations of the drilled holes, see drawing[s].

A large quern-stone, of which the half was absent, was also dug out in the line between the house and the graveyard, and at two-thirds of the distance.

At the bottom of the field, and along the stripe of flat ground adjoining the stream, there is still to be seen the remains of an ancient mill-race. It is nearly filled up. It extends 80 feet in length but beyond either end of that line it is obliterated. No remains can be found of any building attached to it.

Holy Well

In the townland of Cloghmills there is a holy well called Tubberdoney. There had been formerly at it a stone with the print of a saint's knee in it, but it is now destroyed. No rites or ceremonies are performed at it.

There are no military buildings.

Standing Stones, Coves and Discoveries

There is a standing stone, now overturned, in Loughmills. It is 4 feet by 1 foot 4 inches by 2 feet 4 inches.

A fort had been sunk below the ground under the field in which the Kilmandil burying ground is, but opening from the next one there is a cove 80 feet in length and containing 4 rooms, each at an average 20 feet long. They are 3 feet broad and from 4 to 5 feet high, and are divided from each other by low-browed doors, about 2 feet square each. In the ceiling of the first room there is the half of a large millstone inserted. It has evidently been placed there at the time when the cove was built, as it forms one of the roofing stones of the building. It is of the form represented in the margin [drawing]. It is 4 feet along the flat side. The part "a" is plainly and evidently artificial. The original stone appears to have been broken in two and it also would seem that pieces have been chipped from the circumference. The thickness, from the position in which it is placed, cannot precisely be ascertained, but is about 8 inches. No ancient articles have been found in this cave.

From each side of the first room there are 2 very small low-browed doors, each opening into what were apparently originally intended either for air holes or chimneys. They are narrow cavities scooped out of the hard ground of the hill and ascending upwards. They do not come out on the surface of the field, the top having fallen in. There are no stones built upon them.

At the eastern end this cave formerly proceeded further on, but it has there fallen in, the roof having given away [? from front]. It is said by the tenant to have originally extended 160 feet. It passes from south west to north east.

[In] the drawing[s], a circular flat stone with a small hole in the centre, answering much to the description of the "stone coins", as they were called, which were found in a cove in the parish of Skerry, is there represented. It was also found in a cove, situated in the townland of Broughanore but now destroyed; see the Ancient Topography of Skerry.

Some coins were found in the neighbourhood of Kilmandil; see the same drawing.

Map of standing stones of Killagan, scale 3 miles to 1 inch.

Drawings of Antiquities

Rectangular stone with 2 hollows on each side; views with dimensions and longitudinal section.

3 coins found in the neighbourhood of Kilmandil, both faces of each.

Stone hatchet found in Kilmandil, 9 inches long with end view.

Stone found in a cove, full size, with section.

2 arrowheads, full size.

Parish of Kirkinriola, County Antrim

Officer's Statistical Report by Lieutenant
Edward Durnford, December 1832

NATURAL STATE

Name and Situation

The name of Kirkinriola is supposed to be derived
from the words Cill-Coinn-righ-Uladh, "the burying place of Conn, King of Ulster." Kirk is not
Irish, but it is the pronunciation generally given to
this name by the inhabitants.

It is situated in the north east of the barony of
Lower Toome and nearly in the centre of the
county of Antrim, is of a long straggling form,
lying in the direction of about north west by north
of the town of Ballymena, which stands at the
most southern extremity of it.

It is an impropriate curacy in the gift in the Earl
of Mountcashel. The late earl sold the tithes for
4,000 pounds to William Adair Esquire, the proprietor of the manor of Ballymena, but retained
the right of presentation. It is in the diocese of
Connor and province of Armagh, and is
episcopally united pro hac vice to Ballyclug, the
adjoining parish.

In the Ecclesiastical Register part 1, it is stated,
"In the territory called Kilultagh in the Claneboy
district were the rectories of Rasarkin, Kilconriola,
Ballyrobert and Sylvodan, all appendant to
Muckamore Abbey."

Boundaries, Extent and Divisions

It is bounded on the north and north east by the
parish of Dunaghy and grange of Dundermot, on
the east by the parish of Skerry, on the south east
by Racavan <Rathcavan>, on the south by
Ballyclug and on the west by Ahoghill.

It extends in a north west direction about 6
British statute miles and the breadth varies from
2 and a half miles on the south east of the parish
to half a mile on the north west. The parish
contains 6,390 British statute acres.

It is divided into 18 townlands, 16 of which are
in the manor of Ballymena (at one time called
Kilhiltstown, the first proprietor, Sir Robert Adair,
being laird of Kilhilt, a place near Ayr <Air> in
Scotland) and are held by a grant direct from the
Crown by William Adair Esquire, the present
proprietor, who purchased off the quit rents a few
years ago. The remaining 2 townlands, Tullyreagh
and Carnlea, are the property of the Earl of
Mountcashel.

NATURAL FEATURES AND NATURAL HISTORY

Surface and Soil

There are no natural features of country in this
parish worthy of remark. It is of a generally
undulating form, with a good deal of bog in the
flats. It is, however, well cultivated in most parts
and a great deal of bog land is constantly being
reclaimed. About Craigawarren and the north end
of Ballygarvey it is very barren, being chiefly
heath and basalt rocks.

The soil is generally light and gravelly. The
general crops are potatoes and oats, and among
the small farmers a good deal of flax is grown.

Geology

The rocks in this parish are all basalt, of which the
dwelling houses are built. A remarkable detached
boulder of this rock stands in the north west of
Ballymena Town Parks, near the boundary between it and Dunclug. It rises 9 feet high above the
surface of the ground and there are no other rocks
near it. By the inhabitants it is said to be the centre
of the county of Antrim, which appears to be
nearly the case with regard to the length north and
south, but not so near in the breadth east and west.
It is also called by them the Standing Stone.

MODERN TOPOGRAPHY

Towns and Villages

The town of Ballymena (the name is supposed to
be derived from the words Bally-menagh, "the
middle town", or Baile-meodhun-ath, "the
townland in the middle of the ford", or Baile-
maoin-ath, "the townland at the ford or mouth of
the Main") is situated at the southern extremity of
the parish, on a gentle slope from the north bank
of the River Braid (a branch of the Main <Maine>,
which flows into Lough Neagh), over which there
is a stone bridge connecting it with Harryville, a
village in Ballyclug parish. It is a considerable
and increasing town, and from its central situation, is much resorted to by the inhabitants of the
surrounding country.

PRODUCTIVE ECONOMY

Fairs and Markets

There are 2 fairs held annually on the 26th July

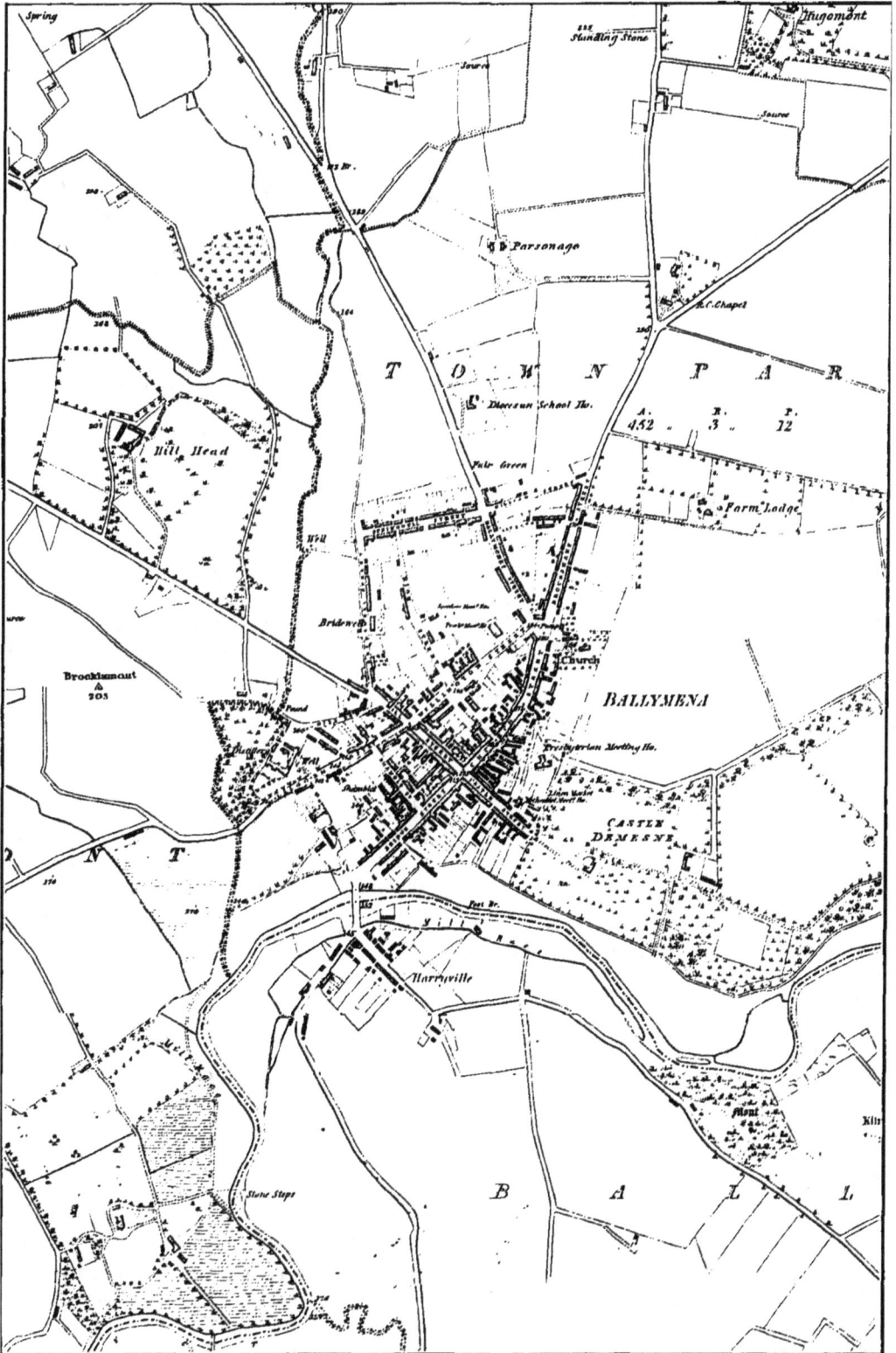

Map of Ballymena from the first 6" O.S. maps, 1830s

and 21st October, and a very extensive market is held every Saturday. These are held by a patent or grant made in the 2nd year of King Charles I to a William Adair Esquire, the ancestor of the present proprietor. The fairs are general marts, but chiefly for the sale of black cattle, and in the markets, in addition to cattle, the chief trade is butter, yarn and linen. Of the latter about 5,000 pieces of 25 yards each are sold every week and of butter about 6,000 firkins are sold annually in the season.

There has been established of late years a pork market on Tuesdays and Fridays from the middle of October to the middle of May, and about 11,000 dead pigs are sold during this season. The corn market is on Wednesdays, but not being a wheat country, it is of no importance. There is little more than a supply of oats for the town passes through it. There is a scale of tolls posted at each end of the town which are authorised by the above grant. It is as follows.

Customs and Tolls

Town of Ballymena. A schedule of the customs demanded and payable to William Adair Esquire by ancient usage in this town, on each of the following articles brought for sale: a boll of malt or oats 2d ha'penny, a load of meal 2d ha'penny, a stand of bread 1d, a load of salt 1d, a load of fruit 1d, a load of wool 2d, a load of timber 1d, a load of fish 1d, a load of cabbage plants 2d, a load of earthenware 1d, a load of empty firkins a ha'penny, a load of wooden bowls 1d, a sack of bran 1d, a sack of beans or peas 1d ha'penny, a sack of eels 1d, a carcass of beef 3d, a cwt of cheese 1d, a mutton 1d, a fat or fed veal 1d, a hog or carcass of pork 1d, a boxcar of potatoes 2d, a sack of potatoes 1d, a hatter's stand 1d, a merchant's stand, covered or uncovered, 2d, a horse bought or exchanged 3d, a cow bought or exchanged 2d, a shoemaker's barrel or stand 1d, a creel or stand with stockings 1d, a firkin of butter retailed 1d, a cwt of butter a ha'penny, a bag of flour 2d, a creel of trout (lake or sea) 1d, a creel of fresh herrings 1d, a car of fresh herrings 2d, a stand with old clothes 2d, a car with small pigs 2d, a live sheep a ha'penny, a stand with pork 2d, 6 lbs of butter a ha'penny.

To be paid by the buyer: a cowhide 1d, a kip hide a ha'penny, a cwt of tallow or fat 4d, a sheepskin unshorn a ha'penny, a half dozen of veal skin 1d, a pig skin a ha'penny.

To be paid at fairs: a merchant's stand covered 6d, a merchant's stand uncovered 4d.

A load of any other articles not before enumerated brought for sale, 4d.

Church

At the north east end of the town is situated the church, which is small but neat and in good repair. It was built in 1707 and constituted by act of parliament (6 Anne ch.21, para.28) "the only parish church in this parish so soon as Sir Robert Adair, the proprietor of the soil, shall have made the necessary conveyance of the ground on which the church is built, with a convenient church-yard."

Meeting Houses

There are 2 very large meeting houses for the Presbyterians, one of which was only built in 1829. This is situated in Wellington Street. There is also a small meeting house for the Seceders and another for the Wesleyan Methodists.

Roman Catholic Chapel

There is a Roman Catholic chapel in the Town Parks, at the meeting of the new road from Broughshane with the road from Clogh. It was built by subscription in 1827, previous to which the nearest chapel was at Crebilly, about 2 miles distant.

Market House

The market house has a small tower and is situated in the principal street, nearly in the centre of the town. Over this is the court house, where the quarter sessions are held in January and July (the alternate ones in April and October are held in Ballymoney). Petty sessions are also held here for the surrounding district once a fortnight.

Bridewell

A bridewell has been recently built (in 1829), which was much wanted. I understood that at one time it was in agitation to have built the county jail at this town, but that Belfast, being so near to Carrickfergus, decided the grand jury on repairing the jail at that place.

SOCIAL ECONOMY

Guy's Free School

There is a free school which commenced in 1821, founded on a charitable bequest by the late John Guy (who bequeathed the profit rent of some houses in the town, about 50 pounds per annum, for this purpose). It is under the superintendence of 5 trustees, the proprietor of the town and the Dissenting minister being 2 of them. There are from 100 to 150 pupils attending it.

There is also another school for the poor under the direction of the clergyman, supported by contributions. This has about 100 pupils attending it.

Mendicity Society and School

The Mendicity Society of the town pay 300 pounds per annum to the poor.

There is a diocesan school which was established in 1830. It is endowed by the clergy of Armagh and Connor dioceses with 120 pounds per annum, and the grand jury of the county presented 1,000 pounds to build the house. The present master is the Reverend Robert Matthews.

Coaches

There are 2 coaches to Belfast every morning (except Sundays), which return in the evening. The mail between Belfast and Derry passes through the town every day from both places and the day coach from Belfast to Coleraine 3 times a week from each place.

Population

By the census of 1831 the population of the town was 4,063.

PRODUCTIVE ECONOMY

Manufactures

The manufacture of linen and spinning of flax is carried on to a considerable extent by the inhabitants at their own houses, as they have a ready sale for it in the Ballymena market.

There are 2 bleach greens in the parish, one situated at the south end of the town of Ballymena and is partly in Ahoghill parish; the other is in Ballygarvey townland. They are both carried on with spirit and are in full work. At the latter a great quantity of the union cloth is manufactured as well as bleached. There are about 60 weavers employed, who work at their own houses.

MODERN TOPOGRAPHY

Roads

The town of Ballymena being centrally situated in the county, many roads radiate from it. Those which traverse the parish are: the mail coach road from Belfast to Derry, which passes through a portion of the parish on its north west boundary.

The road from Belfast to Ballycastle traverses the parish from south to north nearly, as also one from Ballymena to Clogh. The new road to Broughshane and the old one (by Ballygarvey) traverse the south east portion of the parish. These roads are all in good repair as well as several crossroads between them.

NATURAL FEATURES

Rivers

The River Braid forms the south east boundary of the parish and the Ravel river its north east boundary. Both these rivers empty themselves into the Main, which flows into Lough Neagh.

Bogs and Woods

There are several good bogs in the north and centre of the parish which are cut for fuel.

Woods: there are none, but there are some plantations about the Castle demesne and some fine trees about Ballygarvey. There is a plantation of young firs in Craigawarren, but it is of small extent, also some young plantations about the houses of Hugomont and Brigadie near the town.

SOCIAL ECONOMY

Population by Townlands

The population are chiefly descended from the Scotch emigrants. The house called the Castle on the east side of the town belongs to the proprietor of the parish, William Adair Esquire, but this is let as he never resides here, his principal property being in England.

By the census of 1831 the population of the whole parish, including the town of Ballymena, amounted to 7,354. It was as follows by townlands.

Ballymena Town Parks: males 1,958, females 2,105, total 4,063.

Ballygarvey: males 172, females 168, total 340.

Belly: males 70, females 84, total 154.

Bottom: males 64, females 69, total 133.

Carnlea: males 185, females 179, total 364.

Cabra: males 54, females 59, total 113.

Clinty: males 57, females 75, total 132.

Clogher: males 123, females 126, total 249.

Craigawarren: males 250, females 247, total 497.

Derniveagh: males 70, females 70, total 140.

Drumfane: males 113, females 99, total 212.

Drumfin: males 62, females 62, total 124.

Dunclug: males 71, females 72, total 143.

Dungall: males 80, females 72, total 152.

Killyflugh: males 67, females 67, total 134.
Kirkinriola: males 91, females 101, total 192.
Monaghan: males 61, females 66, total 127.
Tullyreagh: males 37, females 48, total 85.

ANCIENT TOPOGRAPHY

Antiquities

The only relic of antiquity in this parish is the remains of a building in the graveyard in Kirkinriola townland. [Signed] Edward W. Durnford, Lieutenant Royal Engineers, 22nd December 1832.

Memoir by James Boyle, October 1835

MEMOIR WRITING

Sources of Information for Memoir

For the Kirkinriola Memoir: it may be satisfactory to state that all the information contained in this Memoir has been derived from the most authentic sources. That relating to the sales of grain, hides, butter and pork has been computed from the sums entered in the weighmaster's book as charged on these <this> articles. The number of cattle has been calculated in a similar manner from the toll gatherer's accounts. The other sales, such as of linen, have been estimated by the most extensive dealers in these articles. The circulation of the Provincial Bank is from the manager, that of the other banks is by estimation. A detailed account of the linen sales (similar to that of the county Derry markets) can, if required, be given. [Signed] James Boyle, January 7th 1836.

NATURAL FEATURES

Hills

This parish occupies the eastern side of the large mass or feature included between the Clogh river at the north, the Main at the west, the Braid at the south and the valley extending between this and the parish of Skerry on the east. Its surface does not present any remarkable features, the highest point, which is near the north of the parish, being only 506 feet above the level of the sea. From this there is general slope southward to the Braid river, where it descends to a level of 140 feet above the sea. There is also a gradual slope eastward, where it declines to an average elevation of 276 feet above the sea. The surface of this parish is greatly diversified, being traversed from north to south by little valleys, and the ridges on

their sides being again intersected by lesser ones. Towards the centre of the parish the basalt appears at the summit of the little hills, and a considerable portion of its eastern side is barren and covered with heath, which gives it but a cheerless aspect. The principal points in the parish are Berkhill, 506 feet, Craigawarren, 498 feet and Cabragh, 413 feet above the level of the sea.

Lakes and Rivers

There are no lakes in this parish.

The principal rivers are: the Braid, which, rising in the parish of Tickmacrevan at an elevation of 650 feet above the sea, pursues a south west course for 9 miles and, ascending to a level of 173 feet, enters on the south east boundary of this parish, separating it from the parishes of Racavan and Ballyclug. After flowing through this parish and passing by the town of Ballymena, it descends to a level of 126 feet and, entering the parish of Ahoghill soon after, discharges itself into the Main river at a distance of 11 miles from its mouth and at an elevation of 110 feet above the sea, and 62 feet above Lough Neagh. Its entire course is 14 miles, its average breadth 58 feet and depth 3 and a half feet. Its bed is pebbly and its banks low except near Ballymena, and the scenery along them in the immediate neighbourhood of that town pleasing. The rest of its course is through an almost level and tame country.

This river is subject to sudden floods which rise to a height of from 3 to 6 feet, doing (in summer) much mischief to the crops along its banks and sweeping off the looser soil. Ditches also are sometimes carried away, its impetuosity in some floods being tremendous. In winter its floods are beneficial as it inundates and enriches the adjacent lands to a considerable extent. It very quickly naturally subsides. Its deposits (in winter) are beneficial.

This river is valuably situated for machinery, irrigation and drainage, and is in several instances converted to the first of these purposes. Its situation also, with regard to Ballymena, is important. Its average fall is 1 foot in 137 feet.

The Clogh river, which takes its rise in mountains in the parishes of Skerry and Ardclinis, at an elevation of about 1,200 feet above the sea, flows north west for 4 miles in a winding manner along the northern boundary of this parish and soon after discharges itself into the River Main, at an elevation of 263 feet above the sea. Its average fall is 1 foot in 49 feet, average breadth 29 feet and depth 2 and a half feet. Its bottom is pebbly and irregular, from the frequent shallows and rapids in it. It is applicable to machinery, irrigation and drainage. For further description of this river, see Rivers, grange of Dundermot and parish of Dunaghy.

Bogs

There are numerous small patches, but no large tracts of bog in this parish. They generally occupy the lower and flatter parts of it, where water seems to have accumulated and, by its stagnation and consequent growth of vegetable matter, to have been the origin of these bogs. Their depth varies from 4 to 12 feet and the subsoil is usually blue clay. From the depth at which timber occurs in these bogs, even in their present state (having been generally cut over), they must at one time have been very deep.

In a tract in the townland of Clinty, at a depth of 5 feet from the present surface, a young growth of fir not more than 3 and a half inches in diameter remains. The stumps only are to be found. They seem to have been burnt down. Oak stumps standing on the clay and a few trunks of the same timber are also found. Fir stumps are found in considerable quantities but there is nothing worthy of description about them.

Woods

There are not now any remains of natural wood in this parish except the small clusters of hazel brushwood on its more rocky parts and the timber found in the bogs.

Climate

The climate of this parish is moist and mild, particularly towards its southern end. Its proximity to the mountains renders it moist, and its low situation and the parallel ridges of the Killymurrys hills on the west, and the greater range of mountains in Skerry and the adjoining parishes on the east, shelter it from all winds except the south, which is particularly prevalent and is generally attended with rain. It is too moist to ripen wheat sufficiently, which is consequently but little sown. Rye is sown in November and reaped about the middle of August. Barley is sown in April and reaped in August. Oats is sown from the beginning of March to the middle of April and reaped in September. Flax is sown in April and pulled in July. Potato planting continues from the end of March to the end of May. The raising of potatoes commences about the middle of September and continues until the end of November. The princi-

pal potato digging takes place generally about Hallow Eve, but much depends on the season.

MODERN TOPOGRAPHY

Towns: Ballymena

The town of Ballymena is situated on the mail coach road from Belfast to Londonderry and near the centre of the county Antrim. It is 29 miles north west of the former of these towns, 132 miles north of Dublin. It is situated in longitude 6 degrees 8 minutes west and latitude 54 degrees 52 minutes north. It is in the diocese of Connor, province of Ulster, county of Antrim, parish of Kirkinriola and north east circuit of assize. The River Braid flows by the southern end of the town, affording an ample supply of water for domestic purposes and also for the manufactories in that quarter of the town. Roads diverge in almost every direction from Ballymena, it being, as it were, the nucleus of the county. Its form is that of an oblong square; its extreme length is half a mile, breadth a quarter of a mile and circumference 1 and a third miles.

Ballymena is seated on the extremity of a feature extending (and gradually declining in height) from the northern end of the parish. Its situation is rather low, the highest point in the town (which is at its north east side) being only 186 feet above the sea. From this there is a gradual fall west and south. That towards the south is the more rapid of the two and terminates at the Braid river, which at the bridge is 136 feet above the sea. The slope westward is gentle and terminates at a little valley which extends along the west side of the town.

From its low situation Ballymena is not discernible at any distance. Its situation is at the western extremity of the valley of the Braid, the view up which from Ballymena is wild and picturesque. There is but little planting about the town, but from the cultivated state of the ground the aspect of the adjacent country is pleasing.

HISTORY

Origin and History of Ballymena

The origin of Ballymena is involved in obscurity, since it is not known as to when it was built or what determined its site. Many traditions and stories concerning it are current, and of them the following are the most probable. It is said that Ballymena derived its origin and name from a ford which was over the Braid where the present bridge [stands], Bally-menagh in Irish signifying "the town on the middle ford."

Another, though less probable, story is told of it. It is said that on the coming of St Patrick to Connor (in the 5th century), the converts there to Christianity become so numerous that Connor church, though enlarged for the purpose, would not contain them, and many persons in Cullybackey being at the same time converted, it was found necessary to erect another church. Both parties wished to have the church built in their own village, but after some time it was built half-way between them, and the houses which were built about it are said to have been the origin of Ballymena.

Bally-mena in Irish signifies "the town in the middle or centre." It is centrally situated, and a stone on the side of the road to Clogh and near the town of Ballymena was formerly supposed to have marked the centre of the county. [Insert marginal note: Mr Hannyngton has furnished a sketch of this stone]. The church just mentioned is said to have stood where the market house now is, but no trace of it or of any monastic or feudal edifice remains.

It is, however, probable that Ballymena is not a place of antiquity and that it was little more than a hamlet when the Adairs first settled in this parish. That family, having come over from Wigtonshire in Scotland, obtained a grant of this parish from Charles I in the beginning of the 16th century. Sir Robert Adair (the first proprietor), who was laird of Kilhilt in Wigtonshire, changed its name to Kilhiltstown and by this it was for some time called, and is so mentioned in old leases. It is certain that Ballymena never was larger or of more importance than at present, as it is every day increasing in size and trade, and more than half the town has been built within the last 20 years. It is said that its site was formerly a barren heath and this has been corroborated by the fact of heath being found under the pavement in Castle Street.

Ballymena never has been distinguished in history. On the 7th June 1798 the town was taken possession of by about 10,000 rebels, who put to death 5 of the inhabitants.

MODERN TOPOGRAPHY

Public Buildings: Parish Church

The public buildings of Ballymena consist of: the parish church, which stands at the northern end of Church Street. It is a plain edifice 66 feet long and 27 feet wide, and has a plain square tower 40 feet high, at its western end. It contains (including the gallery) 55 seats and would accommodate 380 persons. It is, however, much too small, as few of the poorer class can obtain accommodation. It is, however, pretty comfortable. There is a small organ which cost 100 pounds in it, and there are 4 tablets erected to the memory of persons interred near them.

This church was constituted by act of parliament (6 Anne c.21 s.28) "the only parish church in this parish so soon as Sir Robert Adair, the proprietor of the soil, shall have made the necessary conveyance of the ground in which the church is built, with a convenient churchyard." The church was built in 1707 (the ground being given by Sir Robert Adair), Mr Ballantine, architect. In 1798 it was used as a barrack and the woodwork consumed for fuel. In 1822 the tower was built at a cost of 320 pounds, 100 pounds of which was advanced by the Board of First Fruits, to be repaid by instalments.

Presbyterian Meeting Houses

The Presbyterian meeting house in Castle Street was built by subscription in 1730. It is perfectly plain in every respect but in good repair, and consists of a principal aisle 88 feet long and 24 feet wide, and a lesser one 40 feet long and 28 feet wide, at right angles to it. It contains 107 seats and accommodation for 856 persons.

The Presbyterian meeting house in Wellington Street is a substantial capacious building, very simple and similar in its exterior to a cotton factory. It is well fitted up internally. Its dimensions are 68 feet long, 53 feet wide. It contains 120 seats and accommodation for 960 persons. It was erected in 1828 at a cost of 1,000 pounds, which was defrayed by subscription.

Seceding Meeting House

The Seceders' meeting house stands in High Street. It is a plain little building 63 feet long and 33 feet wide. It contains 50 seats and accommodation for 830 persons. It was built by subscription in 1824 and cost 500 pounds.

Wesleyan Methodist Chapel

The Wesleyan Methodist chapel is situated in Castle Street. It is perfectly plain and without pews, long forms being used in their stead. It was erected by subscription in 1816. It might accommodate 130 persons.

Bridge

The bridge is at the southern end of the town and

connects it with the village of Harryville. It is over the Braid river and on the main road from Ballymena to Belfast. It is a plain old structure 146 feet long and 28 feet wide, and consists of 9 semicircular arches.

Market House

The market house stands at the angle of Bridge Street and Mill Street, and near the centre of the town. It is a plain building 2-storeys high. A square tower 90 feet high stands at its eastern gable. This tower bears the date of 1754 inscribed on it and is said to be a more modern erection than the rest of the building.

The market house was built partly by subscription and partly by the proprietor of the estate. The upper part is fitted up as a court house and has 2 jury rooms off it. It is kept in repair by the county but is the property of the landlord. It is used for holding quarter sessions, manor courts, Sunday school, public meetings and assemblies. In the tower is a good clock and a bell, which is rung at 6 in the morning and 9 in the evening for the accommodation of the working class. It, being centrally situated, is also rung for worship at the Presbyterian meeting house on Sundays.

Weigh-house and Shambles

At the angle of Bridge Street and Shambles Street is the weigh-house, in which is the public crane. It is much too small and would require a yard or market place to be attached to it, as on corn market days there is not room in the street opposite to it for the cars laden with grain. This house is 100 feet long, 20 feet wide and 1-storey high. The crane and it are the property of William Gihon, Michael Harrison and James Young Esquires, who in 1813 obtained a grant of the ground from Mr Adair (the landlord) at a yearly rent of 1 guinea and built this house.

The shambles adjoin the weigh-house and are the property of the same persons, who erected them at the same time. They merely consist of a little alley 90 feet long and 7 feet wide, with 14 little stalls or shops along its sides. They are but little used by the butchers. The shambles and weigh-house jointly cost 300 pounds, of which Mr Adair contributed 50 pounds.

Market

In the same street a second market for the sale of meat has just been opened. This is a very judicious measure on the part of the landlord, as the shambles are too small and the street was formerly much obstructed by the numerous cars and stands of meat. This market was until lately occupied as a garden. It is sufficiently spacious and from 25 to 40 cars and stands of fresh and salt meat are exposed in it on Saturdays. Some of these stalls are covered like a tent. The sale of meat continues from 8 in the morning until 9 in the evening, at which time this market presents one of the most extraordinary and grotesque appearances that can be imagined: each car being illuminated by 1 or 2 candles, the glare of which on the carcases of meat and countenances and figures of the bystanders has a most singular effect.

Hotels

There are 5 hotels, to which title only one of these establishments has any pretensions. It is situated in Bridge Street and next to the market house. It is a long-established house and is kept by Miss Courtney. The Derry and Coleraine coaches to Belfast call and change horses at it.

Mrs Brangin's hotel in Church Street is but small; the accommodation otherwise is pretty good. The other hotels are McAuley's in Bridge Street, and Love's and Jack's in Church Street, at each of which whiskey is retailed. Ballymena ought to be able to support a good hotel and there are few towns in which it is more wanting.

Barrack and Bridewell

There is a 2-storey house in Mill Street used as a police barrack. It contains accommodation for 10 men.

The bridewell stands in Bridewell Street, on the west side of the town. It is 70 feet long and 24 feet wide, and consists of the keeper's house in the centre, which is 2-storey. To the right and left of this are a corridor, with 4 cells opening from each corridor. To each of the 2 wards are attached a day room and yard with a pump. Each cell contains a metal stretcher or bench which is used as a bedstead and is calculated to accommodate from 1 to 3 persons. A narrow space or avenue extends around the bridewell, and between it and the exterior wall which encloses all. This wall is 12 feet high and encloses a square 112 feet long and 88 feet wide. The entrance through this wall is by a handsome cut-stone gateway.

This bridewell was built in 1829 at an expense of 1,060 pounds, which was paid for by the county. Mr Kane of Dublin was the architect. It is altogether a very pretty and substantially furnished building, and is kept in very good order and its situation is healthy and airy. It serves to confine the prisoners during the quarter sessions in Ballymena and those on their way to jail from the sessions in Ballymoney. The average number annually confined is 480. The keeper's salary is 20 pounds and the annual allowance for straw, fuel, 35 pounds.

Bank

A handsome and spacious 2-storey house has been lately built in Wellington Street for a branch of the Provincial Bank. It also contains apartments for the manager.

Schoolhouses

The diocesan school stands contiguous to the northern side of the town. It consists of a basement and 2 upper storeys, and presents 2 sides of a square, each of which is 46 feet long and their extreme breadth 20 feet. The house is plain but neat in its appearance and is built of stone and roughcast. Its situation is airy, healthy and cheerful, and there is a spacious playground attached. The apartments of the Reverend Robert Matthews, the headmaster, are in the southern wing.

This school was built pursuant to act of parliament by the grand jury of the county in 1830 and cost 1,000 pounds late Irish currency, Mr Welland of Dublin, architect. It contains accommodation for 16 boarders and 40 day scholars. It is endowed with 120 pounds per annum collected from the clergy of the united dioceses of Armagh and Connor, which sum is given to the headmaster as a salary.

Guy's Free School was built in 1821 at an expense of 450 pounds, bequeathed for the purpose by the late Mr John Guy, together with 50 pounds per annum for its support. It stands in Wellington Street and is a plain 1-storey house 80 feet long and 24 feet wide, and containing a spacious and airy schoolroom and apartments for the master.

The female national schoolhouse stands in High Street. It is a small but neat 2-storey house containing apartments for the mistress and a good schoolroom. It was built in 1833 partly by subscription and partly by the National Board.

Principal Residences

The principal private residences are those of Michael Harrison Esquire in Castle Street, John Patrick Esquire in Broughshane Street, Andrew Gihon Esquire, Galgorm Street, Thomas Casement Esquire in Shambles Street, James Montgomery Esquire in Ballymoney Street and William Orr Esquire in Mill Street. There is nothing worthy of notice or description in the architecture or appearance of any of these residences. They are for the most part very plain and not modern looking.

Ballymena: Streets and Houses

Ballymena consists of 14 streets and 2 lanes containing 297 1-storey, 445 2-storey and 88 3-storey houses. The principal streets are Bridge Street, Church Street and Broughshane Street, which extend for half a mile in a slightly curved line along the eastern side of the town from its northern to its southern extremity, where it terminates at the bridge over the Braid. At the junction of Bridge Street and Church Street this line is intersected at right angles by a street, the eastern end of which is called Castle Street (as it leads to the former residence of the Adair family) and extends for 146 yards. The western end of it is called Mill Street and extends for 220 yards.

From Bridge Street extends Shambles Street, nearly parallel to Mill Street. It terminates at Galgorm Street which, extending from Mill Street, runs nearly parallel to Bridge Street for 264 yards. Wellington Street, forming a continuation of Galgorm Street, extends north west for 286 yards and unites with the extremities of Church Street, Broughshane Street and Ballymoney Street. The latter street diverges in a northerly direction for 210 yards. Alexander Street and William Street cross from it to Broughshane Street. Springwell Street extends westward from Ballymoney Street for 200 yards and terminates at Bridewell Street, which runs along the western side of the town for 308 yards and terminates at Mill Street. High Street extends from Wellington Street to Springwell Street. Mill Row is a dirty narrow lane running from Mill Street into Galgorm Street.

Bridge Street, Church Street, Shambles Street, Castle Street and Mill Street were the first built. The others have been built within the last 20 years. High Street and Wellington Street are still in progress, as are also the lanes called Alexander Street, William Street and Bridewell Street. The latter three, with Springwell Street and Mill Row, are dirty and narrow lanes, though styled streets by the inhabitants.

The general appearance of these streets is unprepossessing and the approaches and outlets of the town, from their filthy state and from the mean description of the houses, must tend to prejudice the opinion of a stranger. Even in the principal streets (except in High Street) no regard whatever seems to be paid to neatness, regularity or uniformity in the erection of the houses. In these streets they are all either 2 or 3-storeys high, built of stone and slated, though many of them are thatched. They are almost exclusively inhabited by shopkeepers and are anything but modern in their appearance. The 1-storey cabins and cottages are in general filthy, untidy and comfortless, though many of them are substantially built and otherwise comfortable. They are mostly thatched, built of stone and consist of 3 apartments.

The streets are narrow, the principal streets not exceeding an average breadth of 36 feet. They are all made of broken whinstone and are very dirty, owing to their being hollow in the centre, their narrowness and the incessant thoroughfare. No attention whatever is paid towards cleansing them. The footways are narrow, badly paved and on a level with the street. They are consequently very dirty and unpleasant, and in wet weather the streets are almost impassable for female pedestrians. It is almost unnecessary to add that Ballymena does not come under the act for cleansing, lighting, paving or watching, though its population would entitle it to it, and in no town is it more required. The inhabitants (chiefly of the lower class) seem opposed to this step.

SOCIAL ECONOMY

Progress of Improvement

There are at present being built in Ballymena 4 3-storey, 24 2-storey and 6 1-storey houses. They are all of stone and lime and slated. The 3-storey and some of the 2-storey houses are situated in High Street. They are of a substantial description and suited for persons in business. The rest are principally in William and Broughshane Streets.

Ballymena has doubled its size within the last 30 years, the western half of the town having been built within that time. There are now 830 houses in it, while by the census of 1832 there were only 691, there being an increase of 139 houses within 3 years. Within that period the greater part of High Street, William Street and Alexander Street have been built. The latter 2 streets are narrow and the houses 2-storey and small, being chiefly inhabited by tradesmen or small dealers. They are built of stone and lime and slated. High Street is tolerably uniform and wide, the houses being of good size and either 2 or 3-storeys high. They are suitable for business or for families of moderate income, and let at from 10 to 30 pounds per annum.

There is still a demand for houses, particularly in the principal streets, where a house is never suffered to remain unoccupied. In these streets, particularly in Bridge Street, Church Street, Mill Street and Castle Street (which are the best situations for business), the houses let at from 13 to 45 pounds per annum and 1 house is let at 55 pounds. Ground lets at, for buildings, from 1s 6d to 2s 6d per foot according to its situation. The usual lease is 61 years and a life.

Quarter and Petty Sessions

Quarter sessions are held in Ballymena in January and July, the alternate terms being held in Ballymoney in April and October. Sums not exceeding 18 pounds 9s 2d upon a bill note or bond, and 9 pounds 4s 7d without a bill note or bond, are recoverable at these sessions. They also have jurisdiction for damages to the amount of 4 pounds 12s 3d. Criminal cases such as riots, rescues, assaults are tried at them, but the offences are rarely of a serious nature.

Petty sessions are held here on every alternate Monday. There are usually 3 magistrates in attendance. Owing to the facility afforded for litigation by these sessions, it is considered that the business at them is increasing, which, it is supposed, would not be the case were offenders more summarily punished.

Manor courts are held here once a month and courts leet twice a year for the manor of Ballymena, Peter Aicken Esquire, seneschal. Sums not exceeding 2 pounds (late Irish currency) are recoverable at these courts.

Ballymena is the residence of the sub-inspector of constabulary and is also the headquarters of that body in this county. There are usually 10 men stationed here.

Population

By the revised census of 1834 the population of Ballymena amounted to 4,063 persons, of whom 1,958 were males and 2,105 females; by the same census 700 Episcopalians, 2,500 Presbyterians, 66 other Dissenters, 757 Roman Catholics and 40 whose religion was unknown. The population was also classed as follows by the enumerator: males over 20 years of age 969, occupiers of land employing labourers 2, occupiers of land not employing labourers 8, agricultural labourers 83, males employed in retail trade or handicraft as masters or workmen 659, wholesale merchants, capitalists, bankers, professional and other educated men 74, labourers employed by these 3 classes and other labourers not agricultural 57, all other males above 20 years old (except servants)

47, total adult males (except servants) 1,899;
male servants above 20 years old 78, male servants under 20 years old 56, female servants 300,
total servants 434.

But the population of Ballymena has increased
considerably since 1832 and, if in a similar state
to that of the houses (which have increased precisely one-fifth), it would now amount to 4,875
persons, and the increase of the different classes
is considered to have been proportionate.

As may be inferred from the above statement,
the inhabitants of Ballymena are almost all engaged in trade, dealing or business of some kind.

PRODUCTIVE AND SOCIAL ECONOMY

Linen Trade

The linen trade (which in no place is carried on
more briskly) affords in its various branches
employment to many and is in fact, from the great
weekly market for the sale of that article, the main
support of the town. It is, besides, the principal
market for the sale of the export linen, and some
of the gentlemen engaged in the linen business in
Ballymena are among the most, if not the most,
extensive purchasers and exporters of linen and
have connections or establishments in New Orle-
ans, Liverpool etc. Many also in this immediate
neighbourhood have from little, realised large
fortunes in the linen trade.

Commercial

The chief part of the population are either shopkeepers or mechanics, the increasing business of
the town being the cause of an increased demand
for shops (for a detailed account of the trades and
occupations see Appendix). There cannot be said
to be 1 private gentleman in Ballymena, as there
is no one who does not exercise some profession
or trade.

The general character of the inhabitants is
extreme industry and attention to business, minding or caring for nothing but what may attend to
their pecuniary advantage. They are almost all of
the middle or lower class and have mostly by their
exertions made their money and rendered themselves comfortable in their circumstances. Strange,
however, as it may appear in a place of so great
trade, there are few (if the linen merchants be
excepted) moneyed men in the town, there actually being not more than 6 or 7 persons worth
2,000 pounds or 13 or 14 worth 1,000 pounds.
This may probably be owing to the small capital
and narrow ideas with which they commenced
business, and their consequent want of spirit or

enterprise. Perhaps it may proceed from their
canny and cautious dispositions which they in-
herit from their Scottish forefathers. It is, however, to be commended in some respects and the
result of it is that there is no safer town for the
banking business, or one where there are fewer
failures.

The shops are very numerous, the main streets
being crowded with them. Many of them are very
good and afford all the necessaries and most of the
luxuries of life, at prices very little higher than
those charged in Belfast. The grocery and woollen shops are particularly good, and there are 2
excellent booksellers' and stationers' shops. Belfast is the principal mart from which the Ballymena
shopkeepers procure their goods.

Amusements: Literature

There are 2 tolerable circulating libraries, Dugan's
and White's, the former containing 672 and the
latter 430 works, such as novels. There is no news
room nor reading room. There was one which was
kept up for 2 years, but given up about a year and
a half ago. Party politics seem to have been the
principal cause of its being abandoned, neither
party being of itself sufficiently strong to support
a news room. There is very little, indeed scarcely
any, taste for literature or science. The people are
all utilitarians and seem to give their undivided
attention to the making of money, and to which
alone they seem to have been bred up. By a
reference to Appendix, a tolerable idea of the
politics and literary taste of the Ballymena people
may be formed.

Societies

The only society is the Ballymena Protestant
Society, which was established here in 1834 and
consists of 102 members. It includes the Protestant clergy, most of the aristocracy of the surrounding neighbourhood and many of the respectable merchants in Ballymena. This society
meets twice a year at supper in Ballymena, but
avoids any unnecessary party display, its avowed
object being the encouragement of unanimity
among Protestants of all denominations and works
(for a statement of its principles see Appendix).
This society is increasing and about to build a
room for holding its meetings in.

Manufactories

Ballymena cannot be properly styled manufacturing or commercial, as its trade, except that in
linen, is chiefly retail. Its manufactories consist

of: the distillery in Galgorm Street, the property of Clotworthy Walkinshaw Esquire. It was established here in 1832 and affords employment to 16 men. It has 2 stills, one of which contains 2,300 and the other 1,000 gallons. The mash tun is 18 feet in diameter and 6 feet deep. The machinery is propelled by a breast water wheel 26 feet in diameter and 3 feet broad, having a fall of water of 21 feet. The machinery of the corn mill attached to this distillery is propelled by an overshot water wheel 18 feet in diameter and 4 feet broad.

There are 2 tanneries: that in Galgorm Street consists of 21 pits and affords employment to 5 men. The other is in Mill Street. It consists of 24 pits and affords employment to 6 men.

There are 3 chandleries: that in Bridge Street employs 5 men, 1 in Church Street employs 3 men, the second in the same street employs 2 men. There is a small rope walk in Broughshane Street; it affords employment to 2 men.

Banks

There is a branch each of the Provincial Bank of Ireland, the Belfast Banking Company and the Northern Banking Company in Ballymena.

The Provincial Bank established a branch here in 1833 and in 1835 built a house for the bank in Wellington Street, Francis Skelly Esquire, manager. It circulates 10,000 pounds weekly.

The Belfast and Northern Banking Companies had agents here until 1834, when they each established a branch bank here. The Belfast Banking Company's office is in Bridge Street, John Patrick Esquire, manager. It circulates about 8,000 weekly.

The Northern Banking Company's office is in Shambles Street, Messrs James and Robert Young, managers. It circulates about 3,000 pounds weekly.

Benefit of Banks

These banks are not only a great accommodation to the linen and other merchants attending the markets in Ballymena, but they have also a very advantageous effect on the country generally, as 2 respectable farmers or others, by joining in a bill, can procure at the banks the means of paying off a pressing demand such as for rent, and can take advantage of the interval between raising the money and lets becoming due to sell their cattle or crops when they may obtain a fair value for them; while on the other hand they might, to meet an emergency, be obliged to sell their property at a loss at a time when the markets are low. A few individuals may indeed be induced to speculate and eventually be ruined on their bills being

dishonoured. The local directors, however, from their knowledge of the country, are in a great measure a check on this and the country must be generally benefitted by the establishment of banks.

The nearest saving bank is that in the village of Gracehill, 1 and a half miles from Ballymena. It formerly was held in Ballymena (for an account of it, see parish of Ahoghill).

Markets

The pork market is held in Ballymena on every Tuesday throughout the season, which continues from the middle of October to the end of May. This market was established in the year 1810 and continues to increase. In the year ending June 1834, 10,909 dead pigs were weighed at the crane and 12,587 were weighed in the year ending June 1835. The pigs are exposed on carts in the public streets. For the rules and regulations of this market, see Appendix.

The butter market is held in similar manner on the same day, but the principal sale is on Saturdays. It also is increasing: 9,153 firkins were sold in the year ending June 1834 and 9,537 firkins in the year ending June 1835.

The corn market was established in the year 1809 and is increasing rapidly. It also is exposed in sacks on carts in the streets.

In the year ending June 1834, 17,154 cwt of oats was sold in Ballymena; of this, 8,000 cwt was purchased by Mr Walkinshaw at the distillery (on Saturdays chiefly, that day being more convenient for the country people, on account of the general market held on it). In the year ending June 1835, 23,317 cwt of oats was sold in Ballymena, and of this, 12,000 cwt was purchased by Mr Walkinshaw. There is not any other grain sold in Ballymena, the country not producing wheat.

Linen Market

The great weekly market is held on Saturdays. This market is increasing and has increased considerably of late years. Armagh was formerly considered the greatest inland market in Ireland, Dungannon the second and Ballymena the third. Now Ballymena is considered equal, if not superior, to Armagh and may probably be considered the greatest inland market in the kingdom. It has of late years almost totally absorbed the trade of the surrounding towns and country. The linen markets of Portglenone, Randalstown, and Ahoghill have merged into it, and much of the fine linen formerly sold in the Belfast market is now brought here.

The quantity of everything exposed for sale has increased. 5 years ago not more than from 4,000 pounds to 5,000 pounds worth of linen was sold in it on a weekly average, while now there is fully 9,000 pounds worth. It includes the qualities worth from 3d to 5s per yard. The webs are exposed for sale by the weavers in the linen hall off Castle Street, where the linen merchants write on them their name and price agreed upon. They afterwards pay for them in rooms in the different inns, or in houses hired for the purpose by the year. 2d is deducted from the price of each web by the buyer. In case he "pays his webs" at an inn, this sum is given to the proprietor for the use of the room, and the merchant gets his dinner and drink for 1 s. But those merchants who buy extensively and reside in the neighbourhood have houses for the purpose and keep the 2d. This, to some, is a matter of consequence, as instances of one family or firm purchasing 1,500 pounds worth of linen in one market is not unusual.

Previous to being sold, the seal master measures the length and breadth of the web and affixes his seal as a guarantee for its being of sufficient breadth, of an equal fineness throughout, and that it is not pasted. For this he receives 2d from the manufacturer. Pasting is a trick resorted to by the manufacturer, who dexterously coats it with a paste of potatoes, starch or white lead to make it appear firmer and closer woven than it really is, by which he may obtain from 1d to 3d per yard more than its real value. On the process of bleaching being commenced the linen, if pasted with white lead, blackens and rots. For this offence the manufacturer and seal master are liable to fines of from 5s to 40s.

The sale of cloth takes place between the hours of 10 and 12 and the payment of it from 12 until 3.

Yarn Market

The yarn market is held in the streets, but principally about the market house. It also has increased considerably of late. 3 years ago there was not more than 400 pounds sold in each market, while now there is 2,000 pounds worth. The yarn is made up in small bunches called hanks, each hank contains 12 cuts and each cut 120 threads. A hank is generally 1 continued thread reeled into a length of about 6 feet, which is therefore the length of the threads in each cut. 4 hanks make a spangle, by which it is usually sold. The number of hanks spun from a lb denotes its quality as to fineness, the finest being the highest priced. The yarn sold in Ballymena market is from 2 to 10 hanks to the lb and fetches from 1s 3d to 3s per

spangle. The yarn market is mostly over by 10 o'clock.

Flax Market

The flax market has increased very rapidly of late. 5 years ago there was not 3 cwt of flax sold in Ballymena market, while now there is an average weekly sale of 600 pounds worth. The reason of this increase is the introduction of mill-spun yarn, which can be produced at a much lower price than the hand-spun yarn, and the consequently increased demand for it. There never was so much flax sown in this country as in 1835, and there is no crop which pays so well. It is sold in the streets and at present fetches from 6s to 10s per stone. The flax crop this year (1835) has paid from 16 pounds to 20 pounds per acre.

Sale of Hides

Hides are sold during the week, but chiefly on Saturdays. In the year ending June 1834, 876 hides were weighed and in the year ending June 1835, 2,448 hides were weighed at the public crane.

Sale of Livestock

Cattle of all kinds are sold on Saturdays in a spacious field enclosed for the purpose by a 6 feet wall. This market was built in 1831 by Mr Adair, the proprietor, and is at the northern side of the town, off William Street. In the year 1833 100 cows were sold in this market on a weekly average. In the year 1834 120 were sold weekly, and in 1835 about 140 weekly.

Horses are not exposed in more than 6 or 7 markets in the year, and then when the ploughing and drawing of manure into the fields is finished. From 4 to 20 horses are exposed in each of these markets. The number of horses exposed on Saturdays is decreasing.

In the year ending June 1834 there were 7,500 pigs exposed for sale on Saturdays, being a weekly average of 144. In the year ending June 1835 there were 7,976 live pigs exposed for sale, being a weekly average of 153.

There is a little increase in the number of sheep exposed for sale, there now being about 20 on average in each market.

There are generally a couple of goats in each market.

Sale of Goods

The sale of bran is increasing: about 30 sacks are now sold weekly.

The sale of meal in the market is decreasing: last year there were about 35 sacks of 3 cwt each sold on a weekly average; this year there have not been more than 30 sacks. This decrease is partly owing to the increased use of baker's bread by the lower class in consequence of the cheapness of that article and also to there being more meal sold in the shops than formerly.

About 12 cwt of flour is sold weekly. The flour, meal and bran are sold in the lower part of the market house.

About 80 cars of potatoes are sold on a weekly average; each car contains from 9 to 10 bushels. They are chiefly sold in Wellington or High Street.

During the season the apple market is very large. On Hallow Eve day 1835 there were 500 sacks of apples in Ballymena market. The quantity of course fluctuates, and declines towards the end of the season. They are sold along the sides of the streets and are principally brought from the parishes of Killead and Drummaul in this county.

The shoemakers' stalls on the market days are ranged along the east side of Bridge Street. There are about 30 of them in each market. The shoes sell at from 3s to 5s per pair and are mostly made of kip leather.

Lime and bricks are sold in Wellington Street. The former is brought from Glenarm and Carnlough on the coast, and also from the lime-kilns in Armoy parish. There are generally 13 cars of it in town on Saturdays and the usual price is 13d per barrel. Bricks are brought from the banks of the Bann. There are generally 15 or 16 cars of them in each market. They sell at from 10d ha'penny to 16d per 100 according to their quality.

Pedlars' stalls with soft goods are ranged along the sides of Castle Street. There are generally 14 of these covered stalls in each market.

Fish are sold at the corner of Bridge Street and Shambles Street. The supply of course varies according to the season. Fine Bann eels from Toome and Portna, the very fine trout and the pullen or freshwater herring from Lough Neagh are sold in abundance in summer. The trout sell for 3d, the eels, according to the size, from 2d ha'penny to 3d ha'penny and the pullen for 2d per lb. Salmon, when plentiful, is brought from the coast and from Belfast, and sells at from 4d to 6d per lb. In winter codfish is well supplied from Carrickfergus, and salt eels and herrings are also sold at that season.

From 50 to 60 carcases of beef and 20 carcases of mutton are exposed for sale in the meat market and shambles on Saturdays. Some very good meat is sold in this market. It rates at from 1d ha'penny to 5d per lb, according to the quantity and season, and mutton at from 3d ha'penny to 5d per lb. There is a good deal of slink, but very little fed veal. There are generally 10 stands of bacon or salt meat in each market. The supply is always greater towards Christmas or Easter. It sells at from 4d to 5d per lb.

The only vegetables are a few loads of cabbages and a few stalls of onions. The latter sell at from 1d to 1d ha'penny per lb.

The foregoing are the articles principally sold in Ballymena market on Saturdays. For an abstract account of the weekly sales, see Appendix. The markets and the fairs are held and the customs levied according to a patent granted in the 2nd year of Charles I to William Adair, an ancestor of the present proprietor.

Fairs

There are 2 annual fairs, one on the 26th July and the other on the 21st October. The latter, however, is inconsiderable. Though these fairs are general marts, still, cattle only are sold in any quantity. The number of cows sold on fair days is commonly about double that on market days. The number of horses varies from 300 to 350. They are of an inferior description and suited only for farming purposes. Pigs are bought up in considerable numbers by dealers for exportation, both at markets and fairs. Black cattle are not in much demand for exportation. Bullocks and beef cattle are sometimes in winter brought from Fermanagh and the west of Ireland to the markets and to the October fair. The number of cattle exposed in the fairs in 1834 and 1835 was much the same, but was an increase on the preceding years.

Pedlar's and other soft goods, with some yarn, constitute the other articles which are principally sold in these fairs.

Supply of Goods

The farmers generally bring their produce to markets and fairs. The supplies of the different articles varies but little throughout the year, there being no gluts nor scarcities of any consequence. At the seasons of seed time and harvest, when the attention of the farmers and manufacturers is turned towards their farms, the supply of linen and yarn is not so abundant, but this continues but for a short time.

Ballymena is well supplied with butcher's meat, milk, butter, eggs and fruit. Poultry are plentiful.

They are sold alive at the doors at low prices. The supply of vegetables is very bad. But few cattle are grazed or stall fed about the town for beef. There is no dairying, no market gardening. Grazing for the cattle of the inhabitants is conveniently situated and lets for about 3 pounds per acre.

Timber of all kinds is brought from Belfast. Pine is the description mostly used. It costs in Belfast from 1s 5d to 1s 6d per cubic foot. The carriage of it from Belfast to Ballymena is 3d ha'penny per cubic foot. Memel timber costs in Belfast 2s 4d per cubic foot and 3d ha'penny per cwt carriage. Slates also are brought from Belfast, where the prices are usually: mill <milled> ton slates 3 pounds 2s 6d per ton, queen ton slates 2 pounds 17s 6d per ton and imperial ton slates 3 pounds 7s 6d per ton. Their carriage from Belfast is from 8d to 10d per cwt. Lime is brought from Carnlough and Glenarm on the coast and from the lime-kilns in Armoy parish. The usual price is 13d per barrel. Bricks are brought from the banks of the River Bann. They usually cost when laid down from 10d ha'penny to 1s 6d per cwt.

Quarries

There are some excellent (though small) basalt and whinstone quarries in the immediate neighbourhood of the town. A white porphyry commonly called Tardree stone is bought from a lately opened quarry in Tardree mountain, in the parish of Connor. It dresses very well and is an excellent stone for building. One large 3-storey house has just been built of it in Ballymena. It costs 4d per cubic foot at the quarry.

Fuel

Turf is the fuel chiefly used in Ballymena. The bogs are conveniently situated and from 6 to 7 loads can be drawn in a day. Turf costs when laid down from 63s to 67s per 100 gauges <gages> (a gauge is a cubic yard). Scotch coal is mostly brought from Glenarm on the coast, which is 16 miles distant. They cost there from 12s 6d to 15s per ton, and English coals cost there from 21s to 22s per ton. The carriage of it to Ballymena is 10s per ton.

Ballymena is well supplied with spring and river water. The air is considered pure and the climate healthy.

SOCIAL ECONOMY

Insurances

The Caledonian Insurance Company have an agent here, but there are very few insurances of any kind.

Combinations and Employment

There cannot be said to be any combinations among the tradesmen. There is an understanding among the tailors not to work under a certain price, and last summer the sawyers struck work and refused to work until they obtained an increase of wages, which was granted. No attempt at outrage or violence was attempted. Artisans and labourers (owing to the numbers employed in the manufacture of linen and as labourers in the bleach greens) are always in constant employment and obtain good wages. They are rather scarce, particularly at seed time and harvest.

Public Conveyances

Ballymena is well circumstanced for public conveyances. A reference to Appendix will more readily afford information on this head. The mail from Dublin and Belfast arrives at 12 noon and is dispatched at 20 minutes past 2 a.m. [p.m?], at which time the mail from Derry and Coleraine arrives.

There are 26 regular carriers or carmen plying from Ballymena to Belfast. They take 3 days to go and return. The charges for carriage vary from 8d to 1s per cwt.

There are neither hospitals nor dispensaries.

Education

The public endowed schools in Ballymena are: the diocesan school, Guy's Free School, the town free school, the female national school, a school partly supported by the London Hibernian Society and a female school supported by a lady. For a description of the diocesan school, see Appendix.

Guy's Free School was opened in 1821. It was built and is supported by funds left for the purpose by Mr John Guy, who, from having been a herdsman, by his extreme parsimony and frugality realised the sum which he has thus bequeathed.

The town free school is free and open to all who chose to go to it. If, from private motives, they wish to pay 1d a week, it is accepted, but not demanded. It is chiefly supported by private subscription, aided by the London Hibernian Society.

The female national schoolhouse was built partly by the board and partly by subscription, and is supported in a similar manner. It contains apartments for the mistress and her assistant.

The London Hibernian Society school is partly supported by that society and partly by the scholars.

The female school, which is supported by the lady (Mrs Harrison), is held in a house given by her. She also pays the mistress 15 pounds per annum.

Mendicity Society

The Mendicity Society was established in the year 1826 (on the 1st February). It has been principally supported by the voluntary contributions of the Ballymena people, aided by an annual contribution of from 30 pounds to 50 pounds from Mr Adair, the proprietor (who is non-resident), a small portion of fines levied at petty sessions and an applotment (by the high constable on the parish) averaging 63 pounds 9s 7d. Annually the annual average of contributions is 191 pounds 9s 7d and of sums derived in other ways 31 pounds. The average annual expenditure is 355 pounds 10s and number of persons assisted 131.

The rates of assistance are from 1s to 3s per fortnight for each person. This is distributed on every alternate Monday at the office of Mr Gihon in Wellington Street. Collectors are appointed for different districts in the town and the collections on Sundays at the Presbyterian meeting house in Castle Street are appropriated to the use of this institution. For details, see Table of Benevolence. The great object of this society is to suppress street begging and in this it has succeeded. A beadle continually patrols the streets to watch beggars or any loose or suspicious characters, and shoplifting is therefore but seldom known.

Clothing Society

The Clothing Society is managed by ladies and was established in 1827. It is supported by voluntary contributions and by the collections made at sermons preached for the purpose in the church and meeting houses. The funds of this society annually average 59 pounds. A small portion of this is derived from fines at petty sessions. About 150 poor persons annually receive clothing from this society (see Table of Benevolence).

Amusements and Character of the People

The Ballymena people are but little disposed for amusement, there being no public amusements nor convivial meetings. In the town there is little society except among families which are connected or intermarried. Party politics seem to operate against the interests of those espousing different opinions and here they are carried to a high pitch. The conservatives are, however, the stronger party. The others number but few of the gentry or upper class.

Strangers will find the town of Ballymena stupid and inhospitable, the people being chiefly engaged in business and solely bent upon making money. There is, however, a good deal of nice society among the neighbouring gentry and clergy, who are hospitable and attentive to strangers.

The Ballymena people are neither polished nor aristocratic in their manners, nor do they possess any taste. The gentlemen in business, though they are wealthy and live comfortably, seem to think that any intercourse with strangers would tend to disturb their domestic arrangements and interfere with their privacy. They therefore take no notice of them. They are rather a moral race (though the number of public houses, there being 107, would lead one to suppose otherwise). They are indeed rather fond of whiskey and too many indulge in it. On Saturday evenings the number of drunkards in the streets is disgraceful, but they are mostly from the country.

Conveyances

There is nothing which will at first strike a stranger more than the number of covered inside jauntings to be seen in the streets of Ballymena. There is scarce a gentleman's family which does not possess one of these conveyances, and here they seem to have superseded the necessity of chaises. There are no saddle horses kept exclusively for that purpose.

There are 4 chaises, 12 jaunting cars and 1 gig, with an equal number of horses, for hire. The charge per Irish mile for chaises is 1s and for gigs and cars 8d for 1 passenger. These conveyances are tolerably appointed and travel at the rate of 5 Irish miles per hour.

Remarks on Improvements

Ballymena has increased and improved and still continues to do so, chiefly owing to the prosperity of the linen trade, the increase of its markets and the consequent increase of the circulation of money among the dealers and persons carrying on business in it; and it may at present be considered one of the most rising and flourishing towns in the kingdom, as its increase in trade is keeping pace with its increase in size.

MODERN TOPOGRAPHY

Public Buildings in the Parish

The public buildings in the parish, besides those

already described under the head of Towns, consist of: the Roman Catholic chapel, which is situated within a quarter of a mile north of Ballymena, on the road to Clogh. It is simple and substantial in its structure, 60 feet long by 27 and a half feet wide, and capable of accommodating 800 persons. It was erected in 1828 at an expense of 475 pounds, which was defrayed partly by contributions and partly by a levy on the congregation, William Deans, architect.

Bridges

The bridges are: that over the Clogh river on the mail coach road from Ballymena to Ballymoney, called the Glaraford bridge, which consists of 1 large circular-segment arch. It is 60 feet long and 17 feet wide. It is not in a very sound state and from its being rather high, narrow and at the angle of the road, requires to be cautiously driven over.

The bridge over the Braid river on the road from Ballymena to Broughshane consists of 4 small semicircular arches and is 62 feet long and 20 wide.

Gentlemen's Seats

The Castle, contiguous to the east side of Ballymena, is now almost in ruins. It formerly was the residence of the Adair family, the proprietors of the estate. It has not, however, been occupied by them for many years. This house is of brick, 2-storey and presents 2 fronts, but in no respect has any pretensions to its name. Its situation is on the summit of a high bank sloping rapidly to the Braid river, both sides of which are beautifully wooded, and about the house there is a good deal of old timber.

The Parsonage, a neat and modern 2-storey house, the residence of the Reverend Hugh Smyth Cumming, the Protestant clergyman, is pleasantly situated near the northern end of the town of Ballymena. It was erected by the Board of First Fruits in 1824 and cost 700 pounds. The situation of this house is cheerful, commanding a view of the picturesque valley of the Braid.

Hougomont, the residence of Captain Harrison, situated in the townland of Bottom, on the road from Ballymena to Broughshane, from the latter of which towns it is distant 1 and a quarter miles.

Brigadie, the residence of John Tracey Esquire, is situated in the same townland, on the same road, and 1 and a half miles from Ballymena. The house is 2-storey and commodious.

Farm Lodge, the residence of Mrs Jones, contiguous to the north side of Ballymena.

Mills and Manufactories

The manufactories of this parish, besides those already described under the head of Towns, consist of: a beetling house, bleach mill and green, the property of Andrew Gihon Esquire and contiguous to the town of Ballymena. The bleach green extends over 11 acres 33 perches. The machinery of the beetling and wash mills is propelled by 2 breast water wheels, each 16 feet in diameter and 5 feet 8 inches broad.

There is a second beetling mill connected with this green. Its machinery is propelled by 2 breast water wheels, one of which is 10 feet 8 inches in diameter and 5 feet broad. The other is 18 feet in diameter and 5 feet broad.

There is another bleach green, beetling and wash mills, the property of Daniel Currel Esquire, situated in the townland of Ballygarvey, about 1 and three-quarter miles from Ballymena, near the road to Broughshane. This green extends over 31 acres 2 roods. The machinery is propelled by 4 wheels, one of which is 16 feet in diameter and 6 feet broad. The others are each 15 feet in diameter and 5 feet broad, all driven by breast water.

These mills are all situated on the Braid river, which affords a constant supply of water. There are no obstructions to the erection of machinery in this parish.

Communications

3 miles of the mail coach road from Belfast to Derry through Ballymena traverse the western side of this parish. Its average breadth is 26 feet. It is not very level, nor is it kept in very good repair. This road is repaired at the expense of the county at large.

4 and a half miles of the main road from Ballymena to Ballycastle through Cloghmills traverse this parish from north to south. Its average breadth is 22 feet. This road is hilly and is kept in but middling repair by the barony through which it passes.

4 and a half miles of the road from Ballymena to Cushendall traverse this parish from north to south. The average breadth of this road is 22 feet. This road is hilly, but might be rendered almost level without being more circuitous. It is also kept in indifferent repair by the barony.

There is a third of a mile of the road from Ballymena to Broughshane in this parish. Its average breadth is 27 feet. This is a well laid out road and kept in good order, but from its being rather low at the centre, the water does not run off it and is generally dirty.

The material used in the repair of these roads is chiefly whinstone, which is abundant and convenient.

The by-roads are sufficiently good and numerous, and are kept in repair by the barony in which they are situated. For an account of the bridges, see Public Buildings.

General Appearance and Scenery

There is little, if anything, in the natural state of this parish to interest the eye. The surface generally is low and undulating, formed of a succession of small oval hills, all nearly of the same character and height; and the general appearance of the country is rather bleak and dreary from the want of wood and hedgerows.

SOCIAL ECONOMY

Early Improvements

The inhabitants of this parish are almost exclusively of Scottish descent, many of them having come over to this country with the family of Adair, who obtained a grant of land in this parish from Charles I. These lands are still possessed by the same family, the town of Ballymena being the property of one of that name. The people in this parish have always been considered as industrious and quiet, being moral and well conducted, and retaining much of the wisdom of their forefathers. The march of improvements has of course extended to them, and they seem in no respect behind any, but rather superior to the inhabitants of some of the neighbouring parishes in general civilisation. They have a disagreeable familiarity and equality of manner, and at the same time a bluntness and independence of ideas. They are very obstinate, averse to innovation, but hospitable and charitable.

The linen trade has been the means of rendering the manufacturing class comfortable in their circumstances and their proximity to such a market as Ballymena, where the farmers can obtain prices very little below those in Belfast for their pork, butter and grain, has certainly contributed to their independence. All classes are comparatively comfortable and independent and at no period has this parish been in a more prosperous state, owing to the improvements in the price of and demand for linen, in the manufacture of which they are chiefly engaged. There are not any extensive farmers, nor many wealthy people among the lower ranks, but they are generally speaking snug and comfortable in their circumstances and manner of living.

Obstructions to improvement: none.

Local Government

There is an excellent magistrate, the Reverend Hugh Smyth Cumming (rector of the parish). His residence is conveniently situated at the Parsonage near Ballymena. He is both firm and respected and possesses the confidence of the people. There are 10 constabulary and their chief constable (who is sub-inspector of the county) stationed in Ballymena. Manor courts are held once a month in Ballymena for the recovery of sums under 2 pounds (late Irish currency) and courts leet once in 6 months for the same purpose, and for applotting sums to be levied on the manor for the payment of bailiffs, the repairs of pounds and similar incidental expenses, Peter Aickin Esquire, seneschal. Quarter sessions are held in Ballymena in January and July, the alternate terms being held in Ballymoney (for further details of these sessions, see Towns).

The criminal business at these sessions is rather on the increase, which is probably owing to the facility afforded for litigation by the petty sessions. It is considered that if the magistrates at the latter would punish more summarily instead of sending many of the minor cases to the quarter sessions, the business would be considerably lightened. The cases tried are, however, comparatively trivial, being mostly assaults, trifling riots and a few rescues.

Petty sessions are held on every alternate Monday in the town of Ballymena. The magistrates in the habit of attending are the Reverend H.S. Cumming, William Gihon, Thomas Birnie and Peter Aickin Esquires. There are generally 3 of these present. No outrages have been committed even within a distant period. There is neither illicit distillation nor smuggling. There are few insurances of any kind and few losses have been sustained by fire.

Dispensary

There is no dispensary. Though the people are generally healthy, still, as there are few towns like Ballymena without a proportionate number of poor inhabitants, a dispensary would be a useful establishment in this parish. No contagious or infectious diseases are prevalent.

Schools

No description of school has tended more towards the improvement of the morals of the people than the Sunday schools, the introduction of which into their parish has been general. The establishment of day schools in this parish is not of a recent date, but those of the present day are of an improved description. They are gladly resorted to by the people, few of whom are unable to read (see Table of Schools).

Poor

The only provision for the poor is the Mendicity Society in Ballymena (see Appendix and Towns). It was established in 1826 and is supported chiefly by voluntary contributions, aided by an applotment on the parish (levied by the chief constable) and a small portion of the fines at petty sessions. Its object is to suppress street begging and to assist the aged and infirm, who receive from 1s to 3s per fortnight on every alternate Monday.

There is a clothing society conducted by a few ladies and supported by voluntary contribution (see Towns and Table of Benevolence) and collections at sermons for the purpose.

There is a sum of between 300 and 400 pounds in the hands of the judge of the consistorial court of the diocese. It was left in 1806 by a Mr Ellis for the support of poor widows in this parish, but there being some difference of opinion as to how it should be distributed, it lies untouched.

There is a sum of 100 pounds in the hands of the Reverend H.S. Cumming (rector of the parish) which was bequeathed in 1802 by a Mr Brown, but as a similar difference of opinion exists with regards to its disposal, it also remains untouched, the interest being annually funded.

The people of this parish are charitable, particularly the lower orders, who seldom withhold their assistance (chiefly in meal or potatoes) from the poor who solicit it. There are, however, comparatively few poor in this parish.

Religion

By the revised census of 1834 there are in this parish 810 Episcopalians, 5,153 Presbyterians (of different denominations), 96 other Dissenters, 1,238 Roman Catholics and 61 whose religion was unknown.

This parish is an impropriate cure in the gift of Earl Mountcashel. The late earl sold the tithes to William Adair Esquire, the proprietor of the estate, but retained the right of presentation. Earl Mountcashel pays the Reverend H.S Cumming (his chaplain), who resides at the parsonage, 30 pounds per annum. This parish is episcopally united to the adjoining one of Ballyclug, the tithes of which, amounting to about 150 pounds per annum, are paid to Mr Cumming. Mr Cumming has also a glebe house and 8 acres of glebe land.

The Presbyterian minister of the meeting house in Castle Street receives a stipend of 100 pounds per annum from his congregation and a regium donum of 100 pounds per annum.

The minister of the Presbyterian meeting house in Wellington Street (a second-class congregation) receives a stipend of between 90 and 100 pounds per annum and a regium donum of 75 pounds per annum. These last 2 congregations are in connection with the Synod of Ulster.

The Presbyterian minister of the Seceder meeting house in High Street receives an annual stipend of 50 pounds and a regium donum of 50 pounds per annum.

The Methodist clergyman receives a salary of [blank] per annum.

It is impossible to find out the different ways in which the priest is remunerated by his flock.

Habits of the People: Houses

The houses of the lower order in this parish are in general more cleanly and comfortable than those in most of the adjoining ones. They are mostly 1-storey, all built of stone and generally thatched. They chiefly consist of at least 2 apartments and are comparatively neat when contrasted with others, being more compact, in better repair and more generally whitened. Their furniture also is of rather a better description. They are generally in clusters of from 3 to 6 and are generally sheltered by a few trees. They still, however, retain the abominable custom of having manure heaps before the door. Their floors are all earthen and they receive light from at least 2 lead windows. One apartment is generally occupied as a kitchen and in the second are the beds and the loom. Internally these houses are usually cleanly and sometimes present a strong contrast to their outward appearance.

Food and Fuel

Meal, potatoes, bacon, herring and milk constitute their principal food. Baker's bread, being now cheap, has in a great measure superseded the uses of that made of oaten meal. Much less meal is used than formerly, and many of the manufacturing families use tea in the morning and few of the old people fail to use it at some period of the day. The bacon or hang beef is fried in a pan with eggs and is used at dinner. Any kind of meat, butter or fat is called "kitchen" or "an accompaniment for potatoes."

They burn good fires, the bogs being conveniently situated, and the fir timber or bog wood found in the bog also serves as a sort of light by which they can spin.

Occupations: Weaving

The parish contains 587 houses, inhabited by 627 families. Of these, 309 families are employed in agriculture, 212 in trade, manufacture or handicraft, all other families 106. The male population amounts to 1,627, the female to 1,664.

There are about 350 persons employed in weaving, 280 of whom manufacture or weave yarn which is given out to them. For this their wages are good, they being paid according to the quality of their work. The females of the family are employed in spinning, though not so much so as formerly, the wages for hand-spinning never exceeding and seldom amounting to 6d per day. It serves, however, to give them employment when they would otherwise be unoccupied. The younger members of a family where there is a loom are employed in winding the yarn on little circular sticks called bobbins. These are put into the shuttle which is used by the weaver. Thus in a family where weaving is carried on, every member of it is engaged in some branch of the process, and a useful spirit and habit of industry is instilled into the younger members of it, by rendering them useful at an age when they would otherwise be idle.

Morality

The inhabitants of this parish are honest, peaceable and industrious. They are rather fond of indulging in whiskey at fairs and markets, and the number of drunken persons to be seen in the streets of Ballymena on fair and market evenings is shameful. Bastards are rather numerous, but this seldom operates to the disadvantage of the female, as there are few instances of her remaining unmarried in consequence of her frailty.

Sunday is properly observed. There may be some confirmed drunkards who frequent public houses on that day, but the majority observe it strictly.

Dress

The inhabitants of this parish dress remarkably well, the females all wearing bonnets, shoes and stockings. They dress with some degree of taste and neatness, and make a respectable appearance on Sundays and at fairs and markets; calico, which constitutes the principal part of their wear, being so very low that good clothes are within the reach of almost all. The men also dress very well

and comfortably. Dark blue is the favourite colour for coats, and their appearance also is respectable. An umbrella is an indispensable appendage to the dress of both sexes.

Marriage and Longevity

The usual number in a family is 5. They do not marry remarkably early. There are always to be found in every townland persons of from 70 to nearly 80 years of age. They in general live to good age, though there are not any remarkable instances of longevity.

Amusements

Dancing, which used to be their principal amusement, is now almost given up. It is indeed their only amusement. The younger people are fond of going to the summer fairs, but they have not the same spirit for amusement as formerly. Hallow Eve is still a little observed by the burning of nuts etc. Easter is but little observed except as a time of idleness, and there are also a few idle days about Christmas <Christmass>, but the observance of these festivals is rapidly wearing away. The boys have a habit of knocking at the doors and then running away for the fortnight preceding Hallow Eve. Cock-fighting is almost wholly given up and is only resorted to by the more profligate, as is also the case with card-playing.

Party politics seem to occupy much of the attention of and run high among all classes, particularly in Ballymena. The Orangemen celebrate the 12th July and the Freemasons the 24th June, by processions.

There are no patrons nor patrons' days, nor have they any local customs, peculiar games, legendary tales nor music. Nor is there anything peculiar in them except their familiarity of manners and ideas of equality, chiefly owing to there being so few of the aristocracy among them, and those persons who, having become gentlemen from having realised large fortunes, still retaining much of their natural and former notions and manners. The inhabitants of most of the adjoining parishes partake of this peculiarity.

Emigration and Migration

There is very little emigration from this parish. The people are generally doing well at home and not more than 10 individuals (on an average) annually emigrate. They embark mostly in spring and go to Canada or the United States of America; few return.

Few, if any, go to the Scotch or English harvests. It is only the very poor and idle who do go, and there are not many of these in this parish.

Remarkable events: none.

Appendix to Memoir by James Boyle

SOCIAL ECONOMY

Newspapers and Periodicals

A list of the newspapers and periodicals in circulation in the town of Ballymena and its vicinity in the year 1835. [Table gives title, number of copies, frequency of publication].

Belfast Guardian, 17, thrice a week; *Belfast Newsletter*, 23, thrice a week; *Belfast Commercial Chronicle*, 18, thrice a week; *Belfast Northern Whig*, 20, twice a week; *Belfast Northern Herald*, 22, once a week; *Londonderry Sentinel*, 1, once a week; *Dublin Evening Mail*, 3, thrice a week.

Periodicals: *Christian Examiner*, 1; *Blackwood's Magazine*, 3; *University Magazine*, 3; *Tait's Magazine*, 12; *Doyle's Farmer's Magazine*, 3; *Saturday Farmer's Magazine*, 12; *Penny Farmer's Magazine*, 12; *Chamber's Journal*, 40; *Penny Journal*, 50; *Orthodox Presbyterian*, 50; *London Quarterly Review*, 2; *Westminster Quarterly Review*, 2; *Edinburgh Review*, 1; *Medical Chirurgical Review*, 3; *Presbyterian Review*, 4; *Lancet*, 1; *Lardner's Cabinet Cyclopedia*, 1; *British Cyclopedia*, 5; *Penny Cyclopedia*, 6; *Musical Library*, 3.

Fine Arts: *Illustrations of the Bible*, 4; *Illustrations of Byron's Works*, 8; *Byron's Beauties*, 2; *Hogarth's Gallery*, 1; *Gallery of the Graces*, 3; *Gallery of Portraits*, 1; *Irish Scenery*, 3; *National Gallery*, 1.

Table of Conveyances

A list of the conveyances plying with or passing through Ballymena. [Table gives conveyance, distance travelled, route, time of arrival, fares, days of plying].

Mail coach from Belfast to Derry, 69 miles; leaves Belfast at 8.30 a.m.; passes through Ballymena at 12 noon; arrives in Derry at 8.20 p.m.; inside fare 16s, outside fare 9s 6d; daily.

Same coach from Derry to Belfast, 69 miles; leaves Derry at 6 p.m.; passes through Ballymena at 2.20 a.m.; arrives in Belfast at 7 a.m.; inside fare 8s, outside fare 4s 6d; daily.

Commerce stage-coach, 23 miles; leaves Ballymena at 4 a.m.; arrives in Belfast at 8.30 a.m.; leaves Belfast at 4 p.m.; inside fare 4s, outside fare 2s 6d; daily except Sunday.

Champion stage-coach from Belfast to Coleraine, 43 miles; leaves Belfast at 1 p.m.; passes through Ballymena at 5.20 p.m.; arrives at Coleraine at 9 p.m.; inside fare 6s, outside fare 4s 6d; Mondays, Wednesdays and Fridays.

Same coach from Coleraine to Belfast, 43 miles; leaves Coleraine at 8 a.m.; passes through Ballymena at 12 noon; arrives in Belfast at 5 p.m.; inside fare 4s, outside fare 6s; Tuesdays, Thursdays and Saturdays.

A 2-horse covered car carrying 10 passengers, 23 miles; leaves Ballymena at 4.a.m.; arrives in Belfast at 8.30 a.m.; leaves Belfast at 4.30 p.m.; inside fare 4s, outside fare 2s 6d; daily except Sundays.

A 1-horse car from Ballymena to Ballymoney, 14 miles; leaves Ballymena at 9 p.m.; arrives in Ballymoney at 12 [mid]night; leaves Ballymena at [blank]; outside fare 2s; daily except Sundays.

2 single-horse cars from Cloghmills, 8 miles; leave Cloghmills at 8 a.m.; arrive in Ballymena at 10 a.m.; leave Ballymena at 4 p.m.; outside fare 1s 6d; Saturdays.

2 single-horse cars from Portglenone, 7 miles; leave Portglenone at 8 a.m.; arrive in Ballymena at 10 a.m.; leave Ballymena at 4 p.m.; outside fare 1s; Saturdays.

A car from Belfast to Ballymena, 23 miles; leaves Belfast at 6 a.m.; arrives in Ballymena at 10.20 a.m.; leaves Ballymena at 4 p.m.; outside fare 3s; Saturdays.

A car from Antrim to Ballymena, 9 miles; leaves Antrim at 8 a.m.; arrives in Ballymena at 10 a.m.; leaves Ballymena at 5 p.m.; outside fare 1s; Saturdays.

A car from Ahoghill to Ballymena, 3 miles; leaves Ahoghill at 9 a.m.; arrives in Ballymena at 10 a.m.; leaves Ballymena at: uncertain; outside fare 6d; Saturdays.

Ballymena Mendicity Society

An account of the receipts and expenditure of the Ballymena Mendicity Society for the years 1826 to 1834.

1826: no account of the year's proceedings has been kept.

1827: sums received this year 352 pounds 3s 11d ha'penny; sums given to paupers 328 pounds 16s 6d; balance in hand 23 pounds 7s 5d ha'penny.

1828: collections 291 pounds 6s; collection in meeting on Sundays 36 pounds 9s; applotments 50 pounds; balance from last year 23 pounds 7s 5d ha'penny; total 401 pounds 2s 5d ha'penny; sums given to paupers 327 pounds 1s; incidental expenses 2 pounds 4s 6d; total expenditure 329 pounds 5s 6d; balance in hand 71 pounds 16s 11d.

1829: balance from last year 71 pounds 16s 11d; collections 291 pounds 18s 10d ha'penny; collection in meeting on Sundays 7 pounds 10d ha'penny; applotments 50 pounds; total 348 pounds 19s 9d; sums given to paupers 303 pounds 6s 9d; incidental expenses 1 pound 16s; total expenditure 305 pounds 2s 9d; balance in hand 43 pounds 17s;

1830: no account of this year's proceedings has been preserved.

1831: balance from last year 62 pounds 10s 6d; collections 187 pounds 16s 9d; collection in meeting on Sundays 15 pounds 19s 9d ha'penny; applotments 76 pounds 10s 11d ha'penny; fines from magistrates 5s; total 339 pounds 19s 9d; sums given to paupers 291 pounds 18s 7d; incidental expenses 2 pounds 8s; total expenditure 294 pounds 6s 7d; balance 45 pounds 13s 2d.

1832: balance from last year 45 pounds 16s 5d; collections 216 pounds 17s 6d; collection in meeting on Sundays 18 pounds 13s 10d; applotments 77 pounds 5s 10d; fines 9 pounds; total 343 pounds 14s 1d; sums paid to paupers 266 pounds 10s 5d; incidental expenses 3 pounds; total expenditure 269 pounds 10s 5d; balance 74 pounds 3s 8d.

1833: balance from last year 74 pounds 3s 8d; collections 185 pounds 10s 11d; collection in meeting on Sundays 16 pounds 18s 9d ha'penny; applotments 77 pounds; fines 22 pounds 5s 7d; total 375 pounds 8s 6d ha'penny; paid former secretary 10 pounds 5s 3d; sums paid to paupers 219 pounds 9s 9d; incidental expenses 2 pounds 14s 6d; total expenditure 232 pounds 9s 6d; balance in hand 142 pounds 19s ha'penny.

1834: balance from last year 142 pounds 19s ha'penny; collections 175 pounds 17s; collection in meeting house on Sundays 26 pounds 1s 1d ha'penny; applotments 75 pounds; fines 15 pounds 16s 11d ha'penny; total 435 pounds 14s 1d ha'penny; paid late secretary 9 pounds 6s 9d; sums paid to paupers 265 pounds 2s 3d; incidental expenses 2 pounds 7s 2d; total expenditure 376 pounds 16s 2d; balance in hand 158 pounds 17s 11d ha'penny.

In the year 1827, 126 paupers received assistance; in the year 1828, 124 paupers received assistance; in the year 1829, 125 paupers received assistance; in the year 1831, 149 paupers received assistance; in the year 1832, 132 paupers received assistance; in the year 1833, 160 paupers received assistance; in the year 1834, 136 paupers received assistance.

Markets

A statement of the average quantity and probable value of the principal commodities sold in the markets of Ballymena for the year 1835.

Weekly sales (on Saturdays): linen 9,000 pounds, yarn 2,000 pounds, flax 600 pounds, butter 402 pounds 12s, hides 23 pounds, oatmeal 40 pounds, flour 11 pounds, bran 13 pounds, apples 30 pounds, cows 450 pounds, horses 80 pounds, pigs 191 pounds 5s, sheep 15 pounds, goats 16s, beef 260 pounds, mutton 20 pounds, potatoes 35 pounds, [total] 13,171 pounds 13s. Weekly sales of pork on Tuesdays (during the season): 358 pigs weighing 716 cwt, worth 25s per cwt, [total] 895 pounds. Weekly sales of corn, chiefly sold on Wednesdays (during the season): 614 cwt, worth on an average 6s per cwt, [total] 189 pounds 4s.

Market Rules

Rules and regulations to be observed in the markets in Ballymena, 27th October 1834.

Pork market: the following deductions to be made from the price of pork where it is liable to the following objections according to the opinion of the buyer, viz. measled pork: lightly, 2s per cwt; moderately, 3s per cwt; much, 5s per cwt; extremely, to be left to the buyer and seller to settle as they can.

Tainted pork: light smelling, 2s per cwt; much, 3s per cwt; very much, 5s per cwt; when slaughtered a length of time, or when sent to the market in consequence of disease or what is termed "fallen" or from accident, left to the buyer and seller to settle as they can.

Blooding in a wrong or injurious direction, 1s per carcass.

Boars: the terms of purchase to be settled between buyer and seller as before.

Butter market: for weighing 1 cask or crock of butter 1d.

Grain market: the following rates for weighing, custom and porterage: 1 cwt 1d, 2 cwt 2d, 3 cwt 3d, 4 cwt 4d, 1 lb tare per cwt. The grain market not to commence before 8 o'clock, to be announced by rings of bell.

Meal market: the following rates for weighing, custom and porterage: a sack of meal not exceeding 2 cwt 3d, tare 1 lb; a sack of meal exceeding 2 cwt 4d, tare 2 lb; a sack of meal exceeding 4 cwt 2 quarters 4d ha'penny, tare 3 lb.

Flax market: the following charges for weighing: under 2 quarters, a ha'penny; from 2 quarters to a cwt, 1d; from a cwt to a cwt 2 quarters, 1d ha'penny.

Hides: the following are the tares deducted from hides: a cow's hide 4 lb, a bullock's hide 6 lb, a bull's hide 8 lb, from 15 to 30 lb, half tare.

Tolls and Customs

A schedule of the tolls, customs demanded and payable to William Adair Esquire by ancient usage in this town on each of the following articles brought for sale, viz. a boll of meal or oats 2d ha'penny, a load of meal 2d ha'penny, a stand of bread 1d, a load of salt 1d, a load of fruit 1d, a load of wool 2d, a load of timber 1d, a load of fish 1d, a load of cabbage plants 2d, a load of earthenware 1d, a load of empty firkins a ha'penny, a load of wooden bowls 1d, a sack of bran 1d, a sack of beans or peas 1d ha'penny, a sack of eels 1d, a carcass of beef 3d, a cwt of cheese 1d, a mutton 1d, a fat or fed veal 1d, a stand with old clothes 2d, a live sheep a ha'penny, 6 lbs of butter a ha'penny, a hog or carcass of pork 1d, a boxcar of potatoes 2d, a sack of potatoes 1d, a hatter's stand 1d, a merchant's stand, covered or uncovered, 2d, a horse bought or exchanged 3d, a cow bought or exchanged 2d, a shoemaker's barrel or stand with shoes 1d, a creel or stand with stockings 1d, a firkin of butter retailed 1d, a cwt of butter a ha'penny, a bag of flour 2d, a creel of trout (lake or sea) 1d, a creel of fresh herrings 1d, a car of fresh herrings 2d, a car with small pigs 2d, a car with live sheep 2d.

To be paid by the buyer: a cow hide 1d, a kip hide a ha'penny, a cwt of tallow or fat 4d, a sheepskin unshorn a ha'penny, a half dozen of veal skins 1d, a pig skin a ha'penny.

To be paid at fairs: a merchant's stand covered 6d, a merchant's stand uncovered 4d, a bag of any other article not before enumerated brought for sale 4d.

There is a discretionary power vested in the custom gatherer to remit the custom on some articles, such as droves of unsold bullocks, by way of encouragement to dealers to come to this market. The customs of Ballymena amount annually to something more than 200 pounds. They are said to be expended by the agent, William Gihon Esquire, in improving the town.

Trades and Occupations

Attorneys 3, architects 4, apothecaries and surgeons 8, bankers 3, bakers 8, barbers 5, butchers 9, blacksmiths 6, bleachers 3, bellhangers 1, bonnet makers 20, booksellers 2, blood-letters 2, clergymen 4, carpenters (house) 7, carpenters (mill) 1, cartmakers 2, curriers 2, coachmakers 1, cabinet makers 3, chandlers 3, carmen 26, clock makers 5, constabulary 10, dressmakers 26, drapers (woollen) 9, dyers 5, delf, glass and china shops 6, flax dressers 1, fruit sellers 11, grocers 36, gardeners 0, gaugers 2, hotel keepers 2, hucksters <huxters> 28, houses of lodging and entertainment 40, hatters 4, hacklers <hecklers> 1, hosiers 3, heddle makers 5, hardware shops 4, haberdashers 14, innkeepers and publicans 107, ironmongers 4, leather cutters 6, milliners 5, mantua makers 4, merchants (timber) 3, merchants (slate) 3, musicians and music master 2, musical instrument makers 2, midwives 2, notaries 1, nailers <nailors> 14, newspaper agents 3, old cloth sellers 4, pork merchants 13, painters and glaziers 11, pawnbrokers 2, physicians 2, pedlars 8, prostitutes 8, paviours 2, paupers 150, rope makers 2, ragmen 5, reed makers 4, shuttle makers 3, shoemakers 5, schoolmasters 5, schoolmistresses 4, saddlers 4, soap boilers 3, sawyers 10, thatchers 2, turners and wheelwrights 4, tailors 17, tanners 2, whitesmiths 2, weavers [blank], [subtotal] 193, yarn buyers 1, brought over 528.

Table of Trades and Occupations

Professions auxiliary to justice, benevolence: physicians 2, surgeons 8, attorneys 3.

Professions auxiliary to commerce: bankers and clerks 7, notaries 1, insurance office 1, coach agents 3.

Trades and manufacturing auxiliary to rural and general production, supplementary to rural production: bakers 8, stocking makers 3, shoemakers 5, tailors 17, milliners 5, bonnet makers 21, dyers 5, hatters 4, chandlers 3, wheelwrights 4, coach and car makers 3, carpenters 7, sawyers 10, cabinet makers 3, coopers 8, masons 11, stone cutters 2, plasterers 3, thatchers 2.

Auxiliary to rural and general production: smiths 8, nailers 14, painters and glaziers 11, saddlers 4, watchmakers 5.

Trades of distribution auxiliary to general production, rural production, luxury, [and] instruction: printers 2, book binders 1, hairdressers 5, flour stores 3, butchers 9, leather sellers 6, woollen drapers 9, spirit sellers 107, sellers of ropes and rugs 7, grocers 37, haberdashers 14, ironmongers 4, china, delf and glass shops 6, timber and stave sellers 3, timber, slates and general sellers 2.

Instruction: stationers 2.

Benevolence: apothecaries (also surgeons) 8. Luxury: pawnbrokers 2.

Ballymena Protestant Society

Principles and intentions: it having appeared to several individuals in this town and neighbourhood that the constitution, that is, as it has been well defined, "that parcel of usages by which the country has been governed from time immemorial", is at present seriously endangered, nay its very existence attacked, by a ruthless and revolutionary party. For example: 1, the repeal of the legislative union between this country and Great Britain has been demanded and absolutely threatened.

2, the house of peers, our only security on the one hand against the exercise of an arbitrary power on the part of the sovereign, and on the other the only bulwark against democratic frenzy, has been assailed of late and the destruction of hereditary peerage imperatively demanded.

3, the religious establishments of England, Ireland, Scotland, by which the preaching of God's word and the administration of Christian ordinances are secured for every subject of the realm, are also marked out for destruction.

4, one of the leading principles of the blessed Reformation, viz. the unrestricted use of the Holy Scriptures at all times and by all persons who may feel disposed to use them, has been authoratively tampered with and practically held as unsound.

It was resolved to establish a society to be called the Ballymena Protestant Society, the object of which should be, by every peaceable and constitutional method in the power of its members, to counteract the efforts now making and likely hereafter to be made for the uprooting of those institutions, in possession of which this country has obtained a high degree of prosperity and glory. The objects of this society being simply to preserve and of course to repair when necessary, they will, at all times, be found ready to co-operate in bringing about every necessary improvement.

I certify that I have read the above statement of the principles upon which the Ballymena Protestant Society is founded, I approve of and will support them all, and am anxious that I should be admitted as a member, signed [blank]. I propose that the above-named be admitted as a member of this society, signed [blank]. I second the above proposal, signed [blank]. Dated this [blank] day of [blank] 183[remaining figure blank].

Ballymena Diocesan School

Course of instruction at the Ballymena diocesan school. [Table gives name and details of headmaster, terms for boarders and other scholars, number of pupils, details of classical authors, authors studied for composition, science and other subjects, general subjects, moral instruction. No free scholars, logic not studied].

The Reverend Robert Mathews A.M., headmaster, appointed on 12th December 1829 by his grace the lord primate. Salary 120 pounds per annum, endowed on the school by the united dioceses of Armagh and Connor, from the clergy of which diocese it is collected.

Terms: for boarders, if over 12 years old, 36 pounds 14s per annum; if not more than 12, 32 pounds 14s per annum; for day scholars of the first, second and third classes, 6 guineas per annum; for day scholars of the fourth, fifth and sixth classes, 4 guineas per annum.

Number of pupils: 1830, 8 boarders, 32 day scholars; 1831, 19 boarders, 42 day scholars; 1832, 16 boarders, 44 day scholars; 1833, 15 boarders, 33 day scholars; 1834, 15 boarders, 26 day scholars; 1835, 16 boarders, 22 day scholars.

Class 1. Classical: Greek, *Homer's Iliad, Xenophon's Cyropoedia* (3 books), *Walker's Lucian*, Greek Testament (4 Gospels and Acts); Latin: *Satires, Odes and Epistles* of Horace, 6 books of Virgil, 4 *Satires* of Juvenal, 2 plays of Terence, 3 books of Livy, Sallust; composition: *Valpy's Elegantiae Latinae*, Latin themes, *Nelson's Greek grammar*. Scientific: mathematics, third and sixth books of Euclid, algebra, equation, involution and evolution; arithmetic, involution, evolution, progressions. *Hinck's Ancient geography, Thomson's Modern geography*. General: mythology, Roman and Grecian history, astronomy, general history, writing. Morals: a lecture on Saturdays. The boys also prepare in *Watt's Scripture history* and the church catechism, as commented on in the *Bristol Tracts society's catechism*.

Class 2. Classical: Greek, *Xenophon's Cyropaedia*, Lucian, *Hinck's Greek grammar*; Latin: *Satires and Epistles* of Horace, 3 books of Livy, 4 *Satires* [of] Juvenal; composition: *Valpy's Elegantiae Latinae*, Latin themes, *Nelson's Greek grammar*. Scientific, mathematics: first and second books of Euclid, surds and fractions; arithmetic: exchange, equations of payment. *Hincks Ancient geography, Thomson's Modern geography*. General: mythology, Roman and Grecian history, astronomy, general history, writing. Morals: a lecture on Saturdays. The boys also prepare in *Watt's Scripture history* and the church catechism, as commented on in the *Bristol Tracts society's catechism*.

Class 3. Classical: Greek, *Walker's Lucian*, John's Gospel of the New Testament, *Hinck's Greek grammar*; Latin: 6 books of Virgil and Sallust, selections from Ovid, *Bryce's Prosody*; composition: *Mair's Latin exercises*. Scientific, mathematics, first book of Euclid, additional multiplication and division in algebra; arithmetic: interest, practice. *Hinck's Ancient geography, Thomson's Modern geography*. General: mythology, Roman and Grecian history, use of the globes, grammar and themes. Morals: a lecture on Saturdays. The boys also prepare in *Watt's Scripture history* and the church catechism, as commented on in the *Bristol Tracts society's catechism*.

Class 4. Classical: Greek, John's Gospel of the Greek Testament and *Hinck's Greek grammar*; Latin: *Sallust's First book of Caesar's commentaries, Valpy's Delectus, Bryce's Prosody, Rudiman's Rudiments*; composition: *Mair's Latin exercises*. Scientific: arithmetic, fractions and common decimals. *Thomson's Geography*. General: English grammar, themes and history, spelling, reading and writing. Morals: a lecture on Saturdays. The boys also prepare in *Watt's Scripture history* and the church catechism, as commented on in the *Bristol Tracts society's catechism*. —

Class 5. Classical: Greek, *Valpy's Delectus, Rudiman's Rudiments, Brice's Prosody*. Scientific: arithmetic, proportion. *Thompson's Geography*. General: English grammar, themes and history, spelling, reading and writing. Morals: a lecture on Saturdays. The boys also prepare in *Watt's Scripture history* and the church catechism, as commented on in the *Bristol Tracts society's catechism*.

Class 6. Scientific: arithmetic, addition, subtraction and reduction. *Thomson's Geography*. General: English grammar, themes and history, spelling, reading and writing. Morals: a lecture on Saturdays. The boys also prepare in *Watt's Scripture history* and the church catechism, as commented on in the *Bristol Tracts society's catechism*.

Class 7. Scientific: arithmetic, addition, subtraction and reduction. General: easy geography, spelling, reading. Morals: a lecture on Saturdays. The boys also prepare in *Watt's Scripture history* and the church catechism, as commented on in the *Bristol Tracts society's catechism*.

Table of Schools

[Table contains the following headings: name, situation and description, when established, income and expenditure, physical, intellectual and moral education, number of pupils subdivided by age, sex and religion, name and religion of master or mistress].

Under the London Hibernian Society, in a house built for the purpose by subscription in the townland of Ballygarvey, established 1832; income: from the London Hibernian Society annually 7 pounds 10s, from pupils 30 pounds; intellectual education: books of the London Hibernian Society; moral education: occasional visits from the clergy, Sunday school, Authorised Scriptures daily; number of pupils: males, 30 under 10 years of age, 14 from 10 to 15, 14 above 15, 56 total males; females, 21 under 10 years of age, 6 from 10 to 15, 27 total females; total number of pupils 83, 4 Protestants, 76 Presbyterians, 3 Roman Catholics; master John Craig, Presbyterian.

Under the London Hibernian Society, in a house built by subscription for the purpose in the townland of Craigawarren, established 1828; income from pupils 12 pounds; intellectual education: books of the London Hibernian Society; moral education, occasional visits from the clergy, Sunday school, Authorised Scriptures daily; number of pupils: males, 6 under 10 years of age, 5 from 10 to 15, 5 above 15, 16 total males; females, 12 under 10 years of age, 1 from 10 to 15, 1 above 15, 14 total females; total number of pupils 30, all Presbyterians; master Ben Johnson, Presbyterian.

Under the London Hibernian Society, in a house built by subscription for the purpose in the townland of Monaghan, established 1833; income: from the London Hibernian Society annually 4 pounds, 24 pounds from pupils; intellectual education: books of the London Hibernian Society, trigonometry, mensuration, book-keeping; moral education: occasional visits from the clergy, Sunday school, Authorised Scriptures daily; number of pupils: males, 4 under 10 years of age, 25 from 10 to 15, 5 above 15, 34 total males; females, 11 under 10 years of age, 5 from 10 to 15, 16 total females; total number of pupils 50, all Presbyterians; master James Thomson, Presbyterian.

National school, in a house built by subscription for the purpose in the townland of Clinty, established 1829; income: from the Board of National Education annually 8 pounds, from pupils 13 pounds; intellectual education: books of the Board of National Education; moral education: occasional visits from the Presbyterian minister, Sunday school, Authorised Version of the Scriptures at stated hours; number of pupils: males, 21 under 10 years of age, 6 from 10 to 15,

3 above 15, 30 total males; females, 11 under 10 years of age, 4 from 10 to 15, 15 total females; total number of pupils 45, 2 Protestants, 36 Presbyterians, 7 other denominations; master William John Hanna, Roman Catholic.

Private school, in a good house built by subscription in the townland of Drumfane, established more than 80 years ago; income from pupils 18 pounds; intellectual education: some of the books of the Kildare Society, *Gough's Arithmetic, Manson's and Universal reader and spelling books*; moral education: Scriptures and Shorter Catechisms daily, Sunday School, visits from the minister; number of pupils: males, 13 under 10 years of age, 3 from 10 to 15, 10 above 15, 26 total males; females, 8 under 10 years of age, 5 from 10 to 15, 14 total females; total number of pupils 40, all Presbyterians; master William McConkey, Presbyterian.

Diocesan school, in a handsome 2-storey house built for the purpose (contiguous to the town of Ballymena) by the grand jury of the county, at an expense of 900 pounds, established 1830; income: from the clergy of the united dioceses of Armagh and Connor 120 pounds; expenditure: headmaster's salary 120 pounds, 1 assistant 35 pounds; physical education: there is a dancing master for 2 quarters in the year and gymnastics; intellectual education: the usual entrance course for Dublin College, also the rudiments of the English language; moral education: on Saturdays the church catechism as commented on in the *Bristol Tract society's catechisms*, a lecture on Saturdays from the master; also an examination in *Watts Scripture history*, in which the scholars prepare; number of pupils: 8 under 10 years of age, 10 from 10 to 15, 32 above 15, total 50, all males, 40 Established Church, 8 Presbyterians, 2 Roman Catholics; master the Reverend Robert Matthews A.M., Protestant, headmaster; [blank] McQuilkin, Protestant, assistant.

Ballymena town free school, situated in a room hired for the purpose in Broughshane Street, Ballymena, established 1832; income: from the London Hibernian Society annually (average) 7 pounds, voluntary contributions of (annually) 16 pounds, [total] 23 pounds, from pupils 16 pounds; expenditure on salaries: to the master and mistress jointly 30 pounds; expenses: house rent paid for teachers' apartments and schoolroom 8 pounds annually; intellectual instruction: the females learn sewing, books of the London Hibernian Society, mensuration, book-keeping; moral education: visits from the clergyman, Sunday school, Authorised Version of the Scriptures daily; number

of pupils: males, 29 under 10 years of age, 68 from 10 to 15, 3 above 15, 100 total males; females, 15 under 10 years of age, 29 from 10 to 15, 1 above 15, 45 total females; total number of pupils 145, 34 Protestants, 79 Presbyterians, 36 Roman Catholics; master [blank] McFarland, Protestant, mistress [blank] McFarland, Protestant.

Guy's Free School, in a house built for the purpose at an expense of 450 pounds, left for the purpose by the late Mr John Guy, established 1821; income: by the late Mr Guy, the sum of 50 pounds, accruing from the rent of 3 houses in Church Street; expenditure: to the master an annual salary of 40 pounds, school requisites, books 10 pounds; intellectual education: reading, writing and arithmetic and cards purchased from the Kildare Place Society; moral education: Authorised and Douai Version daily, visits from the minister, occasional visits from the priest and minister; number of pupils: males, 60 under 10 years of age, 50 from 10 to 15, 110 total males; females, 30 from 10 to 15, 30 total females; total number of pupils 140, 26 Protestants, 80 Presbyterians, 34 Roman Catholics; master John Aikin, Presbyterian.

Female national school, in a good 2-storey house in High Street, built by subscription for the purpose; it contains apartments for the teachers, established 1833; income: from the Board of National Education 10 pounds, from pupils 121 pounds; expenditure: to the mistress 20 pounds and to her assistant 10 pounds, [total] 30 pounds; intellectual education: sewing, books of the Board of National Education; moral education: Douai and Authorised Version of Scriptures daily at stated hours; number of pupils: 46 under 10 years of age, 49 from 10 to 15, 6 above 15, total 100, all females, 34 Protestants, 51 Presbyterians, 15 Roman Catholics; Miss Cameron, Presbyterian, teacher, Miss J. Cameron, Presbyterian, assistant.

Under the London Hibernian Society, in a private house in James Street (the property of the teacher), in the town of Ballymena, established 1832; income: from the London Hibernian Society (annually) 3 pounds, from pupils 35 pounds; intellectual education: books of the London Hibernian Society, elocution, *Jackson's Bookkeeping*, arithmetic; moral education: Authorised Version of the Scriptures daily; number of pupils: males, 20 under 10 years of age, 7 from 10 to 15, 3 above 15, 30 total males; females, 8 under 10 years of age, 7 from 10 to 15, 15 total females; total number of pupils 45, 5 Protestants, 30 Presbyterians, 10 Roman Catholics; master Alexander Patterson, Presbyterian.

Classical and Mercantile School, in an excellent 2-storey house the property of the teacher in Castle Street, established 1820; income from pupils 120 pounds; expenditure: to 1 assistant (with his education) annually 6 pounds; intellectual education: the usual course of classics including Homer, mathematics, algebra, English, arithmetic; moral education: all versions of the Scriptures daily; number of pupils: 20 under 10 years of age, 34 from 10 to 15, 6 above 15, total 60, all males, 10 Protestants, 31 Presbyterians, 19 Roman Catholics; master Charles O'Neill, Roman Catholic.

Mathematical and Mercantile School, in a 2-storey house the property of the teacher in Castle Street, established 1829; income from pupils 32 pounds; intellectual education: all the branches of English and mercantile education, and all the branches of mathematics and algebra; moral education: Authorised Version of the Scriptures and Protestant and Presbyterian catechism; number of pupils, males, 17 under 10 years of age, 13 from 10 to 15, 30 total males; females, 17 under 10 years of age, 2 from 10 to 15, 1 above 15, 10 [sic] total females; total number of pupils 40, 2 Protestants, 8 Presbyterians, 37 Roman Catholics; master John Getty, Presbyterian.

Ladies' day school, in a nice 2-storey house the property of the teachers in High Street, established 1823; income: 35 pounds from societies or individuals, 35 pounds from pupils; intellectual education: music, French, geography, history, needlework, reading, writing, arithmetic; moral education: Authorised Version of the Scriptures daily; number of pupils: 10 under 10 years of age, 2 above 15, total 12, all females, 8 Presbyterians, 3 Established Church, 1 Roman Catholic; mistresses the Misses Balfour, Protestants.

Female day school, in a 2-storey house the property of the teacher in Bridge Street, established 1822; income from pupils 20 pounds; intellectual education: sewing, reading, writing, arithmetic, spelling; moral education: Authorised Version of the Scriptures daily; number of pupils: 6 under 10 years of age, 7 from 10 to 15, 3 above 15, total 16, all females and Presbyterians; mistress Mrs Young, Presbyterian.

Benevolence: Sunday Schools

In an excellent house given for the purpose by Michael Harrison Esquire (in Castle Street), established 1832; income: from Mrs Harrison of Ballymena to the mistress annually 15 pounds; expenditure: salaries 15 pounds; intellectual education: sewing, reading and spelling; moral education: Authorised Version of the Scriptures and

catechisms daily; number of pupils: 4 under 10 years of age, 18 from 10 to 15, 8 above 15, total 30, all females, 6 Protestants, 21 Presbyterians, 3 Roman Catholics; mistress Jane Kidd, Protestant.

Sunday school, held in the Wesleyan Methodist chapel on every Sunday, established 1818; intellectual education: spelling and reading; moral education: Authorised Version of Scriptures and catechisms; number of pupils: males, 21 under 10 years of age, 9 from 10 to 15, 3 above 15, 33 total males; females, 44 under 10 years of age, 18 from 10 to 15, 5 above 15, 67 total females; total number of pupils 100, 31 Protestants, 69 Presbyterians; 12 gratuitous teachers (Protestants).

Sunday school, held in the market house on every Sunday, established 1803; intellectual education: spelling and reading; moral education: Authorised Version of Old and New Testaments; number of pupils: males, 26 under 10 years of age, 11 from 10 to 15, 14 above 15, 41 total males; females, 31 under 10 years of age, 21 from 10 to 15, 7 above 15, 59 total females; total number of pupils 100, 22 Protestants, 71 Presbyterians, 7 Roman Catholics; 16 gratuitous teachers (Protestants).

Sunday school, held in the town free schoolhouse, established 1827; intellectual education: spelling and reading; moral education: Authorised Version of Scriptures and catechism; number of pupils: males, 9 under 10 years of age, 5 from 10 to 15, 3 above 15, 17 total males; females, 11 under 10 years of age, 7 from 10 to 15, 5 above 15, 23 total females; total number of pupils 40, 26 Protestants, 4 Presbyterians; 4 gratuitous teachers (Protestants).

[Overall totals]: income from public societies or benevolent individuals 237 pounds 10s: expenditure: salaries 270 pounds, other expenses 18 pounds; number of pupils: males, 214 under 10 years of age, 203 from 10 to 15, 80 above 15, 487 total males; females, 196 under 10 years of age, 188 from 10 to 15, 33 above 15, 326 total females; total number of pupils 913, 225 Protestants, 375 Presbyterians, 100 Roman Catholics, 7 other denominations.

Benevolence: Establishments for the Indigent

[Table contains the following headings: name, object, management, number relieved, funds, annual expense of management, relief afforded].

13 schools supported wholly or partly by benevolent individuals or societies; object: the removal of ignorance; management: under sundry societies or individuals; number relieved: 958 pupils receiving instruction; funds: from public

bodies 39 pounds 10s, from private individuals 201 pounds; annual expense of management: house rent 18 pounds, salaries to teachers 270 pounds; relief afforded: school requisites, salaries to teachers, free schoolhouses; when founded: at sundry periods.

Mendicity Society, object: the preventing of street begging by affording a support to poor householders; management: by a committee, secretary and treasurer; number relieved: 131 on an annual average; funds from public bodies: applotment on the parish 68 pounds 9s 7d, in other ways 31 pounds, [total] 99 pounds 9s 7d; from individuals: 244 pounds 9s 7d on an annual average; expenses: annual expense of printing 2 pounds 9s; relief afforded: 355 pounds 10s on an annual average distributed; when founded: 1826.

Clothing Society, object: clothing the poor, aged and infirm; management: by a few ladies in Ballymena; number relieved: 150 on an annual average; funds from private individuals: 59 pounds on an annual average; relief afforded: blankets, cloaks, greatcoats, shawls, flannels; when founded: 1817.

Bequest, object: not precisely known; it was bequeathed by a Mr Brown; management: it is in the hands of the rector; funds from private individuals 100 pounds; when founded: 1802.

Bequest, object: the sum of between 300 pounds and 400 pounds was left for the support of poor widows in this parish; management: there being a doubt as to how it should be disposed, it remains untouched in the hands of the judge of the consistorial court; funds from private individuals: between 300 and 400 pounds; when founded: 1806.

Office Copy of Draft Memoir, with Sections by T.C. Hannyngton, J.R. Ward and Another, and Notes by J. Boyle and Lieutenant R.K. Dawson, December 1834

SOCIAL ECONOMY

Ballymena: Table of Trades and Occupations

Forwarded to Lieutenant Larcom, 9th December 1834 [signed] R.K. Dawson, Lieutenant Royal Engineers.

Apothecaries 4, auctioneers 1, blacksmiths 4, butchers 4, bakers 7, barbers 2, coach makers 1, chair makers 1, cobblers 2, clothiers 4, cabinet makers 2, chandlers 1, drapers 10, dyers 2, glaziers 2, grocers 30, hardware shops 4, houses of entertainment for the poor 45, hucksters 9, hatters

1, heddle makers 1, house painters 1, hosiers 1, innkeepers 3, libraries (these belong to the book sellers who let out the books by the month) 2, milliners 14, musical instrument makers 2, nailers 3, plank dealers 4, pawnbrokers 2, rope makers 1, reed makers 4, boot and shoemakers 12, shuttle makers 1, saddlers 5, spirit shops 89, stationers and booksellers 2, tailors 9, turners 2, whitesmiths [2 or 4], watchmakers 8, wheelwrights 1.

NATURAL STATE

Locality

It is situated towards the centre of the county Antrim and on the north east of the barony of Lower Toome. It is bounded on the north by Dunaghy parish and the grange of Dundermot, on the east by Skerry and Racavan, on the south by Ballyclug and on the west by Ahoghill. Its greatest length is 6 and a half miles and breadth [blank] miles, average length and breadth 5 by 5 miles. It contains 6,390 acres 1 rood 15 perches.

NATURAL FEATURES

Hills

The surface of this parish presents no remarkable feature, its highest point being only 506 feet above the level of the sea and the lowest 142 feet. There is a general slope from the north of the parish southward towards the town of Ballymena, and although none of the features of the ground can be called remarkable for their height or boldness, they are so from the unusually complicated forms they exhibit: several small groups of features, whose united base does not cover a square mile, often twisting themselves into as many as 20 or more distinct tops or ridges, thus creating hollows where there are frequently deposits of water or shallow pools. These hills appear to be mostly gravel with here and there a few crags of basalt. There is a good deal of heath on some of the hilly parts of the parish.

Rivers

The Braid river has a pebbly bottom and is subject to very sudden overflows. In November 1834 this river rose 6 perpendicular feet in a few hours and carried away several bridges and flooded its banks to a very considerable extent. When these floods occur in the winter the deposit is beneficial but considerable. Damage is done to the farmer when they occur in the harvest. In the instance of the above-mentioned flood, one farmer lost 20 pounds worth of potatoes and many people lost hay.

Sometimes the whole loose soil or earth is washed completely away, leaving nothing but the heavy clay. Ditches are frequently carried away. Some pieces of the banks, which are made of blue clay and adhere together, weighing half a ton, were rolled for considerable distances in this flood. The winding course of the river is the cause. It subsides in a very short time. No artificial means are employed.

The Clogh river, alias the Ravel water, runs along the north east side of the parish for 4 miles. Its course is exceedingly winding. The general direction of this river from its source is north east to south west till it reaches the east point of this parish, where it turns to the north west till it meets the Main river from the north. It is an inconsiderable stream, running along a pebbly bottom, with frequent shallows and rapids. [Insert marginal note: It is considered a good trout stream].

The Braid river flows for about 2 and a half miles on the south east of the parish, runs in a south west direction and also unites with the Main river. This river is still smaller and shallower than the Clogh river. It unites with the Main about 2 miles south west of Ballymena.

Bogs

There is no large bog in the parish, but in the flats there are several small tracts to be met with in every part of the parish. Although greatly dug for fuel, their layer of peat does not seem near exhausted. They contain as usual a good deal of bog oak branches.

Woods

None: there are a few old trees in the castle demesne at Ballymena which add to the distant views of the town.

Climate and Crops

The climate of this parish is considered colder, more foggy and rainy than that of Belfast, and is not very favourable to the cultivation of wheat. The following is a list of the general seasons for sowing and reaping in the parish.

Wheat: put down during the latter end of October and the beginning of November, and reaped in the latter end of August. Rye: sown in November and reaped latter end of August. Barley: sown in April, reaped at latter end of August. Oats: sown in March or April, reaped early in September. Flax: sown in April, pulled up in July. Potatoes: planted during the months of March, April and May, dug up as early as the 1st August. A potato

requires exactly 91 days to arrive at perfection. [Dawson] The main crop is generally dug in October and November. Memo: it is now the 25th November and still there are 2 or 3 ridges here and there through the parish remaining to be dug.

NATURAL HISTORY

Botany

There is an enormous quantity of a weed called ragweed. It bears a yellow flower, blossoms in June and ripens about the beginning of September. Its seed is like that of the thistle and may be met floating about in all directions in the calm autumnal days. By this means it has spread itself far and wide. When a field is left fallow for a year or two, a plentiful crop of this weed will soon appear. [Insert note by J. Boyle: This is by the country people called "benweed" and on it the fairies are said to ride].

MODERN TOPOGRAPHY

Ballymena Church

Built by Mr Ballantine, the exact cost cannot be found out. In 1707 the body was built in a plain form like the meeting houses of the present day. In 1798 it was used as a barrack and very much injured by all the woodwork being used for fuel. In 1822 the tower was built by William Dean and cost 320 pounds. This sum was advanced by the Board of First Fruits, to be paid by instalments levied off the parish. [Insert note by Boyle: The board only sent 100 pounds, the rest was subscribed]. It is now 1834 and the whole sum has not yet been repaid].

The church is 66 feet by 27, contains 55 seats and affords accommodation for 330 persons. Many more persons would attend if there were a few free seats. Many poor people remain absent, not wishing to intrude on their more wealthy neighbours. There is a small organ in the church.

Meeting Houses in Ballymena

Built by voluntary contributions. There are 4 [crossed out: 2] large meeting houses in the town: 1 in Wellington Street and 1 in Castle Street. The one in Wellington Street is a large new house, built in 1828 by John Legget and cost 1,000 pounds. It is 68 feet by 53, contains 120 seats and has accommodation for 960 persons. The Castle Street house is 69 feet by 24, has 107 seats and affords accommodation for 856 persons. These houses are generally well filled.

There is also a Wesleyan Methodist meeting house in Castle Street, 48 feet by 27. There are no seats or pews in the house and some long forms serve the congregation. There is also a Seceding meeting house in High Street. [Insert note by Dawson: Castle Street house cost [blank], built in the year [blank]; Methodist house cost [blank], built in the year [blank]; accommodation for how many? Seceding house cost [blank], built in the year [blank].

Market House

The ground floor is used as a sale room for oatmeal, potatoes, linen, and in the wet weather affords shelter to numerous dealers in soft goods. The upper room is used as law court, also for public meetings, concerts and other assemblies of the kind. The young ladies of the neighbourhood use it as a Sunday school and devote their Sunday afternoons to the instruction of a number of the poor class of children. There is also a smaller market house in Shamble Street, at which there is a crane at which all the butter, pork, corn and other commodities are weighed at 1d per cwt.

Seceding Meeting House, High Street

This house is 63 feet by 33 and has accommodation for 600 persons [insert query by Boyle: 380].

In this parish there are 1,810 Protestants, Roman Catholics 1,238, Presbyterians 5,159, 96 Methodists, and there are *30 to 40 persons professing no particular creed* and they attend no place of worship. [Insert query by Dawson: How many Seceders? [Answer by Boyle]: Their number is not exactly known, not being distinguished from the great body of Presbyterians in the enumerators' returns].

Shambles

There is a shambles in the town, but they are not made use of by the butchers, they preferring to expose their meat in their own shops. A vast quantity of beef is brought in from the country on Saturdays and exposed on carts and standings erected along the side of the street; also large quantities of salt meat and bacon are disposed of in the same way. The beef thus brought to town is called horse beef, from its being brought to town on the back of a horse, an old sack or other piece of coarse cloth being first thrown over the back of the animal. It is sold for about 3 ha'pence or 2d per lb, some at 1d per lb. November 29th 1834 counted 30 stands on an average, each containing half a cow [insert query by Boyle: 2 cows or carcases],

8 stalls covered with canvas, filled with bacon. A respectable butcher in Ballymena would contract to give good beef at all seasons for the use of military or other body of men, who would consume a quantity at 25s per cwt or 2d ha'penny per lb.

Bridewell

Built in 1829, at a cost of [blank], levied off the county by the grand jury. [Insert memo by Dawson: The exact cost of the bridewell can only be obtained from the treasurer, Mr Stewart of Gracehill near Ballymoney, on the Armoy road]. It contains 8 cells and, according to the regulations, has accommodation for 24 prisoners. Either 1 or 3 persons should be in the same cell. Each person has an allowance for 1 lb of bread and a pint of milk per diem. The average allowance annually to defray this expense is 35 pounds per annum, fuel and straw included. There is only 1 officer: his salary 20 pounds per annum. Average number of prisoners in the year: 480.

Towns: Ballymena

Ballymena, formerly called Kilhiltstown, the first proprietor Sir Robert Adair being laird of Kilhilt, a place near Ayr in Scotland, is situated in the south extremity of the parish, on a gentle slope on the north bank of the Braid river.

It is 22 Irish miles from Belfast, 18 Irish miles from Larne, 10 Irish miles from Antrim, 7 Irish miles from Randalstown, 3 from Broughshane, 13 from Glenarm, 15 from Ballymoney, 24 from Bushmills, 20 from Ballycastle and 16 from Cushendall. [Insert marginal note: These are the reported distances in Irish miles].

The places of public worship consist of a church, 2 Presbyterian meeting houses, 1 Seceding and 1 Wesleyan.

The church is small but neat and in good repair. It was built in 1707 and constituted by act of parliament of 6th Ann[e] c.21 s.28 "the only parish church in this parish so soon as Sir Robert Adair, the proprietor of the soil, shall have made the necessary conveyance of the ground on which the church is built, with a convenient churchyard." [Insert marginal note by Dawson: Query this?].

The market house is in the principal street in the centre of the town and the room over it is the court house. A bridewell was erected in 1829.

MODERN TOPOGRAPHY AND PRODUCTIVE ECONOMY

Banks and Commerce

There is in this town a branch of the Provincial

Bank of Ireland, for which they are now building (1834) a new bank house on a large scale, considering the relative size of the other houses; manager Mr Skelly. There is also a branch of the Northern Bank and another of the Belfast Banking Company. Agents for both have been doing business here for some time back, though they are only now (1834) beginning to fit up the houses for their reception. It has been even projected to make this town contain a branch of the Bank of Ireland, though there are already 3.

This is sufficient proof of the very thriving state of the town, which is more crowded with shops and warehouses of every description than any place of its size in the north of Ireland. The weekly Saturday market for butter, linen, yarn, pigs, black cattle is said to be the largest in Ireland. The quantity of whiskey drunk on the market days here must be enormous and the town is proportionably full of spirit shops.

The streets are dirty and very badly paved, neither are they at all well swept. Great quantities of eels are brought here for sale from the Portna and Toome weirs, and Lough Neagh furnishes the town with fine trout in the season. The streets of this town are not lighted at night. The houses are almost all built of stone. There is a stone bridge over the Braid river which connects Ballymena with Harryville, a small hamlet in Ballyclug parish.

SOCIAL AND PRODUCTIVE ECONOMY

Local Government

Quarter sessions are held in the court house in this town in January and July. The alternate terms in April and October are held in Ballymoney. Petty sessions are also held here once a fortnight.

Markets and Fairs in Ballymena

There are 2 fairs here annually, one on the 26th July and the other on the 21st October. [Insert marginal note: This fair is very inconsiderable]. There is also a weekly market on Saturdays.

At the north end of Ballymena there is a large and good fairgreen, walled in, where cattle are exposed for sale on Saturdays, which is in part a fair and market day in Ballymena. On this day every commodity which the country affords may be had.

There is no regular yarn market. This is held in the principal street opposite one of the hotels. There is a linen market or linen hall in Castle Street. This is used by the linen merchants on Saturday to inspect the linen offered for sale. On such as are approved they place their signature. These webs are afterwards brought to the offices in the town, where they receive the price agreed upon in the market.

Large quantities of ready-made shoes are brought for sale and exposed on stalls and barrels. These are used by the country people and are sold for about 5s a pair and will last a year. Some for women are sold so low as 2s 6d. These shoes are made of kip hide [queried].

The fairs are a general mart but chiefly for the sale of black cattle, and in the markets, in addition to the cattle, the chief trade is butter, yarn and linen. Of the latter, about 5,000 pieces of 25 yards are sold every week, and of butter, about 6,000 firkins during the season. There has of late years been established on Tuesdays and Fridays a pork market from the middle of October to the middle of May. About 11,000 dead pigs are sold during the season.

The corn market is on Wednesdays, but not being a wheat country it is unimportant, the quantity brought for sale scarcely representing what is required for the consumption of the town. The markets are held by a patent or grant made in the 2nd of Charles I to a Mr Adair, the ancestor of the present proprietor.

Conveyances

There are 2 coaches to Belfast every morning (at 4 o'clock), Sundays excepted. The mail coach from Belfast to Derry passes to and fro' every day and the day coach from Belfast to Coleraine [crossed out: every week] [in a different hand] on alternate days, passing from Coleraine on Sundays, Tuesdays and Thursdays and from Belfast on Mondays, Wednesdays and Fridays. [Crossed out: No such weekly coach exists at present, 1834].

Schools

A diocesan school was established in 1830. It is endowed by the clergy of Armagh and Connor with 120 pounds per annum. The grand jury of the county presented 1,000 pounds [insert note by Boyle: late Irish currency] to build the house. There is a free school which was opened in 1821, founded on a charitable bequest by the late John Guy, who bequeathed about 50 pounds per annum for its support, being the profits and rents on some houses in the town.

[Insert queries by Dawson: Average number of scholars? The names of masters and ushers, with their salaries, and anything particular as to the endowment]. [Answer] Diocesan school, Ballymena: the average number of scholars educated in the year 40. Master of the school the Reverend Matthews. There are generally 2 ushers, who receive 31 pounds 10s 6d per year. They reside in the house and have their board free. [Insert additional queries by Dawson: Headmaster's salary? House, when built, at what expense, by whom (contribution and architect), dimensions, materials?] [Answer by Boyle] See Table of Schools for this information.

Guy's Free School

[Insert queries by Dawson: The exact amount of the bequest, to be learnt from executors or trustees? The number of scholars educated? Name, query Grey or Gay? Where are the houses erected? How many of them? The name of the master, his salary and the regulations of his school]. The exact amount of Mr Guy's bequest is 50 pounds per annum, the rent of 3 houses in Church Street, Ballymena, at present occupied by Messrs Dugan, Killan and Wilson. Average number of children educated 150. The master, John Aikin, has 40 pounds per annum and accommodation in the schoolhouse, which is large and commodious. Children of all classes and persuasions are admitted free. The Scriptures are read for 1 hour each day. No catechisms are taught. There is also a female national school under the direction of the National Board of Education; average number of pupils 80, next door to Guy's.

[Insert additional queries by Dawson: When opened? Is there no male national school?].

Benevolence

The Mendicity Society of the town pays 300 pounds per annum to the poor. The town, from its central position, is much resorted to by the inhabitants of the surrounding country and is improving rapidly. [Insert note: Mendicity, Ballymena: The sum of 300 pounds is raised by voluntary contributions amongst the inhabitants of the parish and is distributed on alternate Mondays at the office of Mr Adair, Ballymena. Present report for 1834? What is present state, 1835? Average attendance of mendicants? How much is given to each?]

MODERN TOPOGRAPHY

Public Buildings

There is a Roman Catholic chapel about half a mile [insert correction by Boyle: one-sixth] from

the town. It was built by subscription in 1827. [Insert note: This house was built in 1828 by William Dean, cost 475 pounds. This sum was raised by voluntary contributions at sermons preached for the purpose of raising funds. The rest was levied off the parishioners. The house is 60 feet by 27 and a half feet. It would accommodate 800 persons].

Gentlemen's Seats

[Crossed out: There are few, if any, resident gentlemen about Ballymena or in the town. The greater part of the wealthy people are either linen buyers or linen bleachers, butter merchants, some retired from trades, others still in business. These are a rich but by no means an aristocratic or polished class of persons].

Castle, William Adair Esquire [insert note by Boyle: uninhabited].

Brigadie, John Treacy Esquire.

Hugomont [insert query: Hougoumont? [Answer by Boyle: Hougomont], Hugh Harrison Esquire.

Hill Head, William Gihon Esquire.

Mountpleasant, Reverend Alex Houstan [insert note by Boyle: in Ahoghill parish].

Bleach Greens

There are 2 bleach greens, one on the south side of Ballymena, which extends into the parish of Ahoghill, and another in Ballygarvy townland. There are in all 3 bleaching mills in the parish, 2 beetling and 1 green.

Mills

There is 1 corn mill in Ballymena worked by a wheel of 16 feet diameter, 4 feet breast <brest>, an undershot wheel. There is sufficient water for 2 wheels of 20 feet diameter. The fall of water is 14 feet in this mill-race.

Ballygarvy mills, on the Broughshane road, 1 mile and a half from Ballymena, has 4 wheels: diameter of one is 16 feet, breast 6 feet; the others 15 feet diameter, 4 feet breast, sufficient supply of water at all seasons. [Insert note by Boyle: The fall of water to Ballygarvy mills is 14 feet].

The Green mill, situated in the town of Ballymena, has 2 wheels, 16 feet in diameter, 5 feet 8 inches breast or buckets.

There is another mill on the opposite side of the same street which has also 2 wheels, one 10 feet 8 inches in diameter, 5 feet breast or buckets; the other 18 feet diameter, 5 feet breast or buckets.

All these mills are supplied from the Braid river and have constant supply of water. They are all undershot wheels. There are no disputes relative to water.

Communications

The town of Ballymena being centrally situated in the county, many roads radiate from it. Those which traverse the parish are: the mail coach road from Belfast to Derry, which passes through a portion of the parish on its north west boundary. The road from Belfast to Ballycastle traverses the parish from south to north nearly, as also one from Ballymena to Clogh. The new road to Broughshane and the old one by Ballygarvey traverse the south east portion of the parish. These roads are generally kept in good repair, as well as several cross-roads between them, except in the vicinity of town where they are deep and heavy and full of holes in winter.

ANCIENT TOPOGRAPHY

Standing Stone and Old Church

The only relic of antiquity in this parish is the remains of a building in the graveyard in Kirkinriola townland, also a standing stone which must be several ton weight, erected near the Clogh road on a gentle eminence not more than one-eighth of a mile from Ballymena. It has been thought that this stone was the central point upon which the numerous smaller ones in the county were meant to bear by the ancients, as a means of connecting these supposed landmarks. [Insert note by Boyle: It is said that the old church which forms the subject of the annexed sketch never was completed and that it never was roofed, but this is only a tradition. It is, however, believed].

Plan of old church of Kirkinriola, on the Clogh road, 3 miles north of Ballymena, by T.C. Hannyngton, December 3rd 1834: [ground plan, with orientation and annotations, main dimensions 48 by 24 feet, scale one-sixth of an inch to a yard; detail of window]. This old [church] will soon be pulled down. The stones of the walls are used for headstones for graves.

[Drawing] Portion of west end of the old church of Kirkinriola by T.C. Hannyngton.

MODERN TOPOGRAPHY

General Appearance and Scenery

In the parish of Kirkinriola there is nothing pictur-esque, but when seen from the road leading to Gracehill it is not displeasing to the eye, when contrasted with the high mountains rising on the east side of the parish; but the landscape is miser-ably deficient in trees. The surface generally is low and undulating, formed of a succession of small oval hills, all nearly of the same character and height, and the general appearance of the country is rather bleak and dreary, from the want of wood and hedgerows.

SOCIAL ECONOMY

Early Improvements

The parish is peopled chiefly by the descendants of Scotch emigrants.

Local Government

This town, Ballymena, is the residence of the police inspector of the county, who has a force of [blank] men in the police barracks here. There is also a bench of magistrates.

Dispensaries

There are no dispensaries in Ballymena.

Schools

One free school and 1 diocesan in the town of Ballymena, besides the smaller ones distributed in the parish.

Religion

The parish is an impropriate cure in the gift of the Earl Mountcashel. The late earl sold the tithes to Mr Adair Esquire, but retained the right of pres-entation. It is in the diocese of Down and Connor and province of Ulster, and is episcopally united to the adjoining parish of Ballyclug. The great mass of population are Presbyterian.

PRODUCTIVE ECONOMY

Manufacturing

The manufacturing of linen is extensive, as is also the spinning of flax. The business in the bleach greens is carried on with spirit and are both in full work. The establishments in Ballygarvey townland employ about 60 weavers in the manufacture of union cloth. Great quantities of butter are made in the neighbourhood of the town and brought to market every Saturday.

Rural Economy

The parish is divided into 18 townlands, 16 of which are in the manor of Ballymena and are held direct from the Crown by William Adair Esquire, who purchased off the quit rents a few years ago. The remaining 2 townlands (Tullyreagh and Carnlea) are the property of the Earl Mountcashel. Neither of these proprietors reside in the parish.

The soil in general is light and gravelly. The usual crops are potatoes and oats. The small farmers sow a good deal of flax. Barley and rye with a little wheat are also cultivated.

Uses made of the Bogs

The principal advantage derived from the bogs is the quantity of good turf which they yield. A considerable extent of bog has been lately brought under cultivation and the quantity is increasing every year by very slow degrees.

No spirited draining is carried on in this parish.

Planting

Trees in general thrive well. The castle demesne is ornamented with plantations and there are some fine trees in Ballygarvey townland. There is a plantation of young firs in Craigywarren, also some young plantations about the houses of Hugomont and Brigadie.

Fishing

The Clogh water and the Braid river afford some tolerable trout fishing during the season. The fine fish are much thinned with nets.

SOCIAL ECONOMY

General Remarks

Though a good many wealthy people reside in or near the town of Ballymena, there is very little general society, and the character of the neighbourhood is (as they allow themselves) inhospitality to strangers and indifference to anything but making money. This is not much to be wondered at, as they are all for the most part deeply engaged in trade and they have no idea of anything like public gaieties or amusements. There are several Presbyterian families and they, as well as the Protestants, are pretty well imbued with a spirit of party controversy on religious matters.

The style of country houses in the neighbourhood is small, snug and boxy, generally with young plantations in the immediate vicinity, chiefly of fir, but none of which have sufficient growth to give a richness to the landscape, except towards Broughshane where there are some very luxuriant groves and boskeys <bosquets>. On approaching the town from any quarter, the mountain called Slemish is the most striking object, about 6 miles off in the background, from its singular and abrupt height, formed like a cap picturesquely stuck upon a ridge of hills.

Schools

[Table contains the following headings: name of townland where held, name and religion of master or mistress, free or pay school, annual income of master or mistress, description and cost of schoolhouse, number of pupils subdivided by religion, sex and the Protestant and Roman Catholic returns, societies with which connected].

Sheddings, Dunfane, master James Angus, Presbyterian; pay school, annual income about 35 pounds; Kildare Place Society made a grant of 5 pounds to the master last year; schoolhouse stone and lime, built by subscription, cost 20 pounds to 25 pounds; number of pupils by the Protestant return: 54 Presbyterians, 2 Roman Catholics, 30 males, 26 females; by the Roman Catholic return: 63 Presbyterians, 2 Roman Catholics, 36 males, 29 females; connected with Kildare Place Society.

Parade school, Dunfane, master John McVey, Presbyterian; pay school, annual income 5 pounds; schoolhouse stone and lime, built by subscription, cost 10 to 15 pounds, in bad condition; number of pupils by the Protestant return: 16 Presbyterians, 10 males, 6 females; by the Roman Catholic return: 22 Presbyterians, 15 males, 7 females; associations none.

Craigywarren, master James Black, Presbyterian; pay school, annual income 12 to 15 pounds; schoolhouse stone and lime, good accommodation, built by subscription, cost 20 pounds; the Kildare Place Society granted 10 pounds towards the completion of the schoolhouse and 5 guineas in school requisites; number of pupils by the Protestant return: 44 Presbyterians, 22 males, 22 females; by the Roman Catholic return: 43 Presbyterians, 1 Roman Catholic, 22 males, 22 females; connected with Kildare Place Society.

Clougher, master Robert Gilmore, Presbyterian; pay school, annual income 5 to 6 pounds; schoolhouse a poor barn; number of pupils by the Protestant return: 18 Presbyterians, 2 Roman Catholics, 8 males, 12 females; by the Roman Catholic return: 27 Presbyterians, 3 Roman Catholics, 16 males, 14 females; associations none.

Clentagh, master John Best, Presbyterian; pay school, annual income about 5 pounds; schoolhouse a hired room; number of pupils by the Protestant return: 30 Presbyterians, 10 males, 20 females; by the Roman Catholic return: 30

Presbyterians, 15 males, 15 females; associations none.

Durneveagh, master John Peters, Presbyterian; pay school, annual income 12 to 15 pounds; schoolhouse stone and lime, built by subscription, cost 10 pounds; number of pupils by the Protestant return: 43 Presbyterians, 2 Roman Catholics, 22 males, 23 females; by the Roman Catholic return: 2 Established Church, 40 Presbyterians, 3 Roman Catholics, 22 males, 23 females; connected with Kildare Place Society.

Ballymena, master Charles O'Neil, Roman Catholic; pay school, annual income 150 pounds; schoolhouse a part of the master's dwelling house; number of pupils by the Protestant return: 18 Established Church, 48 Presbyterians, 14 Roman Catholics, 52 males, 28 females; by the Roman Catholic return: 15 Established Church, 50 Presbyterians, 15 Roman Catholics, 59 males, 21 females; associations none.

Ballymena, master James Wasson, Presbyterian; pay school, annual income 20 pounds; schoolhouse a room in master's house; number of pupils by the Protestant return: 18 Presbyterians, 16 males, 2 females; by the Roman Catholic return: 17 Presbyterians, 14 males, 3 females; associations none.

Ballymena, master John Gray, Presbyterian; pay school, annual income 50 pounds; schoolhouse a hired room; number of pupils by the Protestant return: 10 Established Church, 63 Presbyterians, 3 Roman Catholics, 48 males, 26 females [insert note: some error]; by the Roman Catholic return: 12 Protestants, 60 Presbyterians, 6 Roman Catholics, 50 males, 28 females; associations none.

Ballymena, master James McGrogan, Roman Catholic; pay school, annual income 15 pounds; schoolhouse a room in the master's house; number of pupils by the Protestant return: 5 Established Church, 15 Presbyterians, 15 Roman Catholics, 18 males, 17 females; by the Roman Catholic return: 7 Established Church, 17 Presbyterians, 16 Roman Catholics, 20 males, 20 females; associations none.

Ballymena, master Reverend C. Houston, Reformed Presbyterian; pay school, annual income about 20 pounds, rates a guinea to a guinea and a half per quarter; schoolhouse: private dwelling house; number of pupils by the Protestant return: 3 Established Church, 11 Presbyterians, 12 males, 2 females; by the Roman Catholic return: 3 Established Church, 11 Presbyterians, 14 males, 2 females [insert note: some error]; associations none.

Ballymena, master John Hagan, Protestant; pay school, annual income 100 pounds, rates per quarter 2 guineas; schoolhouse a hired room; number of pupils by the Protestant return: 4 Established Church, 10 Presbyterians, 2 Roman Catholics, 16 males; by the Roman Catholic return: 4 Established Church, 10 Presbyterians, 2 Roman Catholics, 16 males; associations none.

Guy's school, master John Aickin, Reformed Presbyterian; free school, annual income 34 pounds 2s 6d, with a house and garden; the maintenance of this school arises from funds vested in trustees of a bequest of the late John Guy; schoolhouse stone and lime, cost 400 pounds or 500 pounds, built by trustees of the bequest of John Guy Esquire; number of pupils by the Protestant return: 23 Established Church, 69 Presbyterians, 28 Roman Catholics, 70 males, 50 females; by the Roman Catholic return: 22 Established Church, 79 Presbyterians, 51 Roman Catholics, 81 males, 72 females [insert note: some error]; the school is supported by funds vested in trustees by bequest of the late John Guy.

Ballymena, mistress Miss H. Balfour, Protestant (ladies' school); pay school, income about 40 pounds; schoolhouse: private dwelling house; number of pupils by the Protestant return: 3 Established Church, 23 Presbyterians, 26 females; by the Roman Catholic return: 3 Established Church, 23 Presbyterians, 26 females; associations none.

Ballymena, mistress Miss Anne Given, Presbyterian; pay school, annual income uncertain; schoolhouse her father's house: number of pupils by the Roman Catholic return: 5 Established Church, 16 Presbyterians, 2 Roman Catholics, 13 males, 10 females; associations none.

Memoir on Ancient Topography by J. Stokes, [1838 ?]

ANCIENT TOPOGRAPHY

Ecclesiastical: Old Churches

An old church is said to have stood on the site of the present market house. It is added that it was built at the time of St Patrick, half-way between Cullybackey and Connor, in order equally to accommodate the inhabitants of both places. No vestiges of it now remain.

An old church stands in the townland of Kirkinriola, on the road from Ballymena to Clogh and at the distance of 2 and a quarter statute miles

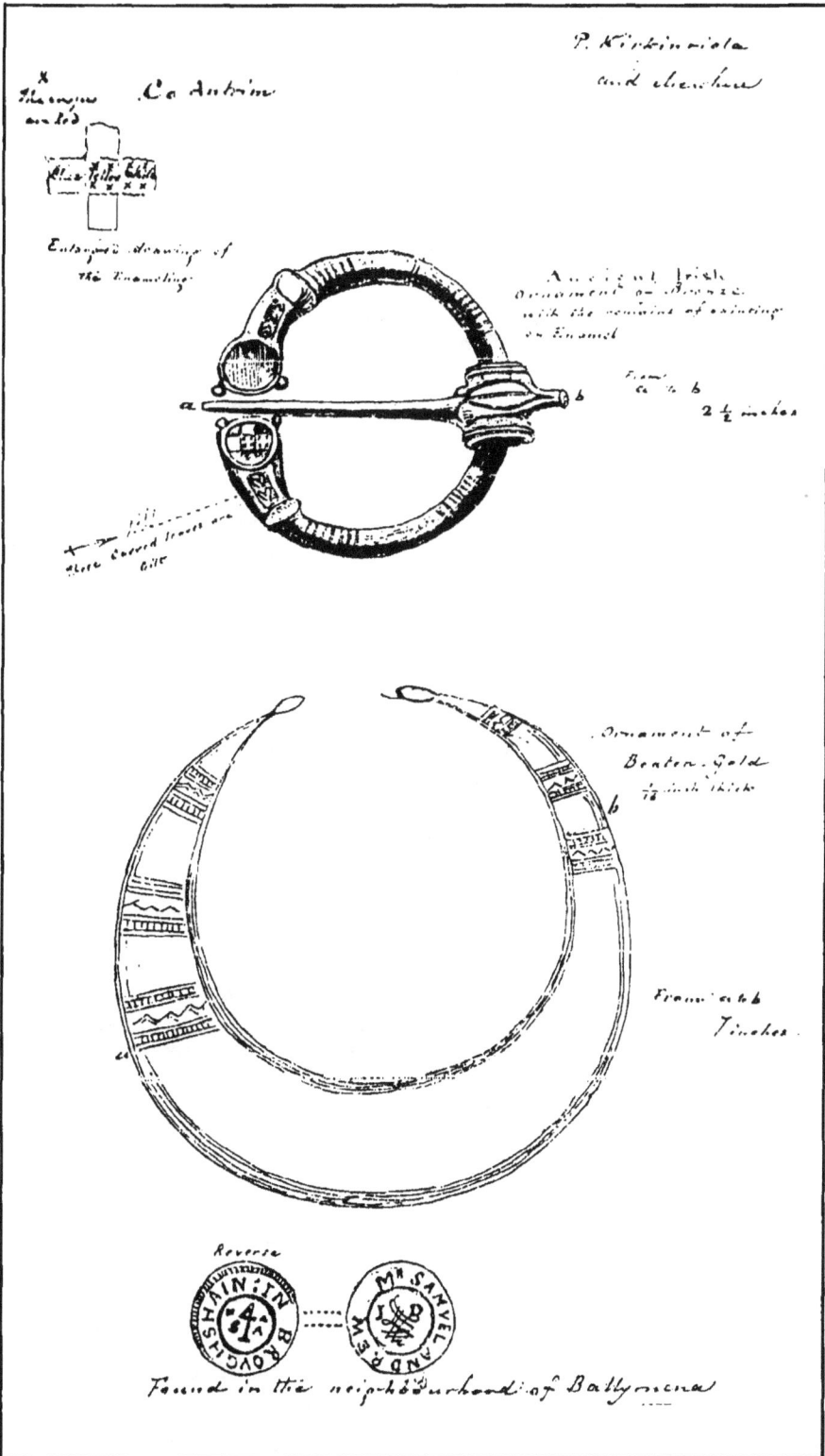

Discoveries from Kirkinriola

from the former town. It is situated in a valley, a few fields to the west of the high road. Its erection was commenced a few years previous to that of the town church, for dates of which see Modern Topography. When the walls were half raised, it was discontinued on account, as it was said, of its being too far from Ballymena, round which place the greater part of the congregation then resided. See drawing[s] for a general view of it. There are neither doorways, nor windows, mouldings or ornaments anywhere visible. It is in the form of a rectangle, 61 feet by 25 and a half feet on the outside, with walls 3 and a half feet thick and from 4 and a half feet to 7 feet high.

From a variety of considerations, it appears probable that on the site of this unfinished building a much older church once stood. First, there is a very strong belief among all the people, both in the immediate neighbourhood and afar off, of its great antiquity, a supposition which is at once contradicted not only by positive information of the recent date of its erection, but also by the indifferent quality of the mortar. It appears then, that the existence of that universal tradition can only be explained by supposing that it was raised upon or near the foundations of an older one.

Secondly, it does not appear likely, if no graveyard whatever had been here prior to 1708, that the persons who were endeavouring to procure a new parish church should have put themselves to the trouble of negotiating <negociating> for and procuring a lot of ground, only to reject it again.

Thirdly, it is probable that the original parish church of Kirkinriola, like many others, was destroyed during the troubles of 1641 and that in this, which is a nearly central situation, it then stood. The wall of the graveyard, however, is not ancient. It appears to be of the same date as that of the church; but perhaps the old graveyard was at that time very much enlarged.

The people attach antiquity not so much to the church as to the burial ground. Many of them then, by a natural transition, invest the former with the age of the latter, taking it for granted that the unfinished walls before them are the true representatives of the old church which they think the burial ground must have had.

There is no tombstone either in the yard or within the walls older than 1700. The oldest is represented in drawing[s] and bears date 1710. It is a fragment, and was found about a foot below the surface in digging the foundations for the burial ground wall of the Raphael family. It is now set in the wall looking into the interior of the small square enclosure of which it consists. There are no crosses of any kind either at this place or in the neighbourhood.

The families buried in the church and churchyard are as follows: Mann, Ross, Knowles, Aikin, Peacock, Gray, Smyth, Perry, Harbison, Robison, Rosborough, Cathcart, Spence, Adair, Raphael, Bell, McCullagh, McFetridge, McCaughy, McMaster, McAdam, McDowell, Grant, Johnstone, Boyd, Anderson, Gordon, Robison, Hume, Gilmor, Strahan. Raphael, a farmer in Ahoghill, is the wealthiest name. The churchyard is still frequently used.

Military Remains

There are no castles in this parish.

Pagan Remains

There are few pagan remains here. No cromlechs or giant's graves of any kind have been met with. There is one standing stone in the townland of Bottom, on the top of a hill commanding a very [insert marginal query: ?]. It is in the southern part of the parish and near the town of Ballymena; see drawing[s].

Forts

As for the Danish forts, their number is rapidly diminishing. On the Ordnance map which is dated 1832 there are 14. In 1837 there are but 10.

The first that are worthy of notice are Drumfane moat and a mound in the townland of Bottom. The former is covered with a rising plantation of young trees, which will have the effect of preserving it from any further dilapidation. It consists of a tumulus about 30 feet high, surrounded with what was originally a ditch and rampart, and having attached on the eastern side the remains of a square fortification. From the top of the tumulus there is a very extensive view towards Lough Neagh; see drawing[s] for plan.

In 1834, at the distance of 20 perches to the north of it, there was found a cave, which, however, is now destroyed. It is a hollow and is in naturally the best situation for concealment of any round about. Some pieces of coin are said to have been found in it. From its retired situation and close neighbourhood to the moat, the idea naturally arises that it was used by the inhabitants of that moat or rath for concealment of their goods during war, even as the tumulus, from its height and steepness, would appear to have been used as a keep or stronghold during a like period.

The mound in the townland of Bottom is represented in drawing[s]. It is an exaggeration of the ordinary form of a Danish fort. The ditch is remarkably broad and the usual enclosure encompassed by it so high as to appear at a distance more like a mound than a fort. Possibly the comparatively defenceless situation in which it stands may explain why such seeming efforts were made to increase its strength. The ground is flat and there is no extensive prospect to give warning of the approach of enemies. The hollow at the top is 4 feet deep.

20 perches to the south of a fort in the townland of Drumfane a large cove was found a few years ago. This fort is of the ordinary form. It stands at the head of a valley and close to a small rivulet.

The ruined fort in the townland of Killyflugh was originally a castle <casiol>. The wall has been razed to the foundations. It is now a circular ring 1 chain and three-quarters from out to out in diameter. The foundations are composed of round stones a foot broad at an average and remaining imbedded in the sod. The average thickness of the wall appears to have been 11 feet. The debris caused by its destruction and fall extends to 6 feet further. The whole place has remained in its present state for the last half century. There is no appearance either within or about it of any cove, but at the distance of 20 perches to the east, round the shoulder of the gently sloping hillside on which it stands, there was one once found. It is now destroyed.

North west of this castle, in the same townland and not many fields off, there stands up on some rugged ground the remains of what had been apparently a building like the Grianan of Aileach <Grienan of Elagh> in the county of Donegal. Drawing exhibits a plan and section of it. The inner ring would seem, by inspection, to have once [been] a wall of about 10 feet thick, containing in its heart a cove running part of the way round. Nothing remains now to indicate those foundations but numerous small hillocks with many imbedded stones. These are disposed to the breadth of 10 feet along the circumference of that ring, except in one part where they are arranged in a double row, leaving a hollow in the middle. This long hollow was most probably a cove. The people say that the inner ring was once a great wall built with very large stones now carried away to build houses in Ballymena. At the spot marked "a", it is said that there was once a cove and that the grassy hole still to be seen there was once the entrance to it.

Other Forts

Dungall Fort, which gives its name to a townland,

is a chain and three-quarters wide at the top. It is 30 feet high above the bottom of the ditch at its foot, and in some parts 40. The ditch itself is 10 feet deep at an average and still contains some water. The circumference of the ditch and fort encloses a Cunningham acre. On the top there is a hollow about 15 feet deep, extending over half its area, of an irregular oval form and shaped like the crater of a volcano. It is believed to be the entrance to a cove. It is situated on the western side of the top. The general appearance of this fort resembles that of the mound in Bottom, only the ditch is not so broad in proportion. It is here about 8 feet wide. The fort is on the summit of a gently rising hill near an excellent stream, but is commanded on every side by higher ground. From there being no rampart along the outer edge of the ditch, as well as from the general appearance of the whole at a distance, it would appear that the whole height of 30 feet had not been raised artificially but that part of it is the body of the hill itself and the remainder the mass excavated from the surrounding ditch.

In the townland of Carnlea, and on the summit of some high ground, there is a very remarkable fort or building, exhibiting in the interior the foundations of several apartments; see drawing[s]. In the western side there is part of an ancient fence and the foundations of some small square huts of earth, much resembling those observed in some parts of the county of Londonderry. See remains of Dungiven and Bovevagh. It has all remained in its present state, time out of mind. The average thickness of the great wall is 10 feet and height 2. The 2 holes are 3 feet deep each. There is no cove in its immediate neighbourhood. None of the walls are more than 2 feet high.

As for the remaining forts, they are all of the usual uninteresting form. No coins appear to have been found in this parish, at least lately. Some quern-stones have been occasionally dug up, as well as wooden vessels of ancient butter from the bogs. There is subjoined a small map showing the several positions of the ancient monuments of Kirkinriola.

[Map] The above map of the area is to the scale of 3 miles to the inch. Only 2 of the forts properly speaking are marked on it: namely Carnlea Fort, see drawing[s]; and the fort spoken of after the description of the mound at Bottom. The former is on the northern part of the map, the latter on the southern.

Drawings

Old church of Kirkinriola.

Stone at Kirkinriola, 1 foot 5 inches high, with sundry letters.

Standing stone in Bottom, 9 feet high, view from the south.

Drumfane moat, plan and section, view from south west, scale 10 chains to 3 inches.

Mound in Bottom, top 68 feet broad, view from south and plan, scale 6 inches to a mile.

Fort commonly called the Castle, in townland of Killyflugh, plan and section, scale 10 chains to 3 inches.

Fort in Carnlea townland, plan and section, scale 106 feet to an inch.

View of Ballymena from the north.

Appendix to Ancient Topography by J. Stokes, March 1838

Drawings

Addenda, March 27th 1838 [signed] J. Stokes.

Ancient Irish ornament of bronze with remains of painting on enamel, diameter 2 and a half inches; enlarged drawing of enamelling.

Ornament of beaten gold 7 inches wide.

Coin or medal, both faces, found in neighbourhood of Ballymena.

2 ancient pins found in the neighbourhood of Ballymena, in possession of Mr Benn, one with decorated head and 2 detail drawings with annotations, 8 and half inches long, the other side view, 4 and three-quarter inches long.

Articles of green glass with knobs of red glass said to have been found buried deep at a standing stone, in the possession of Mr Benn, section drawings with dimensions.

3 arrowheads with dimensions, 1 arrowhead front and reverse with dimensions, parish of Dunaghy.

A sword of brass, broken in 2 pieces, 20 inches long.

Parish of Rasharkin: ornament of gold in the possession of Mr Hamilton, postmaster, Ballymoney, 2 views and section, full size.

Spanish coin found in Finvoy, in the possession of Mr Gordon, watchmaker, Ballymoney.

Kirkinriola parish and elsewhere: small anvil of bronze found near Ballymoney, 2 views with dimensions.

Fragment of ancient mould for casting spearheads, found in the neighbourhood of Ballymena, in the possession of Mr Benn, 2 views with dimensions.

Parish of Rasharkin, County Antrim

Statistical Account by Lieutenant J. Chaytor,
May 1833

NATURAL STATE

Name and Situation

Rath "a fort" and Sharkin is probably a man's
name. [Crossed out: Its interpretation is "rogues'
town", so called from its having been inhabited by
an outlawed people who robbed and murdered to
a great extent about the beginning of the 18th
century. They were a terror to the surrounding
neighbourhood].

In the barony of Kilconway, manor of Oldstone,
county of Antrim and diocese of Down and
Connor.

Boundaries, Extent and Divisions

It is bounded on the north by the parish of Finvoy,
on the east by the River Main, parishes of Killagan,
Ahoghill and grange of Dundermot, on the south
by the parish of Ahoghill, on the west by the River
Bann and county of Londonderry. It extends from
north to south about 5 [miles] and from east to
west about 6 British statute miles. It contains
19, 253 statute acres.

It is divided into 30 portions called townlands,
including the glebe and a detached portion of
Church Tamlaght. The principal proprietors are
Mr Harvey, Mr Caulfield, Mr Smith and E.
McDonald Esquire, neither of whom reside in
the parish. It is mostly let in small farms of 20 to
50 acres on lease of 21 years, 10s to 1 pound
10s per Cunningham acre, with a privilege of
turbary.

NATURAL FEATURES AND NATURAL HISTORY

Surface and Soil

About half of the parish is cultivated. The other is
mostly turf bog and mountain pasture. About the
central and north east portion of the parish the soil
is light and gravelly; that lying along the Bann is
mostly a stiff clay. It is better cultivated and much
more productive than the former. In the north
west division there are several small portions
interspersed with rocks and crags. In one or two
instances they rise into small ranges.

Produce and Turbary

The principal crops are potatoes, oats, flax and
in some places wheat, but it is not generally

cultivated. There is an abundance of excellent
turbary in various parts of the parish.

Geology

In the north east division of the parish, commonly
known by the name Killymorris, townland of
Glenbuck, wood coal is found. The persons who
rent it off the Antrim family are very poor and
have little means of working it. They cut horizon-
tally into the face of the hill in which the coal is
situated, and as yet have not advanced further
than 200 or 300 yards from the opening of the
gallery. The seams of coal are from 1 to 2 feet in
thickness. There is very little raised at present. Of
4 galleries, 2 only are occasionally worked. It is
sold at 6s 8d per ton.

Basalt is the only kind of stone in the parish. Of
it, there are several quarries.

MODERN TOPOGRAPHY AND PRODUCTIVE ECONOMY

Villages

The only village or hamlet in the parish is
Rasharkin. It is situated 1 and three-quarter miles
east of the River Bann. It contains about 260
inhabitants. It holds one fair annually.

Manufactures

Linen is the only manufacture. The spinning and
weaving of this article is the chief support of many
of the peasantry of both sexes. In the south east
corner of the parish, on the Main river, is situated
extensive bleach greens and beetling machinery,
the property of Messrs Birnie and Cunningham.
There are 3 corn mills and 3 flax mills.

Roads

The mail coach road from Ballymoney to
Ballymena passes through the eastern part of the
parish (called Killymorris) for a distance of 4
miles. There are several other roads, some of
which are hilly. They are, for the most part, in
good repair.

NATURAL FEATURES

Rivers

The River Bann, which is the largest in the province of Ulster, bounds the parish on the west for

4 and a half miles. About 1 and three-quarter miles down the river from south boundary of the parish there is a small landing place called Portna, to which place it is navigable for vessels of 50 to 60 tons burthen, which convey the various commodities required by the surrounding neighbourhood from Belfast and Newry by canals into Lough Neagh, and thence into the Bann.

It abounds with salmon, trout and eel. The chief proprietor is Lord Donegall. There is a fishery a short distance below Portna which is rented by Mr Little of Coleraine. It varies in breadth from 180 to 650 feet.

One mile below Portna is situated Kilrea bridge, at which place the breadth of the river is about 230 feet. It is by this river that Lough Neagh empties itself into the sea, which it enters a short distance below Coleraine. Its course along this parish is nearly north north west. The eel fishery was rented a few years ago at 1,200 pounds annum; the present rent is 560 pounds.

The River Main bounds the parish on the east for about 6 and a half miles. It varies in breadth from 20 to 60 feet. It abounds with salmon and trout. There is no fishery on it until it arrives near Lough Neagh, where there is a small one, the property of Lord O'Neill. Its course, as far as it is common to this parish, is nearly south.

Wood

The principal wood in the parish is that in Dunminning, around the dwellings of Mr Birnie and Mr Cunningham. It is a mixture of fir and forest trees. Few of them are full grown.

At Hazlebrook, Daisyhill and in the neighbourhood of the Bann there are some small patches of planting which, with the exception of a few scattered trees around some farmhouses, comprise all the wood in the parish.

SOCIAL ECONOMY

Population

By the census of 1831 the population amounted to 7,981, of which 250 adhered to the Established Church, about 3,300 Presbyterians and the remainder Roman Catholics. There is a church, a chapel and 2 Presbyterian meeting houses. The present incumbent is the Revd Mr Dickson, who resides in the Glebe.

ANCIENT TOPOGRAPHY

Antiquities

The church is of great antiquity. No trace of its erection can be had. It is small and in good repair without spire or tower.

The Glebe House was built in the reign of Queen Elizabeth.

Mr Dickson has found a great many coins of the 12th century in a field near the Glebe House.

There are 19 Danish forts. One of extraordinary size with a double ditch, called Lisnacannon, is situated in the townland of Drumack.

NATURAL STATE

Killymorris

There is a considerable tract of country in this neighbourhood known by the name Killymorris. It comprises the north east part of Rasharkin parish and the adjoining part of the parish of Finvoy. It is distinguished by the terms Scotch and Irish. The former is that part of Rasharkin which is principally inhabited by Presbyterians, the latter by Roman Catholics. It is from the former that the wood coal is obtained. The proper boundary of this district has not been ascertained. The resident Roman Catholic clergyman says the proper orthography is Kieltymorris, which signifies "Morris's wood." [Signed] J. Chaytor, Lieutenant Royal Engineers, 30th May 1833.

Memoir by James Boyle, September 1835

NATURAL FEATURES

Hills

Forwarded to Lieutenant Larcom, 19 December 1835.

The centre of this parish is traversed by the Killymurrys ridge, which extends along the western side of this county from the parish of Ballymoney to near Lough Neagh at its southern side. There is nothing imposing or interesting in the appearance of this ridge nor does it present any striking feature. On the contrary, from its bare and partially cultivated state its appearance is bleak. Its summit, which is nearly flat and covered with bog, averages 550 feet above the sea. Its descent eastward is at first regular and gradual but finally terminates in broken and undulating ground. On its western side its descent is irregular and in many places very abrupt, which is caused by the frequent appearance of the basaltic strata which render this side of the ridge very rough and rocky. The descent on this side is finally terminated in a variety of gently undulating features extending along the edge of the River Bann.

The principal points in this parish are Rabbit Rock, 623 feet and Lisnacannon, 596 feet above the level of the sea.

Lakes

There is part of a small lake in this parish. There are 4 artificial mill-ponds towards its south east side. The portion of the small lake alluded to is intersected by the northern boundary of the parish. It extends over 5 acres 3 roods 28 perches, of which 2 acres 2 roods 15 perches are in this and the remainder is in Finvoy parish.

River Bann

The Bann, which flows between the counties of Antrim and Londonderry, takes it rise from Lough Beg near the south west end of the parish, at an elevation of 46 feet above the level of the sea at low water. From this, after pursuing a northerly course for 7 and a half miles, it descends to a level of 48 feet above the sea and enters on the western boundary of this parish, along which it flows for 4 and three-quarter miles and descends to a level of 26 feet, being an average fall of 1 foot in 1,140 feet. Finally, after an entire and northerly course of [blank] miles and passing through the town of Coleraine, it discharges itself into the sea within the tideway, [blank] miles north of that town.

Its extreme breadth is 660 feet, least breadth 120 feet and average breadth 308 feet. Its greatest ordinary depth (which is towards the south of the parish) is 11 feet, but towards the north of the parish it becomes shallow, particularly at the eel fishery at Portna where its course is interrupted by a ledge of rocks which produce an irregular and trifling fall. Here, for a quarter of a mile, its depth does not exceed an average of 3 feet. South of Portna its bed consists of a whitish and very tough clay, but north of that place its bed is mostly rocky and stony. Its banks are very low and it frequently inundates portions of the level country along them, but seldom does any injury as its deposits are trifling and innocent.

It is not usefully situated for machinery or irrigation. It does not obstruct communication. There are no ferries over it but there are several boats which for a penny will take one person across. It is easily fordable in summer at Portna eel weirs, its breadth there being 320 feet and ordinary average depth 3 feet. The scenery along its banks is by no means cheerful or interesting, a considerable portion of the course being through a bleak heathery bog.

River Main

The Main takes its rise in the parish of Kilraghts, at an elevation of 390 feet above the level of the sea. After flowing for 1 and a third miles it enters on the eastern boundary of this parish, along which it pursues a southerly course for 6 and a quarter miles and descends to a level of 263 feet, being an average fall of 1 foot in 1,177 feet. It finally discharges itself into Lough Neagh 1 and three-quarter miles south of the town of Randalstown, through which it passes after an entire and southerly course of 25 miles.

Its average breadth in this parish is 20 feet and its average depth about 3 feet, but its bed is very uneven and some places very deep. Its course at Dunminning is interrupted by a ledge of rocks which produce a trifling fall. North of this ledge this river is incapable of being applied to machinery, drainage or irrigation as there is not sufficient fall for these purposes, but south of it is very valuable and usefully situated.

It is subject to frequent floods which, north of the fall just mentioned, do serious injury by inundating the almost level plain through which it flows (see grange of Dundermot), but south of it, its floods are harmless as its banks are high and the fall sufficient to carry off the water. Towards the south its banks are high and the scenery along them pleasing, being thickly and tastefully planted.

The parish is well supplied with spring and soft water for domestic use. There are not any mineral nor hot springs.

Bogs

The bogs in this parish are extensive, occupying a considerable portion of the lower ground and almost the entire summit of the ridge. They vary in height from 50 to 600 feet above the sea and 45 to 555 feet above the River Bann. There is scarcely any difference between them and the manner in which timber occurs in them and those in the neighbouring parishes of Finvoy and Ahoghill, and description of them would therefore be a repetition of that of the bogs in those parishes.

Woods

Brushwood is to be found in every townland in the parish, but particularly in those on its western side. Oak and hazel are the most common but birch, ash, holly and alder are also found. The parish has evidently at no very distant period been well wooded and tradition says "that a man could walk on the trees along the Bann from Coleraine to Portglenone." The brushwood and timber in the bog is the only remaining natural wood.

Climate

The climate of the western side of the parish is colder, being exposed to the south west and west winds which prevail here, more subject to fogs and mists from its proximity to the Bann and its less cultivated state, and consequently later than the eastern side. On the latter side sowing commences in the latter end of March and is over by the beginning of May. Potato setting continues during May and the beginning of June. Harvest commences about the end of August and is over by the beginning of October. On the west sides the crops are nearly a fortnight later sowing and about the same time later ripening.

MODERN TOPOGRAPHY

Towns: Rasharkin

There is no town in this parish and the only village is that of Rasharkin, which is situated on the main road from Ahoghill to Ballymoney, from the latter of which towns it is 8 miles. Its situation is uninteresting, being on the acclivity of a rocky, rugged and half-cultivated hill. The village itself is irregular, straggling and dirty, no regard being paid to neatness or uniformity. It contains 36 houses, of which 9 are 2-storey. They are, in general, small, built of stone and mostly thatched. It contains about 180 inhabitants, who are either engaged in dealing, agriculture or as tradesmen (see Table of Trades).

One annual fair is held on 16th November. Horses and cattle of all kinds are sold but not in any number. No tolls are paid. This fair is almost invariably the scene of violent party riots and waylayings, and whiskey is the article for which there is greatest demand.

Rasharkin is rather increasing in size and a few new houses have been recently built. This is probably owing to the increase of dealing for groceries and spirits.

Public Buildings

The Presbyterian meeting house stands contiguous to the village of Rasharkin. It is a plain, well-built house 70 feet long and 30 feet wide, and capable of accommodating about 400 persons. It was built by subscription in 1832 and cost about 400 pounds.

The Seceders' meeting house stands in the townland of Dromore, on the east side of the parish. It is a plain building 40 feet long and 24 feet wide, and capable of accommodating 300 persons. It is just being newly roofed at the expense of the congregation.

The church stands in the townland of Church Tamlaght and near the village of Rasharkin. It is perfectly plain and not in good repair internally. It is 60 feet long and 24 feet wide, and would accommodate about 180 persons. This church is of great antiquity and no trace of erection can be had. A tradition exists that in the year 1641 several persons took refuge in it and were (along with it) all burned.

The Roman Catholic chapel, which stands near the village of Rasharkin and in the townland of Moneyleck, is a singular-looking octagonal building. It is perfectly plain and without seats but a gallery extends round it. Its diameter is 60 feet and it might contain 500 persons. It was built in the year 1789.

The bridge over the River Bann on the road Ballymena to Kilrea consists of 7 semicircular arches which are sprung 7 feet above the ordinary level of the river. It is 240 feet in length from the extremities of the abutments and 21 feet wide within the parapets. This bridge was built about 50 years ago at the expense of the counties of Antrim and Derry. It is perfectly plain but solid, substantial and in excellent order.

Gentlemen's Seats

Hazlewood Glebe, the residence of Revd John Dickson, rector of the parish, is situated in the townland of the Glebe and the village of Rasharkin. The house is 2-storey, pleasantly situated, commanding a fine view of the county Derry and is kept in the nicest order. There is some planting about it. This house was built in the reign of Queen Elizabeth.

Dunminning, the residence of Thomas Birnie Esquire, is a neat, modern and commodious dwelling, prettily situated in the townland of the same name and near the Main river, the banks of which for more than a mile are beautifully varied and clothed with a thriving plantation of fir, larch and some ash and beech, the property of Mr Birnie. There is a handsome lawn and numerous and extensive walks in the plantings.

Dunoyne, the residence of John Cunningham Esquire, is a pretty cottage situated in the townland of Dunminning.

Mills

In the townland of Dunminning are situated 5

extensive beetling mills with their wash mills and bleach greens. 3 of these mills are the property of John Cunningham Esquire. The machinery of the principal one is propelled by a breast water wheel 40 feet in diameter and 7 feet wide. The machinery of the 2 others is propelled each by a breast water wheel 20 feet in diameter and 4 feet wide. The expense of collecting the water and forming dams and reservoirs for these mills has been very considerable.

The 2 beetling mills on the Main river are the property of Thomas Birnie Esquire. The machinery of the principal one, with its wash mills, is propelled by 3 breast water wheels, each 18 feet in diameter and 5 feet broad. The second is propelled by a breast water wheel 13 feet in diameter and 12 feet broad.

The corn mill in Anticur townland is propelled by a breast water wheel 14 feet in diameter and 2 feet broad.

The corn mill in Killycreen townland is propelled by an undershot wheel 12 feet in diameter and 2 feet 2 inches broad.

The corn mill in Magheraboy townland is propelled by a breast water wheel 14 feet in diameter and 2 feet broad.

The flax mill in Dreen townland is propelled by a breast water wheel 14 feet in diameter and 2 feet broad.

The flax mill in Ballydonnelly townland is propelled by a breast water wheel 20 feet in diameter and 3 feet broad.

The flax mill in Gortereghy townland is propelled by a breast water wheel 14 feet in diameter and 2 feet broad.

The corn mill in Ballydonnelly townland is propelled by a breast water wheel 13 feet in diameter and 2 feet broad.

Communications

The main roads are: the mail coach road from Belfast to Derry through Ballymena and Ballymoney, which passes for 4 miles through the eastern division of this parish. It is rather level and is kept in good order at the expense of the county at large. Its average breadth is 24 feet.

The road from Ahoghill through Rasharkin village to Ballymoney, which traverses the western side of the parish: there are 4 miles of it in the parish. It is rather level but not in good repair. Its average breadth is 20 feet.

The road from Portglenone to Ballymoney which joins the former: there are 2 miles of it. Its average breadth is 20 feet, it is tolerably level and in pretty good repair.

The road from Cushendall to Kilrea through Rasharkin: there are 8 miles of this road. It is unavoidably very hilly but it might be rendered much less so and its direction much improved. It is very rugged and in bad order. Its average breadth is 19 feet.

These roads are mostly made of whinstone which is everywhere abundant. The by, cross-roads are sufficiently numerous and pretty good. All are kept in repair at the expense of the barony.

Bridges

The principal bridge is that over the Bann, being the only communication between the parish and the county of Derry. It is 240 feet long between the extremities of the abutments and 21 feet wide within the parapets. It consists of 7 semicircular arches; each spring 7 feet above the ordinary level of the river. It is plain substantial structure and was erected about 50 years ago at the expense of the counties of Antrim and Derry.

The bridge over the Main river at Dunminning is 60 feet long and 19 feet broad, and consists of 3 semicircular arches.

Dundermot bridge, on the mail coach road from Ballymena to Ballymoney and over the Main river, is 60 feet long and 23 feet wide, and consists of 3 small semicircular arches.

The bridge over the Main river, on a road from Portglenone to Ballycastle, is 18 feet wide, 36 feet long and consists of 3 small semicircular arches.

All these bridges are plain but sufficient in every respect. This parish is amply supplied with communications.

General Appearance and Scenery

Along the eastern and western borders of the parish the scenery is very interesting, having all the variety and the advantages of wood, water and diversity in the ground. The interior of the parish is bleak, bare and uncultivated in its appearance, there being nothing interesting in the cultivation of the ground or the habitations of the lower class.

The view of the surrounding scenery from the high ground is very extensive, varied and exquisitely beautiful, extending from Lough Neagh and the Mourne Mountains on the south to the headlands on the northern coast of the county, while the wild and lofty chain of Antrim mountains on the east and the parallel ridge in Derry and Tyrone on the west bound that view. Occasionally glimpses of the Bann can be had, and the fertile grounds along it on the western and the Main on the eastern side of the parish, forming the sides of the valleys watered by these rivers, present a rich and varied prospect.

SOCIAL ECONOMY

Early Improvements

The march of civilisation and improvement, though certainly perceptible in this parish, has been very tardy when compared with that of most of the neighbouring ones, and its inhabitants (particularly those immediately along the River Bann) are in general turbulent, lawless and refractory. There are some along its eastern side who partake of all the peaceable habits of their civilised neighbours, but they form an exception to the rest of the parish. It would seem as if they intended keeping up the spirit of the original name of the parish Magherasharkin, which it still is called by many. The interpretation of this word is "the field of robbers", by whom, it is said, the part of the parish west of Killymurrys hill was formerly exclusively inhabited. [Insert footnote: See notes at the end]. The place seemed well suited to them, as until about a century ago "a bird could hop from bough to bough from Coleraine to Portglenone." So says the tradition of the country, and the immense quantity of brushwood still remaining justifies it.

The inhabitants east of Killymurrys are principally of Scottish descent and probably came over with those in the adjoining eastern parishes, as there is every resemblance to them in manners, habits and dispositions. Those on the western side are partly of Scottish and partly of Irish descent, and the latter occupy what was probably the most lately wooded part of the country and that nearest the Bann. The most prevalent Roman Catholic names are Mooney, Rainey and McConnell. No Scottish names are peculiarly prevalent. The mountain of Killymurrys, as by that name the hilly portion of this parish is known, is distinguished by the subdivisions of Scotch and Irish, the former being inhabited by Presbyterians and the latter by Roman Catholics.

The colonisation of this part of the country by the Scots and the consequent clearing away of the wood may probably have been the first step towards civilising or at all reclaiming it. The people on the western side of it seem to have been too much left to themselves, and that no effort had been made towards their improvement until of late years by the introduction of schools, and they certainly have done some good. Party spirit, however, exists to a great extent in this parish and frequent conflicts and riots occur.

The lower class are in general, particularly about the village of Rasharkin and along the Bann towards Ahoghill, very lawless, fond of whiskey drinking, careless about comfort or neatness, pay no rent and are very disorderly. Some are engaged in weaving but the majority in agriculture. There are some very independent farmers who have comfortable places, but the lower class are not very comfortable in their circumstances.

Obstructions to improvement: none.

Local Government

There is only one magistrate, Thomas Birnie of Dunminning, Esquire, who is both firm and decided, but his residence is inconveniently situated for the western district of the parish as it is very near to its south eastern extremity. There are 6 police in the village of Rasharkin (constabulary). The manor courts and courts leet for the manor are held in the village of Clogh in the parish of Dunaghy. Petty sessions are held on every alternate Monday in the townland of Killydonnelly.

Party riots and waylayings are frequent, both parties equally in fault. On the 12th July 1835 45 shots were fired by the Ribbonmen at some Orangemen, but without effect. Ribbonism is said and universally believed to be extensively carried on.

A person, who had been recently ejected, assembled a number who came by night and pulled up and carried off a large quantity of flax which he had sown on the lands from which he was ejected. This is the only agrarian outrage of recent occurrence but there is every disposition to resist the law and its executors. For the outrage just mentioned there is one person in custody.

Illicit distillation has totally ceased of late years. There is not any smuggling. There are a few fire insurances.

Dispensary

There is no dispensary. The people are in general healthy and free from disease.

Schools

The introduction of schools has of late years become very general in this parish and though they have produced a very perceptible effect in the morals of the rising generation, they are not so generally resorted to as might be wished for; nor are the people on the west side of the parish as anxious for information as their neighbours.

Poor

Except the usual collections on Sundays, there is no regular provision for the poor of this parish.

Religion

By the revised census of 1834 there are, in this parish, 628 Episcopalians, 2,669 Presbyterians, 1,240 Seceders and 2,944 Roman Catholics. The rector of this parish has the tithes of it, the parishes of Finvoy and Kilraghts and the grange of Kildollagh, and also a glebe house and glebe containing 54 acres 1 rood 15 perches. The Presbyterian clergyman has his stipend, the Seceder clergyman his stipend and regium donum, and the priest the usual contributions from his flock.

Habits of the People

The houses of the lower class are all 1-storey and built of stone, mostly thatched and consist of 2 apartments. They are tolerably well lit but are not cleanly nor very comfortable. They invariably possess the prospect of a manure heap before the door. Turf is their only fuel and it is very abundant. Their food consists of meal, potatoes, milk, a little fish and bacon with some baker's bread. The use of tea at breakfast is becoming general. They dress well and comfortably but not quite so neatly as in the more easterly parishes. The Roman Catholics marry rather early, the Protestants not so early. They are tolerably long lived, persons of from 70 to 80 years of age being in almost every townland.

Amusements and Traditions

Their principal amusements are dancing and cardplaying, both of which are on the decline. There is a little cock-fighting at Easter, but they cannot meet at these games without fighting. The Orangemen walk in procession on 12th July, the Freemasons on 24th June and the Ribbonmen have (but not for 2 years) walked on 17th March. They all enjoy themselves in the usual ways at Hallowe'en.

All parties are superstitious and believe in fairies, enchantments. The Roman Catholics are particularly so and still continue (but not so much as formerly) to bathe their children in a rivulet in Carnfinton townland on May Eve to preserve them from the fairies. Wakes are very numerously attended. At those of the Roman Catholics hymns are sung, as also at their funerals.

The latter have many traditions, most of which are not worth noticing. One is "that the first battle ever fought between the English and Irish was on Dunbulkin hill in the townland of Carnfinton and that the last battle between them will also be fought there; but the Irish shall be victorious and that the low ground around the hill shall be raised level with its summit by the bodies of their enemies." This is believed by many who really look forward to such a day.

The hill alluded to is very small and situated at the base and almost close to the mountain between which and it there is a narrow path. It is nearly conical and rises abruptly to a height of 100 feet from its base. Its summit is about 40 yards long and 8 broad. It is covered with rich mould and appears to have been encompassed with a wall. Quantities of human bones, ashes or coins have been found on it and about it, and the mould on it is generally considered to be that of human bodies. Another tradition is "that a bird could hop from bough to bough from Coleraine to Portglenone." This is universally believed and is probable from the quantity of brushwood still remaining.

The Roman Catholics bum fires, when the Protestants allow them, on St John's Eve. Their reason for not permitting this is very absurd though believed by both parties: the Protestants imagine that it is typical of themselves being one day burned or rather, that the Catholics look forward to it.

They have no ancient music, nor is there anything peculiar in their costume.

Emigration

There is not near so much emigration from this parish as formerly, a few years ago 25 families having emigrated in one day. This may be owing to the less encouraging accounts of those who have gone out, though few return. From 30 to 40 persons still annually emigrate to Canada in spring. They are principally of the working class, whose chief inducement to that part of America is probably the cheap passage.

About 100 Roman Catholics annually go to the English or Scotch harvests. They do not take their wives or families with them and return when they are over. Those persons hold no land except a small garden which they always cultivate. This system also is declining, there being less encouragement as to wages for them and numbers this year went only so far as Belfast.

Remarkable events: none.

Rasharkin: Table of Trades

Blacksmiths 3, carpenters 2, constabulary 6,

cooper 1, grocers 6, shoemakers 3, schoolmaster 1, tailor 1, wheelwright 1, total 24.

ANCIENT TOPOGRAPHY

Notes on Parish Name

In throwing down a part of the churchyard wall about 21 years ago, a very curious and extensive artificial cave, said to have been a hiding place for these robbers, was discovered. A respectable farmer living near Rasharkin was present at the time and saw the perfect skeleton of a man, 9 feet long. The cave was destroyed and the skeleton buried. Several silver coins have all been found about it.

In this parish solitary old thorn-trees and bushes are occasionally to be met with in the higher ground and in several instances they are at the junction of 2 or more townlands.

SOCIAL ECONOMY

Table of Schools

[Table contains the following headings: name, situation and description, when established, income and expenditure, physical, intellectual and moral education, number of pupils subdivided by age, sex and religion, name and religion of master and mistress].

Under the Kildare Place Society, in the townland of Bellaghy, in a house built by subscription, established 1810; income from pupils 20 pounds; intellectual education: the books of the society, reading, writing and arithmetic; moral education: occasional visits from the clergy, Scriptures, both versions; number of pupils: males, 28 under 10 years of age, 11 from 10 to 15, 11 above 15, 40 total males; females, 33 under 10 years of age, 7 from 10 to 15, 40 total females; total number of pupils 80, 4 Protestants, 34 Presbyterians, 42 Roman Catholics; master James McWilliams, Roman Catholic.

Under the Kildare Place Society, in the townland of Dunminning, in a house built for the purpose by Thomas Birnie Esq., established 1806; income from pupils 16 pounds; intellectual education: the books of the society, reading, writing and arithmetic, with geometry, Murray's Grammar; moral education: occasional visits from the clergy, Protestant and Presbyterian catechisms and versions; number of pupils: males, 21 under 10 years of age, 9 from 10 to 15, 30 total males; females, 19 under 10 years of age, 3 from 10 to 15, 22 total females; total number of pupils 52, 1 Protestant, 46 Presbyterians, 5 Roman Catholics; master John Berby, Protestant.

Under the Kildare Place Society, in the townland of Church Tamlaght, in a very neat house built by subscription, established 1832; income: the master has a free house built by subscription, 14 pounds from pupils; intellectual instruction: books and cards of the society; moral education: Authorised Version of Scriptures and catechisms; number of pupils: males, 36 under 10 years of age, 3 from 10 to 15, 39 total males; females, 21 under 10 years of age, 3 from 10 to 15, 24 total females; total number of pupils 63, 32 Protestants, 7 Presbyterians, 24 Roman Catholics; master Robert Elder, Protestant.

London Hibernian Society, in the townland of Dromore, in a house built by subscription, established 1832; income: from the London Hibernian Society 2 pounds, 16 pounds from pupils; intellectual education: *Universal and Manson's Spelling book*, arithmetic; moral education: Authorised Version, Presbyterian catechisms; number of pupils: males, 21 under 10 years of age, 5 from 10 to 15, 26 total males; females, 19 under 10 years of age, 3 from 10 to 15, 22 total females; total number of pupils 48, 6 Protestants, 40 Presbyterians, 2 Roman Catholics; master John Watts, Presbyterian.

London Hibernian Society, in the townland of Granagh, in a house built by subscription, established 1830; income: from the London Hibernian Society 4 pounds, 12 pounds from pupils; intellectual education: books of the society, *Universal and Manson's Spelling book, Dublin Reader*; moral education: Authorised Version of the Scriptures, Presbyterian catechism; number of pupils: males, 26 under 10 years of age, 2 from 10 to 15, 28 total males; females, 8 under 10 years of age, 8 total females; total number of pupils 36, all Presbyterians; master Dan Quin, Roman Catholic.

London Hibernian Society, Carnklinty townland, in a private house the property of the teacher, established 1829; income: from the London Hibernian Society 4 pounds, 12 pounds from pupils; intellectual education: *Manson's and Universal spelling, Dublin Reader*, arithmetic; moral education: occasional visits from the clergy, catechism and Authorised Version; number of pupils: males, 31 under 10 years of age, 4 from 10 to 15, 35 total males; females, 9 under 10 years of age, 3 from 10 to 15, 12 total females; total number of pupils 47, 43 Presbyterians, 4 Roman Catholics; master Robert McKee, Protestant.

London Hibernian Society, townland of Drumcon, in a private house hired for the purpose, established 1830; income from pupils 11 pounds;

intellectual education: *Manson's and Universal spelling and reading books*, arithmetic; moral education: Authorised Version, catechisms, the former daily; number of pupils: males, 14 under 10 years of age, 2 from 10 to 15, 16 total males; females, 9 under 10 years of age, 1 from 10 to 15, 10 total females; total number of pupils 26, 3 Protestants, 5 Presbyterians, 18 Roman Catholics; master John Montgomery, Presbyterian.

London Hibernian Society, townland of Ballymaconnelly, in a house built by subscription, established 1832; income from pupils 10 pounds; intellectual education: reading, writing, arithmetic, geometry, their own books; moral education: occasional visits from the clergy, Authorised Version; number of pupils: males, 21 under 10 years of age, 5 from 10 to 15, 1 above 15, 28 total males; females, 9 under 10 years of age, 2 from 10 to 15, 11 total females; total number of pupils 39, 13 Protestants, 18 Presbyterians, 8 Roman Catholics; master John Black, Roman Catholic.

London Hibernian Society female school, townland of Dunminning, in a very nice house built for the purpose by Thomas Birnie Esquire, established 1833; income: from Miss Birnie annually 6 pounds, from the London Hibernian Society 4 pounds, [total] 10 pounds, 3 pounds from pupils; intellectual education: reading, writing, spelling and arithmetic, books of the society; moral education: occasional visits from the clergy, Scriptures daily; number of pupils: 18 under 10 years of age, 11 from 10 to 15, 3 above 15; total number of pupils 32, 30 Presbyterians, 2 Roman Catholics; mistress Mary Bradshaw, Protestant.

Under the Kildare Place Society, in the townland of Dromore and in a private house the property of the teacher, established 1815; income from pupils 12 pounds 10s; intellectual education: the books of the society; moral education: occasional visits from the clergy, Authorised Version; number of pupils: males, 16 under 10 years of age, 4 from 10 to 15, 1 above 15, 21 total males; females, 11 under 10 years of age, 4 from 10 to 15, 15 total females; total number of pupils 36, all Presbyterians; master James Carew, Protestant.

Under the National Board (female), in the townland of Glenbuck, in a neat house built for the purpose by Thomas Birnie Esquire, established 1832; income: from Mrs Birnie 6 pounds per annum and from the Board of National Education 6 pounds per annum, [total] 12 pounds; intellectual education: books of the National Board; moral education: occasional visits from the priest, Scriptures. Douai and Authorised Versions at stated times; number of pupils: 24 under 10 years of age, 4 from 10 to 15; total number of pupils 28, 4 Protestants, 2 Presbyterians, 22 Roman Catholics; mistress Mary Hamilton, Protestant.

[Subtotals]: income from public societies or benevolent individuals 32 pounds, from pupils 126 pounds 10s; number of pupils: males, 215 under 10 years of age, 45 from 10 to 15, 3 above 15, 263 total males; females, 180 under 10 years of age, 41 from 10 to 15, 3 above 15, 224 total females; total number of pupils 487, 63 Protestants, 297 Presbyterians, 127 Roman Catholics.

Private Schools

Private school, in a house built by subscription in the townland of Magheraboy, established 1828; income from pupils 12 pounds; intellectual education: *Manson's and Universal spelling and reading books*, writing; moral education: Sunday school and Authorised and Douai Versions of the Scriptures daily; number of pupils: males, 11 under 10 years of age, 4 from 10 to 15, 15 total males; females, 13 under 10 years of age, 2 from 10 to 15, 15 total females; total number of pupils 30, 2 Protestants, 10 Presbyterians, 18 Roman Catholics; master Patrick Quinn, Roman Catholic.

Private school, in a private house in the townland of Craigs, when established: unknown; income from pupils 7 pounds; intellectual education: *Manson's and Universal spelling and reading books*, writing and arithmetic; moral education: Sunday school and Authorised Version of Scriptures, Shorter Catechism; number of pupils: males, 17 under 10 years of age, 6 from 10 to 15, 1 above 15, 24 total males; females, 6 under 10 years of age, 2 from 10 to 15, 8 total females; total number of pupils 32, 3 Protestants, 29 Presbyterians; master James Getty, Presbyterian.

Private school, in a house built by subscription in the townland of Bellaghy, established 1823; income from pupils 8 pounds; intellectual education: *Manson's and Universal spelling and reading books*, writing and arithmetic; moral education: Sunday school and Authorised Version of Scriptures, Shorter Catechism; number of pupils: males, 13 under 10 years of age, 6 from 10 to 15, 19 total males; females, 8 under 10 years of age, 3 from 10 to 15, 11 total females; total number of pupils 30, all Presbyterians; master Robert Hamilton, Presbyterian.

Private school, in a house built by subscription in the townland of Lisnagarve, established 1832;

income from pupils 7 pounds 10s; intellectual education: *Manson's and Universal spelling and reading books*, writing and arithmetic; moral education: Sunday schools and Authorised Version of Scriptures, Shorter Catechism; number of pupils: males, 11 under 10 years of age, 8 from 10 to 15, 19 total males; females, 8 under 10 years of age, 4 from 10 to 15, 12 total females; total number of pupils 31, 3 Protestants, 24 Presbyterians, 4 Roman Catholics; master James McCaken, Protestant.

Private school, in a house the property of the teacher in the townland of Ballymaconnelly, established 1832; income from pupils 4 pounds; intellectual education: *Manson's and Universal spelling and reading books*; moral education: Douai and Authorised Versions of the Scriptures daily; number of pupils: males, 9 under 10 years of age, 3 from 10 to 15, 12 total males; females, 6 under 10 years of age, 3 from 10 to 15, 9 total females; total number of pupils 21, 3 Protestants, 5 Presbyterians, 13 Roman Catholics; mistress Catherine McMinn, Roman Catholic.

Private school, in a house built by subscription in the townland of Tamlaght, established 1834; income from pupils 6 pounds 10s; intellectual education: *Manson's and Universal spelling and reading books*, writing and arithmetic; moral education: Douai Bible and *Dr Doyle's Catechisms*; number of pupils: males, 16 under 10 years of age, 4 from 10 to 15, 20 total males; females, 9 under 10 years of age, 3 from 10 to 15, 12 total females; total number of pupils 32, all Roman Catholics; master John Welsh, Roman Catholic.

Private school, in his own house in the townland of Killydonly, established 1829; income from pupils 8 pounds; intellectual education: *Manson's and Universal spelling and reading books*, writing and arithmetic; moral education: Sunday school and Authorised Version of Scriptures and Shorter Catechisms daily; number of pupils: males, 13 under 10 years of age, 7 from 10 to 15, 20 total males; females, 6 under 10 years of age, 6 total females; total number of pupils 26, 1 Protestant, 24 Presbyterians, 1 Roman Catholic; master John Bradshaw, Presbyterian.

Private school, in a house the property of the teacher, in the townland of Articarney, established 1832; income from pupils 4 pounds; intellectual education: *Manson's and Universal spelling and reading books*, writing and arithmetic; moral education: Douai Bible and Dr Doyle's Catechism daily; number of pupils: males, 8 under 10 years of age, 4 from 10 to 15, 12 total males; females, 4 under 10 years of age, 1 from 10 to 15,

5 total females; total number of pupils 17, 3 Presbyterians, 15 Roman Catholics.

Sunday school, in the meeting house in Rasharkin village, established 1834; moral education: Authorised Version, Shorter Catechism; number of pupils: 131 males, 69 females, total 200, 24 Protestants, 176 Presbyterians; gratuitous teachers, mostly farmers.

Memoir by J. Stokes

ANCIENT TOPOGRAPHY

Ecclesiastical: Old Church

The parish church is built on the foundations of an ancient one which was destroyed in the rebellion of 1641. From the date 1696 affixed to a Latin inscription on the southern wall and in the interior of the present building, it would appear that it was erected about that time.

This inscription is to the memory of a curate named John Dunbar. There is a tradition that the ancient church was first commenced on the heights above Drumbulkin hill, a situation about half a mile eastward. At this place, all that was erected by day was pulled down at night. After some time the present site was chosen. It is remarkable that this legend is an accompaniment to the history of many other parish churches besides that of Rasharkin.

Of late years, none but Episcopalian families bury in the yard. The names are Scotch and English.

Graveyards

There is an ancient graveyard still used in the townland of Duneany and a few fields distant from the high road between Rasharkin and Clogh. It is very small, containing about 6 square perches Cunningham measure. No one buries in it at present but those who are too poor to pay the sexton at the churchyard. It was formerly the great burying place of the eastern part of the parish. There are 3 tombstones, Catherwood, Blair and Love. The first is the oldest and bears a date between 1600 and 1700. The 2 last numbers are illegible.

An old church is said to have stood at the distance of 200 yards to the south of this yard. Many large stones resembling the quoin-stones <coinstones> of a building were found scattered about the site by the tenants when they came to occupy their farms. Other circumstances, especially the finding of frequent heaps of stones just about that place, have confirmed, to their minds, the vague tradition that always had existed in the country on the subject.

There is another graveyard in the townland of Killycreen, in the centre of a large potato field. It is not surrounded by any fence. It contains about 13 square perches Cunningham measure but was once much larger. The last person buried in it was Una Shiel, who died nearly 100 years ago. It is said that a place of worship also stood here at the distance of 50 yards to the east. A rectangular hollow in the ground marks the site. It cannot now, however, be seen, having been filled up with stones.

A graveyard formerly stood in that part of the townland of Crushybracken called Slaghtaggart. It was so called on account of a priest called Taggart having been murdered and buried here many hundreds of years ago. Latterly, none but stillborn children were interred in it. It is now completely destoyed.

Holy Well

A holy well stands near the village of Rasharkin and close to the rocky hill called Drumbulkin. Children were formerly brought to it on May Eve to be cured of various diseases. It is now forgotten and neglected. It is not known to what saint it had been dedicated.

Military Remains

The only military remains known in the parish are the traces of an entrenchment along the edge of the River Bann, exactly opposite a series of them on the other bank. See the Ancient Topography of the parish of Kilrea, county Londonderry, for a description of them. This one, on the county Antrim side, is very much defaced. It was about 200 yards long and 10 feet wide. It is cut in the side of the bank and, being quite filled up, is now nearly a ledge; but from the manner in which it terminates, it was evidently a trench.

Pagan: Forts and Coves

There is a remarkable fort in the townland of Drumack called Lisnacannon Fort. It is girt with 2 ditches, having between them a rampart of peculiar form; see drawing[s] for plan and dimensions. It is on high ground and surrounded by bog. No ancient articles have been found in it, nor is there any cove known to be at or about it. There are no other interesting forts in the parish.

In the townland of Fehorney there are the remains of a cromlech, but now so tossed about and broken by treasure seekers that all resemblance to its original form is done away with. Almost all the stones are broken. There is a broken fragment 6 feet long said to have been once part of the canopy stone. A long cairn or heap of stones, 130 feet long by about 30 feet wide, contains in its centre, that is, half-way from end to end, the remains of this monument. It seems to have originally covered it. Of this cairn almost all has been removed, leaving only what is sufficient to mark out its length and breadth. Great numbers of small stone-cutting instruments and flint arrowheads were found in it, as well as many quernstones in the adjacent fields.

At the distance of about 500 yards to the south, and near the edge of a small stream, there is a natural ledge in the side of a large rock which is situated in the midst of a group of many others. This is called a giant's chair. There is no tradition connected with it.

Near a flow bog in the townland of Glenbuck there is a fort of ordinary form and size called Pharoah's Fort. Within it, and at the distance of 17 feet from the most northern parapet, there is a cave of considerable dimensions; see drawing[s]. [Insert footnote: This distance refers to the mouth of the cove]. The fort itself is 72 feet in diameter.

There is a cove in the townland of Anticur; see drawing[s]. It is now mainly destroyed.

On the western side of an ordinary earthen fort in the townland of Dromore, which is in diameter 107 feet, there is another. It runs north and south, is 24 by 2 and a half feet.

There are some others in the parish but stopped up and uninteresting.

Standing Stone

In the townland of Duneany there is a standing stone about 50 paces west of the road from Ballymena to Ballymoney. It is 3 feet 10 inches by 2 feet by 1 foot.

Silver and Brass Objects

Very few miscellaneous articles have been picked up. Mr Birnie of Dunminning has the most important. See drawing[s] for a horse ornament in his possession, found in the townland of Glenbuck, just at that part of the bed of a rivulet where it had worked its way underground. He had also a remarkable and richly finished silver ornament, intended apparently to go round the neck. It was lately in the possession of Major Sirr of Dublin.

He has sold his collection. Mr Birnie's ornament was picked up in Killyconaway. In its vicinity many silver coins of Henry VIII's reign were discovered. These are not now to be had.

A brass bar, in shape and size resembling the instrument called the crowbar, was found on the top of Drumbulkin hill many years ago. It was given away to Alexander McNeil Esquire of Ballycastle.

Several coins of the dates usually found in this part of the country have been obtained at different times. One from the townland of Bellaghy is represented in drawing[s].

Derivation of Place-names

It may not be amiss to mention that the small rocky hill called Drumbulkin was formerly called Rasharkin, from having been the residence of a robber called Sharkin. The tract of ground in which Hazlebrook, the rector's residence, is situated was called in Irish the "bard's quarter", as the robber was also a poet. This rocky hill stands but 2 fields distance from the eastern side of the village and immediately at the foot of the steep declivity of a larger and more extensive one that rises above it. In shape and form it much resembles Dungonnell Fort in the parish of Dunaghy. It is of the same height. On the top, however, there cannot be perceived any remains of the fortification, cove or dwelling.

Both Hazlebrook and Drumbulkin are close to the village of Rasharkin.

Drawings

Map of the standing stones etc. of Rasharkin, scale 3 miles to 1 inch.

Lisnacannon Fort, ground plan and section, with dimensions and orientation, scale half chain to an inch.

Ornament, stirrup-shape, found in Glenbuck, main dimensions 7 by 5 and a half inches, and section; brass pin found with the ornament, full size.

Cove in Pharoah's Fort, 36 by 12 feet; cave in Anticur, 30 feet by 24 feet; ground plan with orientation, scale 20 feet to 1 inch.

Coin found in Bellaghy, 2 views, full size.

Fair Sheets by J. Bleakly, September and October 1837

Graveyard and Cove

There is an ancient graveyard in the townland of Duneany, on the farm of Robert Love, about 60 paces north of the road leading from the mail coach road to Rasharkin. There is only 3 tombstones in the graveyard. The oldest is to the memory of Catherwood. This is said to have been the chief burial ground for this part of the parish before the Presbyterian meeting house was built.

There is a cove, artificial, but closed up, about 40 perches north east of the above graveyard on the same farm and same townland. 27th September 1837.

Forts

There is a fort of earth and stones, very conspicuous, on the farm of Mrs Blair in the townland of Duneany. The fort is all grown over with brushwood but nothing remarkable about it.

There is also one of earth on the farm of Daniel McCaw in the same townland, about 45 paces south west of the same road, but part is dug away. 29th September 1837.

Caves

[Ground plan, main dimensions 36 and half feet by 12 feet, roughly "L" shape with orientation]. The above cove is situated on the north side of a fort of earth and stones called Pharoah's Fort, but now on the farm of Patrick Magowan in the townland of Glenbuck, east of the flow bog a short distance. The first room at the east end is 18 and a half feet long by 3 feet wide and 4 feet high. The mouth is 1 foot 7 inches high by 2 feet wide. The second room is 18 feet long by 3 and a half high by 2 wide. The entrance to this room is 1 and a half feet high by 1 foot wide. The room at the south end is 12 feet long by 2 and a half feet high by 2 feet wide. Entrance to this room is 10 inches high by 1 and a half feet wide. The fort is undisturbed and 72 feet in diameter. The cave is 17 feet from the north parapet; *well worth drawing*. 5th October 1837.

Gingling Hole

The Gingling Hole is situated in a natural rock on the farm of James Gasten in the townland of Duneaney, above a stream which divides it from Croshnabrackin.

Fort

Fort of earth in Dromore, near the road leading to Rasharkin, on the farm of Alexander Rodgers but part dug away. 6th October 1837.

Carn of Stones

There is a curious carn of large and small stones, about 2 cart-loads, lying at the north west face of a small rock on the farm of Alexander Catherwood, on the Foreign mountain in the townland of Glenbuck. The carn is 5 feet in diameter and 2 feet high. The face of the rock against which the stones are placed is also 5 feet high.

Tradition says these stones have been several times carted away from the face of the rock on one day and on the next day all collected together in their old place, supposed by some supernatural beings. William Harkness and Robert Lynn states they have frequently scattered them and that they were collected together the next day in the same place, and that they had placed one of the stones on the leaf of a bible at night and that it remained undisturbed until the next day. Information obtained from William Harkness and Robert Lynn, farmers. 9th October 1837.

Standing Stone

There is a standing stone about 50 paces west of the mail coach road leading from the Ballymena road to Ballymoney, on the farm of Frank McCaw in the townland of Duneaney. This stone is 3 feet 10 inches high by 2 feet wide and 1 foot thick. 10th October 1837.

Cove

There is an artificial cove a few paces north of Robert Park's house in the townland of Anticor, which is of this shape: [ground plan, main dimensions 30 feet by 24 feet, "L" shape, with orientation] but the stones are now taking away to build, and nearly demolished. 11th October 1837.

Forts

There is a fort of earth on the farm of John Boyle in the townland of Anticor, on the top of a hill above the mail coach road leading from the Ballymena road to Ballymoney, but nothing remarkable about it.

There is also a fort of earth on the farm of James McWilliams in the townland of Bellaghy.

There is also one on the farm of Thomas Caldwell in the same townland, near the flow bog in a marshy bottom, very small.

There is also one on William Gosten's farm in Killycreen. 12th and 13th October 1837.

Coves and Forts

There is a cove on the farm of William Arbothnot which runs nearly north at his house in the townland of Bellaghy, but also closed up, in a potato field near the road leading to Ballymoney.

There is also one on Robert Shearer's farm but closed up in the same townland; also a fort on James McWilliams farm, same townland.

Coin

A small ancient coin of sixpenny magnitude, but very thin, found by James Anderson this year, 1837, in a potato field in Bellaghy townland; see specimen. 14th October 1837.

Forts and Caves

There is a very conspicuous fort of earth on the farm of Hugh Reed in the townland of Dromore, a short distance west of the road leading from the mail coach road to Ballymoney. This fort is 107 feet in diameter with only one trench. There is an artifical cave near the west side of this fort which runs nearly north and south, 24 feet long by 3 and a half feet high and 2 and a half feet wide. The mouth is 1 foot 4 inches high by 2 feet wide, only one room. 16th October 1837.

There is also a fort of earth in a marsh at the west edge of a flow bog on the farm of Thomas Caldwell, in the townland of Bellaghy.

There is a fort of earth on the farm of Hugh McAtaggart in the townland of Gortahar, but part is dug away; also one of earth on the farm of George McHendry in the townland of Magheraboy, which is his garden. 17th October 1837.

Spear and Crow Iron

A spear of brass was found by Alexander Kilpatrick in a flow bog in 1837. 18th October 1837.

A brass crow iron is said to have been found by John Boorman on Drumbulkin hill in the townland of Carnfinton, on the top of the hill, but was given away to Alexander McNeil of Ballycastle. 18th and 19th October 1837.

Drumbulkin Hill

Drumbulkin is a rocky hill, the top of which is said to be artificial and is in shape like Dungonnell Fort. It is situated a short distance east of the village of Rasharkin, in the townland of Carnfinton. Bones and ashes have been discovered on the top with human teeth. From Robert Elder, schoolmaster at Rasharkin.

Church

The church, which is situated at the south end of the village, is said to be the oldest house in the village and is said to have been burned during the

'41 war, at the burning of which only 2 lives were lost. It has no other ornament outside than a belfry. It is 61 and a half by 25 and a half feet long. About the year 1800 it was reduced in length by 16 feet by the Revd William Ravencroft, prebendary of Rasharkin at that time. The walls are not thicker than those of a modern building.

The following monumentum is placed in the south wall near the communion table [inscription]: "Hic iacet Johan Dunbar cler[icus] qui berris [verris] in celum [coelum]; micravif [migravit] 28 die 7 [Septem]bris anno dinni [domini] 1696."

There is another monument at the north side to the memory of Margaret McNeill and children, 1723. 20th October 1837.

Graveyard

There is an ancient graveyard about 200 perches west of the mail coach road leading to Ballymoney, on the farm of Robert Dickey in the townland of Killycreen. It was much larger but is every year digging away. The last person buried was Unna Shiel, but no tombstone; died about 100 years ago. Tradition says a place of worship was here, which is very probable as there is a spot near the graveyard which has the appearance of a place where ruins might have been. Last spring a large quantity of human bones have been dug up near the graveyard by the proprietor.

Derivation of Rasharkin

The parish of Rasharkin is said to have taken its name from a noted robber named Sharkin, who used to reside near the village where the minister now resides, called Hazlebrook, formerly called Carabard or the "bard's quarter", as Sharkin was a great poet. The rocky hill above the village was then called Rathsharkin, now called Drumbulkin. From the Revd Peter McMullin, parish priest of Rasharkin, and [blank] Birnie Esquire. 21st October 1837.

Graveyard

There is an ancient graveyard on the farm of Frank McFerran in that part of the townland of Crushybracken called Slaght Taggart, from a priest named Taggart who is said to have been killed and buried in a stone grave or coffin in this graveyard. About 10 years ago the grave was dug up, in which 6 flags which contained his ashes was found and are now put into a building. None but stillborn children were buried here, but the

whole graveyard is long since demolished. From William Harkness and Frank McFerran, farmers.

Arrowheads

Hugh McCandle in the townland of Crushybracken has 2 arrowheads; one is a flint and very perfect, the other is of the same material as the stone hatchets found by the proprietor in 1837 on his farm. 26th October 1837.

Dane's Pipe

A Dane's pipe was found in this year 1837 in a field near the house of Thomas Shearer, and by him, in the townland of Killycowan (see specimen).

Lisnacannon and Other Forts

There is a very conspicuous fort of earth and stones called Lisnacannon in the townland of Drumack, on the farm of John McAllister, which has 3 large trenches and is nearly circular, perfect in shape and undisturbed.

There is also a fort of earth on the farm of James Smith, same townland, but laboured inside; also one on the farm of John McCauley, townland of Dreen, but almost dug away; also one on the farm of Robert Hindman, townland of Killydonnelly. 27th October 1837.

Coffin Stone

This stone is nearly the shape of a coffin, situated in an island in a marsh about 500 yards south east of Lisnacannon Fort, on the farm of Andrew Disart in the townland of Drumack. The stone is lying almost flat and is 4 and a half feet long, 1 foot 8 inches broad and 1 foot thick. [Signed] John Bleakly.

School Statistics

Table of Schools

[Table contains the following headings: name of townland where held, name and religion of master or mistress, free or pay school, annual income of master or mistress, description and cost of schoolhouse, number of pupils subdivided by religion, sex and the Protestant and Roman Catholic returns, societies with which connected].

Carnfinton, master Robert Elder, Protestant; pay school, annual income 24 pounds; schoolhouse stone, lime and slated, cost 20 pounds;

number of pupils by the Protestant return: 9 Established Church, 23 Presbyterians, 8 Roman Catholics, 21 males, 19 females; by the Roman Catholic return: 9 Established Church, 23 Presbyterians, 8 Roman Catholics, 21 males, 19 females; the Reverend J. Dickson gives the master 2 pounds, the parish school.

Dromore, master James Carew, Presbyterian; pay school, annual income 2s 1d to 4s 4d per quarter; schoolhouse stone and lime, cost 8 pounds; number of pupils by the Protestant return: 38 Presbyterians, 1 Roman Catholic, 30 males, 9 females; by the Roman Catholic return: 39 Presbyterians, 1 Roman Catholic, 26 males, 14 females; connected with the Kildare Place Society, H. Robinson Esquire, patron.

Dunminning, master John Burby, Established Church; pay school, annual income 32 pounds; schoolhouse stone and lime, cost 20 pounds; number of pupils by the Protestant return: 1 Established Church, 42 Presbyterians, 6 Roman Catholics, 23 males, 26 females; by the Roman Catholic return: 2 Established Church, 37 Presbyterians, 4 Roman Catholics, 23 males, 20 females; connected with the Kildare Place Society, the schoolhouse built by subscription, Hugh Birnie Esquire, patron.

Kinlinty, master Samuel Marr, Presbyterian; pay school, annual income 6 or 9 pounds per annum; schoolhouse held in a barn; number of pupils by the Protestant return: 21 Presbyterians, 15 males, 6 females; by the Roman Catholic return: 2 Established Church, 26 Presbyterians; associations none.

Killydonnelly, master Samuel Bradshaw, Presbyterian; pay school, annual income 10 pounds; schoolhouse held in his own kitchen; number of pupils by the Protestant return: 3 Established Church, 20 Presbyterians, 15 males, 8 females; by the Roman Catholic return: 20 Presbyterians, 1 Roman Catholic, 13 males, 8 females; associations none.

Lovestown, master Neill Boyle, Roman Catholic; pay school, annual income 8 pounds per annum; schoolhouse held in a barn; number of pupils by the Protestant return: 12 Presbyterians, 6 Roman Catholics, 15 males, 3 females; by the Roman Catholic return: 11 Presbyterians, 9 Roman Catholics, 10 males, 10 females; associations none.

Bellaghy, master James Hamilton, Established Church; pay school, annual income 22 pounds; schoolhouse stone and lime, cost 30 pounds; number of pupils by the Protestant return: 38 Presbyterians, 4 Roman Catholics, 21 males,

21 females; by the Roman Catholic return: 31 Presbyterians, 5 Roman Catholics, 20 males, 16 females; connected with the Hibernian Society and Reverend Mr Wilson, the schoolhouse built by subscription.

Glenbrook, master John Dempsy, Roman Catholic; pay school, annual income 12 pounds; schoolhouse stone and lime; number of pupils by the Protestant return: 3 Presbyterians, 19 Roman Catholics, 16 males, 6 females; by the Roman Catholic return: 6 Presbyterians, 17 Roman Catholics, 9 males, 14 females; Thomas Birnie Esquire built the schoolhouse.

Gortahare, master James Adair, Roman Catholic; pay school, annual income 12 pounds; schoolhouse: house falling down; number of pupils by the Protestant return: 13 Presbyterians, 2 other denominations, 11 Roman Catholics, 16 males, 10 females; by the Roman Catholic return: 1 Established Church, 16 Presbyterians, 3 other denominations, 15 Roman Catholics, 23 males, 12 females; associations none.

Glenbrook, master Pat Walsh, Roman Catholic; pay school, annual income 8 pounds; schoolhouse a vacant cabin; number of pupils by the Protestant return: 4 Established Church, 13 Presbyterians, 3 other denominations, 16 Roman Catholics, 20 males, 16 females; by the Roman Catholic return: 4 Established Church, 12 Presbyterians, 19 Roman Catholics, 22 males, 13 females; associations none.

Magheraboy Dranach, master John Black, Roman Catholic; pay school, annual income whatever he can get; schoolhouse stone and lime; number of pupils by the Protestant return: 33 Presbyterians, 1 Roman Catholic, 18 males, 16 females; associations none.

Culmore, master Archibald Greer, Presbyterian; pay school, annual income 16 pounds; schoolhouse built for a porter's lodge; number of pupils by the Protestant return: 7 Established Church, 14 Presbyterians, 2 other denominations, 3 Roman Catholics, 17 males, 9 females; by the Roman Catholic return: 7 Established Church, 11 Presbyterians, 6 Roman Catholics; associations none.

Antidoney, master Daniel Quinn, Roman Catholic; pay school, annual income 12 pounds, schoolhouse stone and lime, bad accommodation, cost 30 pounds; number of pupils by the Protestant return: 30 Presbyterians, 11 males, 19 females; by the Roman Catholic return: 7 Established Church, 23 Presbyterians, 23 Roman Catholics; associations none.